Hatred in Print

'Often, conflict is founded on a difference of perception that the other has of the situation of his adversary. Your identity is not defined in opposition to another identity. If this is the case, then it means that you have very little confidence in yourselves.'

John Hume, Peace Nobel Prize winner, addressing the Corsican nationalists gathered at Bastia on 14 February 1999, 'La leçon de pacifisme d'un Prix Nobel irlandais aux nationalistes corses', *Le Monde* (Tuesday 16 February 1999), p. 1.

Hatred in Print

Catholic Propaganda and Protestant Identity during
the French Wars of Religion

LUC RACAUT

Ashgate

Published by
Ashgate Publishing Limited   Ashgate Publishing Company
Gower House   131 Main Street
Croft Road   Burlington VT 05401–5600 USA
Aldershot
Hants GU11 3HR
England

Ashgate website: http://www.ashgate.com

British Library Cataloguing in Publication Data

Racaut, Luc.
   Hatred in Print: Catholic Propaganda and Protestant Identity
   during the French Wars of Religion.
   (St Andrews Studies in Reformation History)
   1. Catholic Church—France—Apologetic works—History and
   criticism. 2. Hatred—Religious aspects—Christianity.
   3. France—History—Wars of the Huguenots, 1562–98.
   I. Title.
   274.4'06

Library of Congress Cataloging-in-Publication Data

Racaut, Luc.
   Hatred in print: Catholic propaganda and Protestant identity
   during the French Wars of Religion/Luc Racaut.
      p.   cm. (St Andrews Studies in Reformation History)
   Includes bibliographical references and index.
   ISBN 0–7546–0284–2 (alk. paper)
   1. Counter-Reformation—France. 2. Huguenots—Controversial
   literature—History and criticism. 3. France—History—Wars of the
   Huguenots, 1562–98—Propaganda. I. Series.
   BR370.R33   2002
   274.4'06—dc21

                                                    2001048709

ISBN 0 7546 0284 2

This book is printed on acid-free paper

Typeset in Sabon by Manton Typesetters, Louth, Lincolnshire, UK and printed in Great Britain by MPG Books Ltd, Bodmin, Cornwall.

Contents

St Andrews Studies in Reformation History

The Magnificent Ride: The First Reformation in Hussite Bohemia
Thomas A. Fudge

Kepler's Tübingen: Stimulus to a Theological Mathematics
Charlotte Methuen

'Practical Divinity': The Works and Life of Revd Richard Greenham
Kenneth L. Parker and Eric J. Carlson

*Belief and Practice in Reformation England: A Tribute to
Patrick Collinson by his Students*
edited by Susan Wabuda and Caroline Litzenberger

*Frontiers of the Reformation: Dissidence and Orthodoxy
in Sixteenth-Century Europe*
Auke Jelsma

*The Jacobean Kirk, 1567–1625:
Sovereignty, Polity and Liturgy*
Alan R. MacDonald

John Knox and the British Reformations
edited by Roger A. Mason

*The Education of a Christian Society:
Humanism and the Reformation in Britain and the Netherlands*
edited by N. Scott Amos, Andrew Pettegree and Henk van Nierop

Tudor Histories of the English Reformations, 1530–83
Thomas Betteridge

*Poor Relief and Protestantism:
The Evolution of Social Welfare in Sixteenth-Century Emden*
Timothy G. Fehler

*Radical Reformation Studies:
Essays presented to James M. Stayer*
edited by Werner O. Packull and Geoffrey L. Dipple

*Clerical Marriage and the English Reformation:
Precedent Policy and Practice*
Helen L. Parish

Penitence in the Age of Reformations
edited by Katharine Jackson Lualdi and Anne T. Thayer

The Faith and Fortunes of France's Huguenots, 1600–85
Philip Benedict

Christianity and Community in the West:
Essays for John Bossy
edited by Simon Ditchfield

Reformation, Politics and Polemics:
The Growth of Protestantism in East Anglian Market Towns,
1500–1610
John Craig

The Sixteenth-Century French Religious Book
edited by Andrew Pettegree, Paul Nelles and Philip Conner

Music as Propaganda in the German Reformation
Rebecca Wagner Oettinger

John Foxe and his World
edited by Christopher Highley and John N. King

Confessional Identity in East-Central Europe
edited by Maria Crăciun, Ovidiu Ghitta and Graeme Murdock

The Bible in the Renaissance:
Essays on Biblical Commentary and Translation
in the Fifteenth and Sixteenth Centuries
edited by Richard Griffiths

Obedient Heretics: Mennonite Identities in Lutheran Hamburg
and Altona during the Confessional Age
Michael D. Driedger

The Construction of Martyrdom in the
English Catholic Community, 1535–1603
Anne Dillon

Baptism and Spiritual Kinship in Early Modern England
Will Coster

Editorial note

In the footnotes, references to sixteenth-century books are to the edition that was actually consulted. Where the first edition predates this, this is indicated in the bibliography. The name of printers is added to the bibliographical references to sixteenth-century books when known. Sometimes the name of the author, printer, the place or date of publication does not figure on the title-page and when it was possible to identify this by other means, this is indicated between square brackets. When it was not possible to identify the printer, the place or date of publication, this information is simply omitted. When the author was not identified, the reference is marked with 'Anon.' for anonymous in the first instance and omitted in later references.

Copyright acknowledgements

Some material used in this book forms part of a doctoral thesis entitled 'Hatred in Print: Aspects of Anti-Protestant Polemic during the French Wars of Religion' that was awarded by the University of St Andrews in May 1999. Sections of this book were published as articles:

'The cultural obstacles to religious pluralism in the polemic of the French Wars of Religion', in K. Cameron, M. Greengrass and P. Roberts, eds, *The Adventure of Religious Pluralism in Early-Modern France* (Bern: Peter Lang, 2000), pp. 115–27.

'Accusations of Infanticide on the eve of the French Wars of Religion', in M. Jackson, ed., *Infanticide: Historical Perspectives on Child Murder and Concealment, 1550–2000* (Aldershot: Ashgate, 2002), pp. 38–61.

'The polemical use of the Albigensian Crusade during the French Wars of Religion', *French History*, XIII: 3 (Oxford: Oxford University Press, 1999), pp. 1–19.

'Religious Polemic and Huguenot Self-Perception and Identity, 1554–1619', in R. Mentzer and A. Spicer, eds, *Society and Culture in the Huguenot World, 1559–1685* (Cambridge: Cambridge University Press, forthcoming), pp. 29–43.

These sections are reproduced with the kind permission of the copyright holders.

Acknowledgements

I would like to thank Professor Mark Greengrass (University of Sheffield) for providing the initial inspiration for this project; Professor Andrew Pettegree (University of St Andrews, Reformation Studies Institute) for supervising the thesis which formed the basis for this book; Professor Robert Knecht (University of Birmingham) for invaluable advice and feedback; Dr Tom Freeman (Institute of Historical Research) for advice on Foxe's *Acts and Monuments*; Dr Irena Backus (Institut pour l'Histoire de la Réformation de Genève) for advice on Genevan Apocalypticism; Brandon Hartley (University of Arizona) for feedback on misogyny and the world upside down; Dr Ingeborg Jostock (European University Institute) for help on censorship in Geneva; Dr Fiona Campbell (Newnham College, Cambridge) for her help with the *Flügschriften*; Professeur Alain Tallon (Université de Paris IV, Sorbonne) for his help with the cardinal de Lorraine; Professor Ray Mentzer (University of Iowa) for showing interest in my work; the staff of the Herzog August Bibliothek (Wolfenbüttel), the Society for the Study of French History and the Bibliothèque de la Société pour l'Histoire du Protestantisme Français for logistical support; members of the St Andrews Reformation Studies Institute who provided me with advice and guidance; Dr William Naphy (University of Aberdeen), Dr Andrew Spicer (University of Exeter), Dr Peter Maxwell-Stuart (University of Aberdeen), and Dr Penny Roberts (University of Warwick) for friendship and help. Finally, I reserve my deepest gratitude to my family for supporting me in more ways than one.

List of abbreviations

BHR	*Bibliothèque d'Humanisme et Renaissance*
BSHPF	*Bulletin de la Société de l'Histoire du Protestantisme Français*
CF	*Cahiers de Fanjeaux*
FH	*French History*
P&P	*Past and Present*
SCJ	*Sixteenth-Century Journal*
THR	*Travaux d'Humanisme et Renaissance*

Introduction

The French Wars of Religion remains an area of the European Reformation that benefits from lively debates and new insights. None has been more interesting than the discussion surrounding Denis Crouzet's *Les Guerriers de Dieu*.[1] Crouzet has been praised for bringing religion back into the history of sixteenth-century France but also criticized for applying a selective reading of the sources.[2] When the historiography of the French Wars of Religion had been largely dominated by the Protestant side of the story, Crouzet redressed the balance by drawing from both Protestant and Catholic sources. The importance of print culture, in the forming of opinions and patterns of behaviour, can no longer be set aside. Although the case for the importance of printing in the Protestant Reformation has been made over and over, the Catholic side of the story has been largely ignored. This book is an attempt to redress the balance of play by exploring the production and impact of Catholic propaganda.

Our modern perception of the Reformation is a tribute to the Protestant skill in rewriting history. With the Enlightenment, Catholicism came to epitomize obscurantism and superstition, and Protestantism became a herald of progress. The proponents of the budding discipline that was history adopted this line wholeheartedly. This legacy is still with us today, to the point where Protestantism is still the subject of sustained and, on the whole, sympathetic attention. Calvin's own works have pride of place in the historiography and, to a lesser degree, so do those of his lieutenants and supporters who promoted their views in print.

The Catholic writings of the period, in contrast, have attracted comparatively little interest and even less study. This constitutes an important lacuna in the historiography of the French Wars of Religion and is, to some extent, a paradox, since it was the Catholic cause that ultimately prevailed in France. For all the energy and polemical zeal that accompanied the Huguenot movement in the middle years of the sixteenth

---

[1] Denis Crouzet, *Les Guerriers de Dieu: La violence au temps des troubles de religion vers 1525–vers 1610*, 2 vols (Paris, 1990).

[2] Notably by Larissa J. Taylor, *Heresy and Orthodoxy in Sixteenth-Century Paris: François Le Picart and the Beginnings of the Catholic Reformation* (Leiden, 1999), pp. 190, 200–202, 205; Kathleen A. Parrow, 'From Defense to Resistance: Justification of Violence during the French Wars of Religion', *Transactions of the American Philosophical Society*, LXXXIII (1993), pp. 12–13.

century, its eventual achievement was limited, certainly in terms of its original ambitions. That this was a surprise to contemporaries, on both sides of the confessional divide, is well attested, even as hopes on both sides rose and sank with the ebb and flow of the fortunes of war.

The question of why France ultimately remained a Catholic country has not been properly addressed, and to do so fully is beyond the ambition and scope of the present volume. Rather, this study hopes to contribute to the discussion by putting forward what it argues was a determining factor to the majority's continuing adherence to Catholicism. The large body of Catholic literature, which has been for the most part ignored by historians of the Reformation, contributed strong and persuasive arguments to the Reformation debate. The extent to which these arguments have been largely set aside, despite their obvious qualities and the quantity in which they were produced, warrants further explanation.

There has been a recurrent association, among religious historians, between print, heterodoxy and literacy. The Enlightenment and its heir, nineteenth-century positivism, have produced the notion that the Reformation ushered in an era of progress for mankind. Although the earlier notions of progress were largely contested in the twentieth century, the association between Protestantism and progress has stuck. This is reminiscent of the theory of Max Weber who, in his much debated essay 'The Protestant ethic and the spirit of Capitalism', makes the Protestants the agents of the introduction of *Zweckrationalität* into the world.[3] The word *Zweckrationalität* can be translated loosely as denoting instrumental reason that is geared towards the pursuit of defined goals, or, to put it more prosaically, the means to an end.[4] Although Weber was writing about Lutheranism and nineteenth-century American sects, his conclusions were applied by historians to Protestantism as a whole. As a herald of 'progress', Protestantism was identified with rationalism and positivism, which are the hallmarks of nineteenth-century historiography. These values were a looking-glass that distorted the historians' reading of events and had a long-term influence on future historiography. In many ways the historiography of the Reformation still suffers from this prejudice, as noted by Mark Greengrass: 'Historians have tended to write the history of the French Reformation through the eyes of the protagonists of change.'[5]

---

[3] Max Weber, *L'éthique Protestante et L'esprit du Capitalisme, Les Sectes Protestantes et L'Esprit du Capitalisme* (Paris, 1965).

[4] E. Gellner, 'L'animal qui évite les gaffes, ou un faisceau d'hypothèses', in P. Birnbaum and J. Leca, eds, *Sur L'individualisme* (Paris, 1991), pp. 25–44, p. 40.

[5] Mark Greengrass, 'The Psychology of Religious Violence', *FH*, V: 4 (1991), pp. 467–74, p. 467.

Printing is therefore inextricably linked with the emergence of the Reformation and, at first glance, the coincidence of the two 'revolutions' may curtail further objections. The fact that printing had already reached maturity as a trade and means of communication by the time the Reformation had taken hold, however, is too often forgotten. The association between printing and the Reformation was established predominantly by scholars of the Lutheran Reformation. It seems that, in the Empire, printing worked as a decentralizing force which was served by the political fragmentation and extensive urbanization of this region of Europe. The Lutheran movement merged in time with a wider movement of disaffection, among the urban semi-literate élite, which carried it like a tsunami wave. Printing, and particularly the *Flügschriften* in the first instance, was the chosen medium for the expression of this disaffection and coincident ideological and religious message. Consequently, the association between printing and Reformed ideology originates in a symbiotic relationship that emerged in the first decades of the Lutheran Reformation. This 'German paradigm' has much to answer for the predominant view that the Reformation went hand in hand with such innovations as printing.

Although Protestants are almost universally recognized as heralds of progress, in France they conspicuously failed to convince the large French majority who remained Catholic. This calls for a reassessment of the seemingly universal equation between the success of the Reformation and print. France could not be any more at odds with this paradigm. Before the Reformation had made inroads into France, the printing presses had already been harnessed by what posterity has dubbed the 'forces of reaction'. In the sixteenth century, Paris was the largest printing centre in the kingdom as well as the royal capital. Within Paris, print shops were clustered around the institutions that provided them with their livelihood: the University of Paris, the Parlement and the Crown. The Renaissance historians have conjured up a picture of printing workshops haunted by forward-looking humanists. Conservative theologians, lawyers and clerks on Crown business, however, were more likely to be their best clients.[6] The sixteenth-century French book was dominated by three institutions which remained conservatively Catholic throughout the sixteenth century.

The large body of Catholic material that these institutions fostered has nonetheless received little attention. In the absence of a usable bibliography of sixteenth-century French Reformation material, it is

---

[6] Denis Pallier, 'Les réponses catholiques', in Roger Chartier and Henri-Jean Martin, eds, *Histoire de l'Édition Française*, 3 vols (Paris, 1983), I, pp. 327–47, p. 328.

very difficult to reconstruct the full picture of the confessional debate.
Given the imbalance in the historiography, the work of a large number
of very prominent Catholic figures, such as Antoine de Mouchy, Robert
Ceneau and René Benoist, has been virtually ignored. By contrast, the
work of relatively obscure secondary figures of the Protestant movement has been recently edited and published.[7] Those Catholic authors
who have been the subject of some scholarly attention are systematically denigrated even by those who have studied them. Thus, Giese,
author of a bibliography of Artus Désiré: 'He distinguished himself less
for his intellectual qualities than for the violence and intransigence of
his attitude.'[8] I should like to argue, having read a substantial proportion of these men's writings, that such judgements spring from an
historiographical bias rather than familiarity with the sources. The
intellectual qualities of two of these authors, Antoine de Mouchy and
Robert Ceneau, were noted at Trent by an Italian cardinal who suggests
that these were men of exceptional talent.[9] Far from being marginal
figures of the Church, these polemical authors were pillars of the establishment and represented the 'conservative party' identified with the
Faculty of Theology and the Parlement of Paris.

The distinctions that were drawn between Protestant and Catholic
mentalités are largely arbitrary and flow from the Enlightenment identification of the Reformation with reason and of Catholicism with
superstition. As will be argued in the following chapters, this identification clearly transpires in the historiography of the French Wars of
Religion. The material analysed provides numerous examples of the
cross-fertilization between the Catholic and Protestant mental worlds
which essentially drew from the same sources. For example, anti-Protestant arguments developed in France during the French Wars of Religion
were later used in the context of polemic with Calvinists in Lutheran
Germany.[10] These arguments do not belong to any confession in particular but were used indiscriminately by one group against another.

---

[7] The publishing house Droz has made a virtue of editing these texts. For a recent
example see the anonymous *Discours merveilleux de la vie, actions et deportements de
Catherine de Medici, Royne-mère* edited by Nicole Cazauran (Geneva, 1995), which is
'the most vitriolic attack' on Catherine de Medici according to R. J. Knecht, *Catherine
De' Medici* (London, 1998), p. 285.

[8] Frank S. Giese, *Artus Désiré Priest and Pamphleteer of the Sixteenth Century* (Chapel
Hill, 1973), p. 35; Crouzet, *Guerriers de Dieu*, I, pp. 61, 75, 191; II, p. 287.

[9] Alain Tallon, *La France et le Concile de Trente (1518–1563)* (Rome, 1997), pp. 741–
2.

[10] See the work of Bodo Nischan, *Lutherans and Calvinists in the Age of Confessionalization* (Aldershot, 1999), p. 215 and *Prince, People, and Confession: The Second
Reformation in Brandenburg* (Philadelphia, 1994), p. 53.

It can be argued that the French Wars of Religion were lost and won by the ability of Catholics and Huguenots to create and to block competing narratives and representations of each other. The Protestant representation of Catholicism is more familiar to the modern reader because it achieved greater notoriety with time. One of the tenets of this book is that Catholic representations were nonetheless more successful in the short term in fostering distrust and hatred of the Protestants.

Catholic printing at this time is characterized by the increasing number of works in the vernacular, split equally between theological defences of tenets of the faith and offensive (in both senses of the word) attacks on the character of the Protestants themselves. It is with this latter category, overlooked in the historiography because of its distasteful and embarrassing nature that this work is primarily concerned. In a 1980 article, Wylie Sypher made inroads in the jungle of a polemical genre which had been previously ignored by historians of the French Wars of Religion. Although wrongly suggesting that this historiographical oversight had been caused by a 'scarcity of surviving work', he duly noted the disdain of many historians for this genre which 'deliberately wallowed "in triviality, in filthy vulgarity"'.[11] Wylie Sypher brought the names of Antoine de Mouchy, Gentian Hervet, René Benoist, Jean de la Vacquerie, Antoine du Val, Jean Gay and Artus Désiré to the attention of the academic community. The significance of these authors has since been acknowledged by historians, and has motivated much of this research.[12]

Catholic polemic was at once grounded in tradition, drawing from familiar arguments which had been available to previous generations of writers, and contemporary, demonstrating the ability to exploit and respond to every twist and turn of new circumstances and events. The majority of the polemical material which forms the central focus of this study had not been read since the sixteenth century, even where its existence was known. The themes developed in the analytical chapters have been drawn from a sample of about a hundred titles, overwhelmingly Catholic in persuasion, all of which were published prior to the massacre of St Bartholomew's Day.

From the mid 1550s and throughout the French Wars of Religion a rhetoric of exclusion was spun by Catholic authors who concentrated on portraying the Protestants in the worst possible light. Catholic theologians were exasperated by a royal policy, wavering between repression

---

[11] Wylie Sypher, G., 'Faisant ce qu'il leur vient a plaisir: The image of Protestantism in French Catholic Polemic on the Eve of the Religious Wars', *SCJ*, XI (1980), pp. 59–84 (pp. 61–2).

[12] Crouzet, *Guerriers de Dieu*, I, pp. 201–6.

and pacification, that was unable to re-establish religious concord. The period leading up to the Surprise de Meaux in 1567, and the abandonment by Catherine de Medici of the policy of conciliation, was crucial for the development and success of the Protestant cause.[13] The ability of Catholics, unfettered by censorship, to produce anti-Protestant material in vast quantities during this period should be taken into account in assessing the failure of the French Reformation.

Chapter 1 is devoted to a discussion of the differences between the French and German Reformations in terms of the vernacular and censorship. The next two chapters are concerned with the problem of violence in the French Wars of Religion and the impact of Catholic polemic on the emerging public opinion. Chapters 4 and 5 explore the portrayal of Protestantism and the Protestant response in the opening years of the French Wars of Religion. The next chapter addresses the use of the 'world turned upside down' and the reversal of gender roles to undermine the impact of the Reformation. The last two chapters outline the recourse in polemic to the topos of the Albigensians and their subsequent adoption as Protestant martyrs.

---

[13] Olivier Christin, 'From Repression to Pacification: French Royal Policy in the Face of Protestantism', in P. Benedict, G. Marnef, H. van Nierop and M. Venard, eds, *Reformation, Revolt, and Civil War in France and the Netherlands, 1555–1585* (Amsterdam, 1999), 201–14.

CHAPTER ONE

Print, censorship and the vernacular during the French Wars of Religion

In a seminal article, 'The Advent of Printing and the Protestant Revolt', Elizabeth Eisenstein argued that Protestantism had successfully harnessed the relatively new medium of printing, whereas Catholicism had not.[1] This model was borne out by work on the Lutheran Reformation, the conclusions of which were applied to the Reformation as a whole. In the dedication of Jean-François Gilmont's *La Réforme et le Livre*, a tribute is paid to the Reformed book and those who contributed to the 'progress of humanity'.[2] This implies that Catholics contributed little to the book revolution, a view that has been passed on to us through several generations of historians. In the nineteenth century, for example, the Baron de Ruble described the Faculty of Theology of Paris as composed of 'doctors pickled in scholastic, little to be feared in itself, had it not ruled over an army of scribes and imps ... always ready to break the public peace'.[3]

The history of the Reformation in France has largely been written from the point of view of the agents of change.[4] For the same reason the history of the French religious book is dominated by the role of Geneva and the Protestant movement. I should like to challenge Eisenstein's premise, at least as far as France is concerned, that the Protestants were

---

[1] Elizabeth Eisenstein, 'The Advent of Printing and the Protestant Revolt: A New Approach to the Disruption of Western Christendom', in R. M. Kingdon, ed., *Transition and Revolution: Problems and Issues of European Renaissance and Reformation History* (Minneapolis, 1974), pp. 235–70.

[2] J.-F. Gilmont, *La Réforme et Le Livre: l'Europe de l'imprimé, 1517–v.1570* (Paris, 1990).

[3] Baron de Ruble, 'L'Arrestation de Jean de Hans et le Tumulte de Saint-Médard (Decembre 1561)', *Bulletin de la Société de l'Histoire de Paris et de l'Ile de France*, XIII (1886), pp. 85–96, p. 87.

[4] Greengrass, 'Psychology of Religious Violence', p. 467; also J. K. Farge, *Le Parti Conservateur au XVIe siècle: Université et Parlement de Paris à l'époque de la Renaissance et de la Réforme* (Paris, 1992), p. 25: 'En raison d'une absence d'étude scientifique des élites et des institutions conservatrices du seizième siècle, les historiens ont parfois été amenés à faire leurs les opinions des hommes "nouveaux" ... Si l'on ajoute à cette négligence le danger omniprésent pour tout historien d'adopter la perspective de son propre siècle, on se trouve alors menacé de mésestimer les traditionnalistes, et de les juger tout simplement comme ennemis des "lumières" et du progrès. On court ainsi le risque de prendre à tort l'histoire d'une mentalité minoritaire pour l'histoire de l'époque entière.'

better at harnessing the new medium of printing than the 'forces of reaction'. French Catholics were in a much better position than their German counterparts to fight back against the Reformers. A very fierce campaign of anti-Protestant polemic was the Catholics' answer to what Robert Kingdon called 'the flood tide' of evangelical books from Geneva.[5] French Catholic print in the vernacular has been understudied and underestimated by many historians of the French Wars of Religion. Its quantity and impact was considerable and it enabled French Catholics to compete on an equal footing with the Genevan Reformers.

From the outset, the University and the Parlement of Paris reacted very quickly to the spread of the evangelical message in France. The Faculty of Theology condemned Luther in 1521 and remained vigilant throughout the first half of the sixteenth century. The printing of vernacular bibles, the hallmark of the Reformation, was banned in 1525.[6] An index of books forbidden by the theologians, backed by the Parlement, was issued in the 1540s.[7] At the same time, the Edict of Fontainebleau transferred the repression of heresy from the ecclesiastical courts to the secular courts.[8] In 1547, Henri II recognized the authority of the Faculty of Theology to dispense authorizations to print on religious matters. The co-operation between King, Parlement and Faculty of Theology reached its high-water mark in 1551 with the Edict of Châteaubriant. This piece of legislation reinforced the co-operation between University and Parlement, as permission to print could be issued only with approval of the Faculty of Theology. A *privilège*, which had been a tool in the hands of the Parlement to protect the book trade, had to be printed on the frontispiece of the book. For works of theology, this had to be accompanied by a *permission* which gave the work the official stamp of theologians of the University of Paris.[9]

Nevertheless, the degree of co-operation between these three institutions and, as a result, the effectiveness of censorship should not be

---

[5] Robert Kingdon, *Geneva and the coming of the Wars of Religion in France, 1555–1563* (Geneva, 1956), p. 93.

[6] J. K. Farge, *Orthodoxy and Reform in early Reformation France: the Faculty of Theology of Paris, 1500–1543* (Leiden, 1985), pp. 213–19.

[7] Francis Higman, *Censorship and the Sorbonne: a bibliographical study of books in French censured by the Faculty of Theology of the University of Paris, 1520–1551* (Geneva, 1979), pp. 49–50, 52.

[8] William Monter, *Judging the French Reformation: Heresy Trials by Sixteenth-Century Parlements* (London, 1999), p. 85.

[9] Alfred Soman, 'Press, Pulpit, and Censorship in France before Richelieu', *Proceedings of the American Philosophical Society*, CXX (1976), pp. 439–63 (p. 454).

overestimated. The Crown often found itself at odds with the Parlement and the University, notably regarding questions of religion. The Concordat of Bologna (1516), which had granted the King considerable powers over Church government, did much to antagonize the theologians.[10] The Parlement was renowned for its conservatism and its attachment to the liberties of the Gallican Church that the Concordat was perceived to jeopardize.[11] These divisions grew stronger as the religious problems escalated and the Crown sought a solution beyond mere persecution. Recent scholarship has shown that the Crown came to disagree with the theologians and members of the Parlement on how best to restore religious concord.[12] Members of the University and the Parlement thought that the best way was to exterminate the Protestant heresy, while the Crown sought temporary measures of conciliation, to ultimately fall back on a legal solution.

The emergence of what Olivier Christin has called 'an impartial state' based on the 'autonomisation of political reason', however, could only be achieved through the control of the printing press.[13] In the process the Crown came into conflict with the self-styled upholders of orthodoxy, the University and the Parlement. The censoring powers of the Parlement and the University of Paris had been strengthened during the reign of Henri II but were increasingly challenged by his successors. The conservatism of the Parlement had been enhanced with the purge culminating with the execution of Anne du Bourg, suspected of heresy, in March 1560.[14] The Parlement openly came into conflict with the Crown when Catherine de Medici appointed Michel de L'Hôpital as chancellor in June 1560. L'Hôpital was unpopular among the members of the Parlement who disagreed with his conciliatory views and regarded his promotion as arising from Catherine's sudden change of policy.[15]

[10] Farge, *Orthodoxy and Reform*, p. 228.

[11] Jean du Tillet, *Memoires et advis de M. Jean du Tillet, protonotaire et secretaire du Roy tres chrestien, greffier de sa cour de Parlement faict en 1551 sur les libertés de l'église gallicane* (Paris, 1551).

[12] Mario Turchetti, 'Religious Concord and Political Tolerance in Sixteenth- and Seventeenth-Century France', *SCJ* XXII: 1 (1991), pp. 15–25; Marc Venard, 'Catholicism and Resistance to the Reformation in France, 1555–1585', in P. Benedict, G. Marnef, H. van Nierop and M. Venard, eds, *Reformation, Revolt, and Civil War in France and the Netherlands, 1555–1585* (Amsterdam, 1999), pp. 133–48.

[13] Olivier Christin, *La paix de religion: L'autonomisation de la raison politique au XVIe siècle* (Paris, 1997), p. 16.

[14] J. H. Shennan, *The Parlement of Paris* (London, 1968), p. 207.

[15] Seong-Hak Kim, 'Michel de L'Hôpital: The Visions of a Reformist Chancellor during the French Religious Wars', *Sixteenth-Century Essays and Studies*, XXXVI (Kirksville, 1997).

At a time when the views of Church, Parlement and Crown converged, censorship was fairly straightforward. On the eve of the French Wars of Religion, however, this was no longer the case. A case in point is a book that had been approved by the Parlement and the theologians but was offensive to the Crown.[16] In October 1561, this inflammatory anti-Protestant book provoked the reaction of the English ambassador in Paris, Throckmorton, who asked for it to be removed from circulation.[17] In compliance with the ambassador's remonstrance, Montmorency issued an order forbidding printing without the authorization of the King or his council, thus conflicting with the prerogatives of the Parlement and the Faculty of Theology.[18]

This order came in the wake of the refusal of the Parlement of Paris to ratify the edict of pacification of January 1562 that included unprecedented measures of conciliation.[19] The King had authorized Montmorency to have the Edict of January immediately printed by Charles Langelier although the Parlement had refused to ratify it.[20] On this occasion, the Crown chose to disregard the traditional prerogatives of the Parlement – which was a stepping stone towards gaining control of the printing press.[21] In 1563 this trend was reinforced by an edict of Charles IX forbidding the printing of books which did not bear royal permission endorsed by the chancellor.[22] In 1566 it culminated in the Edict of Moulins which gave the Crown sole control of the *privilège*. Theoretically, the Crown could turn its powers of censorship, originally designed to stem the flow of Protestant books, against disaffected Catholics who disapproved of the royal policy of conciliation. But it seems that even the Edict of Moulins was unsuccessful in curbing the production of anti-Protestant material in Paris or elsewhere. During the ascendancy of the Holy Catholic League, the Edict of Moulins was rendered largely

---

[16] Jean Gay, *Histoire des scismes et heresies des Albigeois conforme à celle du present: par laquelle appert que plusieurs grands princes, & seigneurs sont tombez en extremes desolations & ruynes, pour avoir favorisé aux heretiques* (Paris, 1561).

[17] Joseph Stevenson, ed., *Calendar of State Papers, Foreign series, of the reign of Elizabeth, 1561–1562*, IV: 833 (London, 1866), p. 503.

[18] Geneviève Guilleminot, 'Religion et politique à la veille des guerres civiles: Recherches sur les impressions françaises de l'année 1561', 2 vols (unpublished thesis, Ecole des Chartes, 1977), I, p. 11.

[19] Geneviève Guilleminot-Chrétien, 'Le contrôle de l'édition en France dans les année 1560: la genèse de l'édit de Moulins', in P. Aquilon and H-J. Martin, eds, *Le Livre dans l'Europe de la Renaissance: Actes du XXVIIIe Colloque international d'Etudes humanistes de Tours* (Nantes, 1988), pp. 378–85.

[20] Eugénie Droz, ed., *Chemins de l'Hérésie*, 4 vols (Geneva, 1970–76), I, p. 375; III, p. 407; and Pallier, 'Les réponses catholiques', p. 340.

[21] Guilleminot-Chrétien, 'Le contrôle de l'édition en France', pp. 382–3.

[22] Soman, 'Press, Pulpit, and censorship', p. 454.

ineffectual as the powers of censorship reverted back to the hands of the Parlement.[23] The conflict over jurisdiction meant that censorship remained largely ineffectual until the beginning of the seventeenth century.[24]

The Parlement and the University of Paris dominated the Reformation debate, competing with the Crown as well as the heterodox publications that were produced in Geneva. Until the dismissal of the chancellor Michel de L'Hôpital in 1568, the Crown, under the aegis of Catherine de Medici, pursued religious concord through dialogue.[25] In doing so, it attracted the wrath of traditionalists, lawyers in the Parlement and theologians in the University, for whom any form of dialogue, conciliation, or tolerance was anathema. Unlike in Germany, it was these self-same traditionalists who had most influence on the French book trade, both as to the amount of material published in the vernacular, and in their powers of censorship. This 'conservative party' resisted the Crown's measures of conciliation at every turn, through printed remonstrances addressed to the King, sermons from their most acclaimed preachers, and in numerous works of polemic lambasting the Protestant faith. It is this material, for the most part underresearched, that constitutes the principal source for this book.

Heralding the development of the League which openly turned against the Crown, these pamphlets were as much a protest literature as were Protestant productions. Increasingly, the anti-Protestant pamphlets were directed against the royal policy of conciliation. Preachers such as Simon Vigor and Jean de Hans did not refrain from speaking openly against the edicts of pacification that, they argued, betrayed the true religion. The pamphleteer Artus Désiré even resolved to appeal to the King of Spain, a former enemy of France, in the spring of 1561.[26] The end of the second war of religion in 1568 and the Edict of Longjumeau provoked a considerable reaction amongst Catholic authors.[27] From 1568 until

---

[23] Denis Pallier, *Recherches sur l'Imprimerie à Paris pendant la Ligue, 1585–1594* (Geneva, 1976), pp. 20, 37.

[24] Soman, 'Press, Pulpit, and censorship', pp. 457, 463; Jeffrey K. Sawyer, *Printed Poison: Pamphlet Propaganda, Faction Politics, and the Public Sphere in Early Seventeenth-Century France* (Oxford, 1990), pp. 5, 25, 46.

[25] Olivier Christin, 'From Repression to Pacification: French Royal Policy in the Face of Protestantism', in P. Benedict, G. Marnef, H. van Nierop and M. Venard, eds, *Reformation, Revolt and Civil War in France and the Netherlands 1555–1585* (Amsterdam, 1999), 201–14.

[26] Edouard de Barthélemy, ed., *Journal d'un curé Ligueur de Paris sous les trois derniers Valois* (Paris, 1866), pp. 41, 43; Giese, *Artus Désiré*, pp. 25, 28–30.

[27] Simon Vigor, *Oraison funebre prononcee aux obseques, de treshaute, tres-puissante, & tres-catholique Princesse, ma Dame Elizabeth de France, Royne des Espagnes, prononcee en l'Eglise nostre Dame de Paris, le XXV. du mois d'Octobre 1568* (Paris, 1568), sigs F2ᵛ, H4ʳ; Giese, *Artus Désiré*, pp. 168, 179, 180.

the massacre of St Bartholomew in 1572, the Crown was openly attacked by a number of authors, notably Artus Désiré, René Benoist and Simon Vigor.[28]

If censorship was unable to curb the excesses of Catholic polemic, it had an adverse effect on the Protestant productions. In Germany, Robert Scribner remarked that the Catholic response was 'too meagre and too limited to have any large-scale or long-term impact' – a view that is often found in the historiography.[29] In France, however, the situation is reversed: Protestant printing was apparently not in a position to compete quickly and effectively with Catholic attacks on the Reformation. Geneva has been rightly identified as the source of the Calvinist message in print. On the other hand, it is clear that Calvin and the Geneva city council were unwilling to engage Catholic polemic on its own terms and it was left to clandestine printing centres within France to do this. Because of the tight censorship that was operated in both Paris and Geneva, the badly needed Protestant response was limited in its scope and efficacy.

There were good political reasons why Calvin's Geneva was ill-equipped to answer the French challenge. In the very sensitive period immediately preceding the French Wars of Religion, Calvin himself was busy fighting his own enemies within Geneva and establishing himself in the face of other Reformed centres. As Calvin gained control of the city of Geneva, there was a hardening of the Calvinist ecclesiology which is typified by the execution of Michel Servet. At the same time, Calvin was also struggling to distinguish his theology from other Protestant strands, Lutheran and Sacramentarian. As late as 1558, Calvin complained that 'in France they make no distinction of parties, but group under the name of Sacramentarians, all who do not approve of the sacrifice of their mass'.[30] Geneva was mostly concerned with domestic matters and the internal debate within the Reformation, and could not hand over its printing presses to the controversialists who sought to defend the Protestant cause in France.

Calvin's own attitude towards polemic was ambiguous, especially after the bruising effects of the Nicodemite controversy and the debate with Westphal over the sacraments in the 1550s. It can be inferred from his response to doctrinal disputes with other Reformed centres that

[28] Barthélemy, ed., *Journal d'un curé Ligueur*, p. 134.

[29] Robert W. Scribner, *For the Sake of Simple Folk: Popular Propaganda for the German Reformation* (Oxford, 1994), p. 239.

[30] Jules Bonnet, ed., *Letters of Calvin*, 4 vols (New York, 1972), III, p. 404.

Calvin entered the debate reluctantly and only out of necessity, and preferred to leave the most virulent attacks unanswered.[31] For example, the question of the sacraments was the source of much debate among Reformed theologians, and Calvin became involved only unwillingly in order to calm things down:

> For my own part, I had endeavoured in all my writings with simplicity to aim at such moderation as might be calculated to satisfy all persons of plain good sense. But when I had striven to bring about a good understanding among all the parties, some wrong-headed polemics with their importunity have drawn me on by force to the contest.[32]

The internal debate within the Reformation, notably regarding the sacraments, played a divisive role and prevented Reformers from answering contemporary attacks effectively. Catholics exploited this apparent division among Reformers and argued that the Reformation was nothing but division and dissension.[33] Calvin was frequently challenged personally by Catholic authors, but there is no evidence that he responded to any of these challenges.[34] If Calvin himself was reluctant to engage in polemic against the Catholics, the Geneva council was equally reluctant to be seen as encouraging confessional divisions within France. The independence of Geneva as a Protestant city-state had been won from the Duke of Savoy with the help of the city of Berne, itself a member of the Swiss confederation which kept good relations with France.[35]

---

[31] Jean-François Gilmont, *Jean Calvin et le Livre Imprimé* (Geneva, 1997), pp. 371–87. Gilmont includes a very helpful table of Calvin's publications which demonstrates that the focus of his writings shifted in the 1550s to biblical commentaries. I am grateful to Professor Pettegree for pointing this out to me.

[32] Bonnet, ed., *Letters of Calvin*, IV, p. 404. The context of this letter is undoubtedly the publication of Joachim Westphal's, *Apologia confesiones de coena contra coruptelas ed calumnias Ioannes Calvini* (Oberursel, 1558). I owe thanks to Dr Mark Taplin for this reference.

[33] Stanislas Hozius exploits the division between Calvin and Westphal in *Des sectes et heresies de nostre temps: traicte composé premierement en Latin, par reverend Pere en Dieu monseigneur Stanislas Hozie, Evesque de Varme en Pouloigne, dedié au roy de Pouloigne, & nouvellement mis en François* (Paris, 1561), pp. 81–3.

[34] Notably Antoine du Val, *Les contrarietez & contredictz, qui se trouvent en la doctrine de Iean Calvin, de Luther & autres nouveaux evangelistes de nostre temps* (Paris, 1561), sig. A1ʳ. Du Val refers to two editions of Calvin's *Institution de la religion chrestienne*, one published in Geneva in 1545 and a clandestine French one dated 1557; Gay, *Histoire des scismes et heresies des Albigeois*, pp. 2, 25; and Nicolas Durand, *Lettres du Chevallier de Villegaignon sur les remonstrances, a la Royne Mere du Roy la souveraine Dame, touchant la Religion* (1561), sig. B3ʳ.

[35] Paul Chaix, *Recherches sur l'imprimerie à Genève de 1550 à 1564* (Geneva, 1978), p. 80.

The city council was therefore very careful that no books printed within Geneva carried any ambiguous messages of dissension, which would discredit its political credibility.[36] Censorship was tightened as a result of the perceived role of Geneva in the political events in France.[37] In January 1561, Charles IX issued an official complaint to ask for the stemming of the flow of books which were sent into France from Geneva. This complaint, triggered by the recent conspiracy of Amboise, alleged that the books had encouraged sedition.[38] In a very carefully worded letter to the King, Calvin denied knowledge of the conspiracy and condemned any Genevan citizens or ministers who might have been involved.[39] Until his death in 1564, Calvin discouraged armed rebellion as he was still hoping that the Reformation in France could gain political legitimacy.[40] In a recent paper, Philip Benedict has brought new light to the discrepancies which lay between Geneva's official upholding of royal authority and the involvement of Protestant ministers in acts of rebellion. He argues that the image of Protestantism (which has been reproduced largely in the historiography) as basically law-abiding is the result of careful engineering on the part of the Genevan authorities.[41]

Recipients of the censorship exercised in Geneva include Crespin's *Histoire des Martyrs* in 1554, at a time when Geneva was uncomfortable with the word 'martyr', as implying political disobedience (the first Christian martyrs had refused to pay homage to the Emperors).[42] Others include Conrad Badius' *Satyres de la cuisine du pape* (1560) which was seen as being too inflammatory.[43] Virulent anti-papal material found another outlet in Lyon, particularly in the year 1562 when the city was briefly in the hands of the Protestant forces.[44] But even in Lyon, censorship was exerted, as is shown by the burning of a tract that was deemed

---

[36] Gilmont, *Jean Calvin et le Livre Imprimé*, pp. 315–51.

[37] Catherine Santschi, *La Censure à Genève au XVIIe siècle* (Geneva, 1978), pp. 16, 25–6.

[38] Kingdon, *Geneva and the coming of the Wars*, pp. 34, 93.

[39] Bonnet, ed., *Letters of Calvin*, IV, p. 167.

[40] W. Nijenhuis, *'Ecclesia Reformata': Studies on the Reformation*, 2 vols (New York, 1994), especially 'The limits of civil disobedience in Calvin's latest known sermons: the development of his ideas of the right of civil resistance', II, pp. 73–97.

[41] Philip Benedict, 'The Dynamics of Protestant Militancy: France, 1555–1563', in P. Benedict, G. Marnef, H. van Nierop and M. Venard, eds, *Reformation, Revolt, and Civil War in France and the Netherlands, 1555–1585* (Amsterdam, 1999), pp. 35–50.

[42] J.-F. Gilmont, *Bibliographie des éditions de Jean Crespin 1550–1572* (Verviers, 1981), pp. 47–8.

[43] H. A. Shaw, ed., *Conrad Badius and the Comedie du Pape Malade* (Philadelphia, 1934), pp. 42–3.

[44] Gilmont, *Jean Calvin et le Livre Imprimé*, pp. 335–6, 338, 344.

too contentious in 1563.[45] The work of Pierre Viret, which could be construed as encouraging iconoclasm, was camouflaged under the title of earlier works which had already been approved.[46] Calvin's close associates Nicolas des Gallars and Antoine de la Roche Chandieu were given relatively free rein to vent their anger against the persecutions in France. François Hotman and Augustin Marlorat wrote extensively in defence of the Protestant cause after the failure of the conspiracy of Amboise, responding directly to Catholic pamphlets. It should be noted, however, that these works were not printed in Geneva, or at least did not bear the Genevan imprint. Polemical authors used false imprints to circumvent censorship and the ban that had been imposed within France against Genevan books.

In these clandestine pamphlets, Catholic attacks were answered point by point, following key events, like the affair of the rue St Jacques, the conjuration of Amboise or the massacre of Vassy. For this reason the polemic had to be produced quickly and locally, within France rather than in Geneva. The bulk of anti-Catholic propaganda produced around the tumult of Amboise, for example, reflects first-hand knowledge of the events and was probably produced locally. The repeated dedication to Catherine de Medici also suggests that the pamphlets were intended to have an impact at Court. The danger of printing and disseminating these tracts was considerable. For example, Hotman's *Epistre envoyée au Tigre de la France* created such outrage that a scapegoat was singled out and hanged. Contemporary accounts relate how a bookseller and printer, Martin Lhommet, was found in possession of a copy and tortured to reveal the identity of its author. When he was about to be executed, not having confessed to anything, a merchant from Rouen attempted to moderate the fervour of the crowd of onlookers. The crowd turned on the unfortunate merchant who was saved by the city watch only to be thrown in prison and to be executed in turn on the spot where Lhommet had died.[47]

As a result, the onus of the Protestant response to Catholic polemic is marked by anonymity and clandestinity. Authors and printers, to avoid detection and arrest, often remained unnamed and their pieces were

---

[45] R. Kingdon, *Geneva and the Consolidation of the French Protestant Movement 1564–1572* (Geneva, 1967), p. 140.

[46] For instance Pierre Viret, *De la vraye et fausse religion, touchant les voeus et les sermens licites et illicites: et notamment touchant les voeus de perpetuelle continence, et les voeus d'anatheme et d'execration, et les sacrifices d'hosties humaines, et de l'excommunication en toutes religions* ([Geneva], 1560); Stuart Foster, 'Pierre Viret and France, 1559–1565' (unpublished Ph.D. thesis, University of St Andrews, May 2000).

[47] Charles Read, ed., *François Hotman: Le Tigre de 1560* (Geneva, 1970), pp. 9–12.

usually short and badly printed; many were also very bitter in tone, as they were written by those who had suffered personally from the persecution in France. Nicolas des Gallars was in Paris at the time of the affair of the rue St Jacques and wrote to Calvin for guidance.[48] This is also the case of Antoine de la Roche Chandieu who was able to write his history of the persecution of Paris from first-hand experience. The polemical tracts of François Hotman, who seems to have been driven by a personal hatred of the Guise family and was implicated directly in the conspiracy of Amboise, were printed on illegal printing presses, carefully omitting the names of both place of publication and printer from the title-page.[49] All this points to a culture of rebellion that ran parallel to Geneva's refusal to be implicated in events in France. This situation changed somewhat after the beginning of the war when Protestants gained cities and *places de sûreté*. But the precariousness of the Protestant holdings within France – which changed hands several times in the course of the wars – curtailed any attempts to compete with what Paris or Geneva could produce. For example, the Protestant printing press of La Rochelle, established in 1563 by Barthélemy Berton, 'printed almost nothing but political pamphlets ... mediocre in typographic quality because it had a very limited font and had to keep using the same deteriorating type again and again'.[50] French Reformed polemic was therefore of a very different nature from its Lutheran counterpart. This is not reflected in the historiography which has predominantly concentrated on Geneva, while largely ignoring the efforts of Protestant authors within France.

The use of the vernacular that was made during the French Wars of Religion also disqualifies further comparisons with Lutheran Germany. With the Edict of Villers-Cotterêts (1539), François I made French the official language of the Crown and thereafter all royal edicts were printed in French rather than Latin. The edict also had a profound impact on the legal profession, which began to use French rather than Latin, in court and in treatises of law. Although it is difficult to provide an estimate, royal edicts form a sizeable proportion of books that have been inventoried so far by the French Book Project. The Church, usually

---

[48] Robert M. Kingdon, ed., *Registres de la compagnie des pasteurs de Genève au temps de Calvin*, 12 vols (Geneva, 1962–95), II (1962), pp. 128–34.

[49] [François Hotman], *L'Histoire du tumulte d'Amboyse advenu au moys de Mars, M. D. LX.* (1560); Read, ed., *Le Tigre de 1560*.

[50] Robert M. Kingdon, *Myths about the St. Bartholomew's Day Massacres 1572–1576* (London, 1988), p. 24.

opposed to the use of the vernacular, was very quick to react to the new taste for books in French, especially in the second half of the sixteenth century.[51] The widespread use of the vernacular by French Catholic theologians alone should be enough to dispel any comparisons with the Lutheran Reformation.[52]

Luther's use of the vernacular was geared towards bringing his message to as many people as possible, but particularly to the unlearned, as a reaction to university learning. Scholars of the Lutheran Reformation have argued that, to a certain extent, the appeal to the unlearned was a rhetorical convention that was used by Luther in the face of the monopoly of the Church on learning.[53] The words used in this context are problematic as the 'unlearned' points to illiteracy in Latin and not necessarily to lack of learning. The association between the laity and Latin 'illiteracy' justified the use of the vernacular in the eyes of the Reformers but was problematic for the Catholics who always felt obliged to justify their departure from Latin. The use of the vernacular in religious discourse was never intended for the illiterate (in the modern sense) but for the *illiterati*: an élite literate in the vernacular but not in Latin. The historiography of the Reformation nonetheless associates the use of the vernacular with a liberating movement of the 'masses', a 'democratization' of religion. Peter Matheson has recently argued that the Reformation was a liberating movement for the common man and woman and that polemic was the literature of the 'underdog'.[54]

On the whole, both Catholics and Protestants were concerned with the impact of polemic on the 'unlearned'. This idea reproduced contemporary rhetoric often found in Catholic polemic that the Protestants were catering to the unlearned and the *femmelettes* (silly women). The fear of social upheaval dominated the Catholic criticism of the Reformation. From the Peasants' War of 1525 onwards, the spectre of a 'revolution' turning the world upside down was brandished by the Catholics as one of the dangers of the Reformation. In France, numerous pamphlets argued, especially after the conspiracy of Amboise, that the aim of the Protestants was to abolish the monarchy and establish a commonwealth where everything was shared in common (and first of

---

[51] Francis Higman, 'Premières réponses catholiques aux écrits de la Réforme en France, 1525 c. 1540', THR, CCCXXVI (1998), pp. 497–514.

[52] Mark U. Edwards, Jr, 'Catholic Controversial Literature, 1518–1555: Some Statistics', *Archiv für Reformationsgeschichte*, LXXIX (1988), pp. 189–205.

[53] Bob Scribner, 'Heterodoxy, literacy and print in early German Reformation', in P. Billen and A. Hudson, eds, *Heresy and Literacy 1000–1530* (Cambridge, 1994), pp. 255–78, pp. 265–7.

[54] Peter Matheson, *The Rhetoric of the Reformation* (Edinburgh, 1998), pp. 7, 22–3.

all women).[55] Whether this was more than a literary and rhetorical device, the use of which can be traced back to the Middle Ages, remains to be shown. One cannot ignore, however, the concern for the 'opinion of the common man' expressed on numerous occasions on both sides of the confessional divide.[56] Unlike German Catholics, the French were quick to respond to Protestant material in the vernacular justifying their stance, like Antoine du Val in 1559: 'so that no one, particularly the simple ignorant, is abused by such books'.[57] In a sermon, printed in 1561, René Benoist spelt out the reason for upholding the Catholic faith: 'Many more people are firm in the belief of the true presence of Christ in the host than those who hold the contrary. ... Moreover this number includes those who are instructed and maintained in truth by the holy spirit, namely the simple and the poor.'[58]

This sermon was given on the feast day of Corpus Christi of 1560, at a time when this statement was challenged by the enthusiasm and daring of the Protestant movement. Although Catholic theologians were alarmed by the increasing numbers of Protestants, they seldom swayed from the second statement: faith was upheld by the 'simple'.[59] According to this view it was necessary to write in the vernacular so that the 'simple', who were most at risk from heretical conversion, would be instructed. Whether Catholics responded to the influx of Protestant books coming from Geneva, or perpetuated a tradition begun by the likes of François le Picart and Nicole Grenier, the preoccupation with the 'masses' was a leitmotiv of the French Wars of Religion.[60] As Artus

---

[55] René Benoist, *Brieve Response a quelque remonstrance faicte a la roine mere du Roy, par ceux qui se disent persecutez pour la parolle de Dieu* (Paris, 1561), sig. A6ᵛ; [Marlorat, Augustin], *Remonstrance a la royne mere du Roy, par ceux qui sont persecutez pour la parole de DIEU. En laquelle ils rendent raison des principaux articles de la Religion, & qui sont aujourdhuy en dispute* ([Paris], 1561), sig. B6ᵛ.

[56] Edmond Auger, *Sommaire des Heresies, abus, impietez et blasphemes qui sont en la Cene des Calvinistes, & nouvelle Religion pretendue reformee* (Paris 1568), sigs E4ʳ⁻ᵛ.

[57] Antoine du Val, *Mirouer des Calvinistes et Armure des Chrestiens, pour rembarrer les Lutheriens & nouveaux Evangelistes de Genéve (sic)* (Paris, 1562), sig. A2ᵛ.

[58] René Benoist, *La Manière de cognoistre salutairement Jésus Christ* (Paris, 1561) sig. D1ᵛ.

[59] Francis Higman, '"Il seroit trop plus decent respondre en Latin": les controversistes catholiques du XVIe siècle face aux écrits réformés', *THR*, CCCXXVI (1998), pp. 515–30.

[60] Larissa Taylor, *Soldiers of Christ: Preaching in the Late Medieval and Reformation France* (Oxford, 1992); R. E. Hallmark, 'Defenders of the faith: the case of Nicole Grenier', *Renaissance Studies*, XI: 2 (1997), pp. 123–40. Hallmark's opening remark is typical of the way Catholics are perceived in the historiography (p. 123): 'In both France and Germany, Catholic apologists were slower – and obviously more reluctant – to respond in the same vein. French exponents of orthodoxy were even more leaden-footed than their German counterparts, though their response was not perhaps as tardy as has sometimes been suggested.'

Désiré wrote: 'Heresy needs to be destroyed in France by French books; one book in the French language will be more fruitful than thirty in Latin.'[61]

Catholics probably misunderstood and overestimated the impact of the Protestant printed book on the masses: it was the literate élite that were most at risk of being converted to Protestantism. It is very difficult to gauge the effect that printed polemic had on the population at large. By all accounts, printed books had only a small audience predominantly composed of the urban élite. It could be argued that the Catholic fears concerning the Calvinist teaching reaching the unlearned were unjustified. There was a great difference in tone between the Lutheran and Calvinist movements that can be explained by a general shift in the Reformation's attitude towards university learning. Lutheranism was at first imbued with anti-intellectualism that was later associated with social protest.[62] There definitely was a revolutionary element in the *Flügschriften*, where the university-trained Catholic was confounded by the simplicity of the common man self-taught in the Scriptures. Here is the transcription of a dialogue published in 1524 by Hans Sachs, typical of the *Flügschriften* genre, between a Canon and a shoemaker:

> Canon: ... the laity should not be dealing with Scripture ... where do you lay folk want to learn all this? Most of you cannot read.
> Shoemaker: Christ said, John 6, 'They will be taught by God'.
> Canon: There must be some sort of ability involved too, or what use would the universities be?
> Shoemaker: Which university did John go to?[63]

After the dramatic outcome of the Peasants' War in 1525 and the subsequent denunciation by Luther of radical movements such as the Anabaptists, the fashion of the *Flügschriften* had passed. Criticism of university learning was increasingly associated with the radical Reformation and was used by the Catholic opponents of Luther to drag down the whole Reformed edifice.[64] Robert Scribner has shown that, to a certain extent, the 'man in the street' was a myth, a rhetorical device

---

[61] Giese, *Artus Désiré*, p. 125.

[62] Geoffrey Dipple, *Antifraternalism and Anticlericalism in the German Reformation: Johann Eberlin von Günzburg and the Campaign against the Friar* (Aldershot, 1996), pp. 214–15.

[63] Hans Sachs, *Disputation zwischen einem Chorherren und Schuchmacher darin das wort gottes / und ein recht Christlich wesen verfochten würdt* (1524). I am grateful to Dr Fiona Campbell (Newnham College, Cambridge) for this reference and the translation.

[64] Carlos Gilly, 'Das Sprichwort "Die Gelehrten, die Verkehrten" in der Toleranzliteratur des 16. Jahrhunderts', in Jean-Georges Roth and Simon L. Verheus, eds, *Anabaptistes et dissidents au XVIe siècle, Actes du colloque international d'histoire anabaptiste 1994* (Baden-Baden, 1987), pp. 159–72.

conjured up by the Lutherans to gather support among the semi-literate urban élite. Nonetheless it provided grounds for the Catholics to accuse the Reformation of being anti-intellectual; for example, John Eck in his *Lieux communs* (1539): 'It seems that the Lutheran heretics simulate disputation ... not before the lettered and learned in theology: but in front of the lay unlearned and vulgar.'[65]

In reaction to this criticism, Reformers moved away from the *Flügschriften* and its connotation of radicalism in order to save the essential tenets of the Reformation. This change in tone is best illustrated by the controversy surrounding Sebastian Castellio. Castellio had voiced criticism at the execution of Michel Servet and published *De l'impunité des hérétiques* (1554) which was condemned in Geneva.[66] His work still bore the mark of the radical Reformation, which had been repudiated by the second generation of Reformers. In his translation of the Bible published in Basel in 1555, Castellio pitched the word of God against 'worldly wisdom' and cited the German proverb 'the more learned the more wicked'.[67] The condemnation of Castellio is symptomatic of a clear departure from the radicalism of the early years of the Reformation.

The difference between these two different intellectual worlds was reflected in the use of language. As much as Luther had used the language of the 'man in the street' to disseminate his message, the language of Genevan Reformers was the language of the literate élite. Calvin surrounded himself with men of great literary merit, such as Theodore Beza who had competed on the Parisian scene with the likes of Joachim du Bellay and Ronsard before the Reformation.[68] Francis Higman has argued persuasively that the dissemination of Calvin's vernacular writings contributed to the refining of the French language.[69] By modern standards, Calvin's French is remarkably concise and easy to read compared with that of other contemporary authors. But this reflects our own perceptions rather than contemporary ones, as Larissa Taylor has suggested: 'Modern readers have more in common with

---

[65] John Eck, *Les lieux communs de Jean Ekius, contre Luther* (Lyon, 1551), sig. D7r.

[66] The response from Geneva was very fierce, notably Jean Calvin, *Declaration pour maintenir la vraie foy ... contre les erreurs detestables de Michel Servet* (Geneva, 1554); Jean Calvin and Theodore Beza, *Responses de Jean Calvin et Theodore de Bèze aux argumens et calomnies d'un qui s'efforce de renverser par tous moyens la doctrine de la providence secrete de Dieu* (Geneva, 1559).

[67] Quoted in Gilly, 'Die Gelehrten die Verkehrten', p. 169; Scribner, 'Heterodoxy, literacy and print', p. 266.

[68] K. Cameron, K. M. Hall and F. Higman, eds, *Théodore de Bèze: Abraham sacrifiant* (Geneva, 1967), p. 46.

[69] F. Higman, 'Linearity in Calvin's thought', *THR*, CCCXXVI (1998), pp. 391–418.

educated sixteenth-century humanists than with "le menu peuple".'[70]
The linearity of Calvin's French, which has been observed by Francis
Higman, heralds the predominance of our own written culture. The
written facilitates the construction of linear, rational thoughts such as
dominate our own mental world; but sixteenth-century media were still
dominated by the oral, and the written was only starting to change the
way people formulated thoughts.

Although, from the point of view of systematic theology, Calvin's
Institution de la religion chrestienne (1541) remained in a league of its
own, Reformed polemic was far behind what the Faculty of Theology
was able to produce. Although French Catholics were incapable of
competing with Calvin in devising theological treatises in French, their
use of a less refined language allowed them to reach a wider audience.
Authors notably from the Sorbonne preferred Latin but did not refrain
from using the vernacular in extremely crude attacks against Protestantism. In their own words, their use of the vernacular was justified by the
need to reach the unlettered who could not understand the finer points
of theology. Unfortunately for the Reformers, these crude attacks found
a ready audience among the Catholic majority who remained insensitive
to Calvin's *Institution de la religion chrestienne* or other works of
systematic theology available in French. By contrast, Calvin and other
prominent Genevan theologians, although very keen to use French in
their works of theology, failed to respond effectively to these attacks.
This task, which was deemed to be of secondary importance, fell to less
prestigious members of the Company of Pastors, notably to the body of
largely anonymous ministers who were sent to France.

The unsuitability of the German model for the French Reformation
could not be any better demonstrated. Whereas, in Germany, the evangelical authors out-published their Catholic opponents many times over,
in France, Catholic authors matched and often bested their Protestant
opponents in terms of output throughout the religious wars.[71] In Germany, Catholic authors were hard pressed to find publishers, but in
France the orthodox cause enjoyed the whole-hearted support of the
printing industry. In Germany, Luther was opposed by a small number
of theologians who moved away from Latin only with the greatest
reluctance, whereas in France the vernacular was adopted from a very
early stage. The nature of censorship in France favoured the production

---

[70] Taylor, *Soldiers of Christ*, p. 228.
[71] Authors such as Pierre Doré and René Benoist were extremely prolific. Information
from the St Andrews French Book Project files.

of virulent Catholic material, which benefited from the patronage of the University and the Parlement of Paris. The Protestant response, on the other hand, was seriously curtailed by the vulnerable political position of Geneva.

CHAPTER TWO

The problem of violence
during the French Wars of Religion

The violence of the French Wars of Religion, particularly the massacre of St Bartholomew's day, has always excited the imagination. Alexandre Dumas' novel *La Reine Margot*, that was spectacularly adapted to the screen by Patrice Chereau in 1993, is only one of many fictional accounts that this event inspired.[1] What struck the imagination of Dumas – and still fascinates the spectator of the film *La Reine Margot* – is the seemingly unprovoked violence directed at French Protestants. The press of Huguenots in the entourage of Henri de Navarre being thrown on the spears of the Paris watch or the random killing of innocents in the streets, makes a vivid impression on the viewer. Images, albeit cinematic ones, make a stronger impression than contemporary accounts of the massacres or journals of the period, and the spectator cannot help wondering how this could ever happen. In trying to answer this question, historians of the French Wars of Religion are faced with a particularly knotty problem which has generated a lively debate.

For the sake of brevity, only the historiography of the past 30 years, since publication of Janine Garrison's *Tocsin pour un massacre* (1968), will be reviewed here.[2] Characteristically for this period, the antagonism between Catholics and Protestants has been interpreted along social and economic lines, like grain riots, as a manifestation of a 'class war'. The victims of the St Bartholomew's Day massacre were described as rich Huguenots who were resented for their wealth rather than their religion. This school of thought derives from the premise that there was a social factor in the adherence to Protestantism, a theory which has been the subject of much controversy and debate. The consensus now seems to be that the evidence is much too sketchy to confirm the predominance of any one social group in the make-up

---

[1] Alexandre Dumas, *La Reine Margot* (Paris, 1845); P. Joutard, J. Estèbe, E. Labrousse and J. Lecuir, eds, *La Saint-Barthélemy: Ou les résonances d'un massacre* (Neuchâtel, 1976), pp. 116–17.

[2] Janine Garrisson-Estèbe, *Tocsin pour un massacre ou la saison des Saint-Barthélemy* (Paris, 1968).

of French Protestantism.[3] Historians have even questioned the relevance of social factors, as religion seems to be coming back centre-stage
in the historiography of the French Wars of Religion.[4]

In her seminal article 'Rites of Violence: Religious Riot in Sixteenth-
Century France', Natalie Davis departed from the traditional explanations
of religious riots.[5] She challenged the idea that violence was motivated
by class conflict and suggested that there was a cultural facet to violence, which had been overlooked. Davis turned for the first time to the
ritual signification of the violence of the French Wars of Religion. She
suggested that popular violence was inspired by official acts of violence
perpetrated on criminals and heretics in public executions, that in many
ways the crowd felt that it was merely extending the mechanism of
justice by taking the law into its own hands. This occurs, Davis argues,
when official mechanisms for the persecution of heresy are seen to be
failing and the crowd appropriates them for itself. The timing of religious riots does not coincide with the rise in grain prices, which was
one of the arguments of the 'traditional explanation', but with religious
rituals. The violence itself is described as ritual, the elements of which
are borrowed from public executions, liturgy and popular culture. To
quote Davis's own definition of the rites of violence:

> I would suggest that they can be reduced to a repertory of actions,
> derived from the Bible, from the liturgy, from the action of political
> authority, or from the traditions of popular folk justice, intended
> to purify the religious community and humiliate the enemy and
> thus make him less harmful.[6]

Davis also notes a distinction between Catholic and Protestant violence
in that the Catholics attacked the physical body of their victims whereas
Protestants were more interested in objects and symbols. In this sense
priests would have been the victims of Protestant attacks, not as individuals but as symbols of authority of the Roman Catholic Church.

The publication of 'Rites of Violence' provoked a reaction from
Janine Garrisson who defended the traditional explanations of religious
riots, notably the role of conjectural accidents.[7] One of Garrisson's

---

[3] Mark Greengrass, *The French Reformation* (Oxford, 1987), pp. 46–7.

[4] Mack P. Holt, 'Putting Religion Back into the Wars of Religion', *French Historical Studies*, XVIII (1993), pp. 524–51.

[5] Natalie Zemon Davis, 'The Rites of Violence: Religious Riot in Sixteenth-Century France', *P&P*, LIX (1973), pp. 51–91.

[6] N. Z. Davis, *Society and Culture in Early Modern France* (Oxford, 1995), pp. 155, 169, 173–4, 178.

[7] Janine Estèbe, 'Debate: The Rites of Violence, Religious riot in Sixteenth-Century France, A Comment' followed by N. Z. Davis 'A Rejoinder', *P&P*, LXVII (1975), pp. 127–35.

strongest criticisms is that Davis excluded from the massacres the urban poor who, she argues, were the most likely to be affected by social and economic factors. Based on the assumption that social origin was not a factor in the adherence to Protestantism, Natalie Davis argued that Protestants were representative of all sections of urban society; Garrisson, however, defended the idea that Protestants represented the élite and that class differences would have been a particular motivation in the urban massacres. Nonetheless, Garrisson does agree with Davis that there is a noticeable difference between Catholic and Protestant violence, and adds that Protestant violence is pedagogic and demonstrative whereas Catholic violence is more purgative. Tentatively, Garrisson writes that Catholics killed Protestants because 'they were not as others were, because they were different', which may not be as simplistic as it seems. Both agree that the difference between Catholic and Protestant violence could be ascribed to culture.

These approaches – the socio-economic represented by Garrisson, and the cultural represented by Davis– despite their differences, have something in common. Both attempt to provide a 'rational' explanatory framework for the otherwise incomprehensible violence of the French Wars of Religion, as though the incomprehensibility of violence would be mitigated if its perpetrators had good economic or social motives. This paradigm is summarized by Natalie Davis who provides an alternative explanation to the social-economic ones:

> To social historians it is the seeming irrationality of most sixteenth-century religious riot that has been puzzling … . Finally we may see their violence, however cruel, not as random and limitless but as aimed at defined targets and selected from a repertory of traditional punishments and forms of destruction.[8]

A more recent contender for the explanation of religious violence, however, has chosen to do away with reason altogether by pointing out that in all attempts to explain religious violence, the word 'religious' had been ignored. Denis Crouzet dismisses the need to produce a rational explanation for religious violence, because as violence for God, with God and in God it belongs to a realm which operates beyond reason. To him, there are no motivations for the massacres of the French Wars of Religion, other than religious ones. For this reason Crouzet is very critical of all the approaches mentioned above and dismisses them as symptomatic of 'a history without God'. Crouzet criticizes the social interpretations of religious violence, denying its 'religious' specificity.

---

[8] Davis, *Society and Culture*, p. 154.

Denis Crouzet has elaborated, in his *Guerriers de Dieu*, an overarching theory which aims at explaining the astonishing violence of the Wars of Religion, as well as the appeal of the Reformed faith. His analysis is a refutation of the 30 years or so of social historiography which has attributed religious violence to social or political tensions. His view, in short, is that the degree of violence of the French Wars of Religion can be explained only through the understanding of the 'discourse' of the times. The answer is not to be found in the social, political or confessional tensions of the 1560s, but in the eschatological literature which had gathered momentum during the previous 40 years. This 'genre' of eschatological writings would have driven the 'anguish', which he argues pervaded the religious life of the laity, to a head, culminating in the physical expression of these emotions through religious violence, on both sides of the confessional divide.

Crouzet rightly points out that the study of pamphlet literature so far has been one-sided and that far too little attention has been paid to Catholic authors. His work also challenges the historiography of the French Wars of Religion in another important way: the prominent role that Crouzet gives to 'prophets of the Apocalypse', touches upon the problem of interpreting contemporary sources, and particularly printed ones. Emphasis on printed sources as a barometer of contemporary discourse brings new light to old problems, particularly the problem of violence.

The centrality to Crouzet's thought of Thomas Illyricus, an eschatological preacher contemporary to Luther, is demonstrated by the fact that he features in both *Les Guerriers de Dieu* and *La nuit de la Saint-Barthélemy*. Crouzet seems to ascribe much potency to the preaching of a man whose influence, he argues, could be felt more than two generations after his death. Illyricus started preaching in 1518 at Condom, attracting his audience in tens of thousands, and preached subsequently in Bordeaux and Toulouse against the newly publicized ideas of Luther. In *Les Guerriers de Dieu*, Crouzet had linked the violence of the 1550s and 1560s in the south of France to the preaching of Illyricus;[9] in *La nuit de la Saint-Barthélemy*, Crouzet outlines a movement that culminates with the massacre of St Bartholomew's Day and, again, begins with the preaching of Illyricus at Condom in November 1518.[10]

The eschatological anguish that Crouzet describes so eloquently would have had its root in the religious uncertainties of the final decades of the fifteenth century, finding its full expression in the confessional conflicts

---

[9] Crouzet, *Guerriers de Dieu*, I, pp. 515, 526.

[10] Denis Crouzet, *La nuit de la Saint-Barthélemy: un rêve perdu de la renaissance* (Paris, 1994), p. 15.

of the sixteenth century. His narrative account of the events themselves is interspersed with extracts of Catholic propaganda, and Biblical references, in a bid to show the relevance of 'stereotypes of a collective memory of prophetic writings'. A certain coherence is outlined between the descriptions of the Huguenots in Catholic sermons and polemic and violence carried out in urban massacres.[11] Crouzet painstakingly establishes a 'rationale' which would account for the apparent irrationality of the religious violence, without resorting to social or cultural explanations.

Crouzet describes France in the sixteenth century as a civilization of anguish where everyone was afraid of the Last Judgement; he explains the rise of Calvinism by the fact that it provided a *désangoissement* to its adherents whose anxiety was relieved. This argument finds its roots in the works of Jean Delumeau, who argued that Luther's *sola fide* was a remedy to anguish, and more particularly in those of Alphonse Dupront.[12] One obvious implication of this argument, which is left unexplored, is that Catholicism could no longer fulfil this role; another is that people were more afraid of the end of time in the sixteenth century than at any other time in the history of Christendom. It seems difficult to accept the specificity of the sixteenth century in terms of its eschatology, since no period of history (including our own) is devoid of apocalyptic fears.

The civilization of astrological anguish described by Crouzet predates the sixteenth century by several centuries, as millenerianism was a central aspect of medieval Christianity.[13] What is specific to the sixteenth century is that apocalypticism found new means of expression in print which were unavailable to the medieval peddlers of doom, as Crouzet's impressive bibliography testifies. Crouzet argues that the success of this genre is an indication that France was a 'civilization of astrological anguish' even before the beginning of the Reformation in France.[14] This numerical approach is problematic at best as the selection of a particular genre of printed literature to the exclusion of any other might lead to gross generalizations if taken out of context. As it has been lucidly pointed out by Mark Greengrass:

---

[11] Crouzet, *Guerriers de Dieu*, I, p. 247.

[12] Jean Delumeau, *Naissance et affirmation de la réforme* (Paris, 1965), pp. 48, 55; J. Delumeau, *La Peur en Occident, XIVe–XVIIIe siècles* (Paris, 1980); Steven Ozment, *Reformation in the Cities: The Appeal of Protestantism to Sixteenth-Century Germany and Switzerland* (London, 1975), p. 42; on Dupront, see Jacques Revel and Lynn Hunt, eds, *Histories: French Constructions of the Past* (New York, 1995), pp. 173–9.

[13] Greengrass, 'Psychology of Religious Violence', p. 472.

[14] Crouzet, *Guerriers de Dieu*, I, p. 131.

> When citing from such a vast mass of published materials over
> such a long chronology, it is easy to construct a plausible argument
> on the basis of small extracts from the text rather than to reflect
> the flavour of a text as a whole – or to rest too much by way of
> explanation upon one small point of reference.[15]

A complete bibliography of sixteenth-century French vernacular books
is currently in progress at the St Andrews Reformation Studies Institute.[16] Preliminary statistics suggest that almanacs and astrological
prophecies were not as prominent in the printed literature of the sixteenth century as Crouzet implies.[17] Furthermore, his emphasis on the
eschatological undertones of certain works has been questioned by
other historians, notably by Larissa Taylor in the case of François
Picart.[18] Other authors such as Antoine de Mouchy, Robert Ceneau,
Esprit Rotier, Jean de La Vacquerie and Antoine du Val are described by
Crouzet as members of an 'intelligentsia of prophets of violence'.[19] The
following chapters, however, will show that these authors relied primarily on stereotypical representations of the heretic (borrowed from
scriptural, patristic and medieval sources) rather than on eschatology to
inspire fear and hatred of the Huguenots.[20]

A different reading of these authors reveals that they were at once
more prosaic and less subtle than Crouzet suggests; they pursued their
own agenda, calling for the persecution of Protestants, but seldom
resorted to eschatology to justify their views. For example, de Mouchy
was a senior member of the Faculty of Theology who defended the
Gallican Church against the onslaught of the new religion. The instrumental role that is ascribed to him by Chandieu and Beza in the
persecutions preceding the Wars of Religion conjures up the image of a
medieval inquisitor rather than a 'prophet of the apocalypse'.

Crouzet was successful in putting eschatological anguish on the
historiographical map of the French Wars of Religion, but whether it
was as central as he makes it is a matter for serious consideration. Our
own fears of a global ecological disaster at the dawn of a new millen-
nium should convince us that no historical argument can be built on the

---

[15] Greengrass, 'Psychology of Religious Violence', p. 473.

[16] Some of the early findings that this project has made possible can be found in
Andrew Pettegree, Paul Nelles and Philip Conner, eds, *The Sixteenth-Century French
Religious Book* (Aldershot, 2001).

[17] Francis M. Higman, *Piety and the People: Religious Printing in French, 1511–1551*
(Aldershot, 1996), pp. 8–12.

[18] Taylor, *Heresy and Orthodoxy*, pp. 190, 200–202, 205; Parrow, 'From Defense to
Resistance', pp. 12–13.

[19] Crouzet, *Guerriers de Dieu*, I, pp. 201–2.

[20] Crouzet, *Guerriers de Dieu*, I, pp. 191, 202, 205.

specificity of any period of history in respects of millenarianism. One could argue that apocalypticism has been part of human culture ever since men realized they were mortal: it is a lot easier to contemplate the end of all things than it is to contemplate one's own.

The work of David Nicholls, linking urban massacres with public executions, adds to Natalie Davis's rites of violence, in suggesting that judicial, ecclesiastical and royal institutions had greater responsibility in provoking violence than had previously been thought. Nicholls has argued in an article entitled 'The Theatre of Martyrdom' that the violence of urban massacres was inspired by repertories of actions found in public executions. Nicholls sharpens Davis's hypotheses by showing in detail how the actions of the crowd mirrored the officially sanctioned acts of cruelty known as the theatre of execution or martyrdom and he describes how trials of heresy were staged to provide the spectacle of the humiliation of the heretic. The theatre of execution borrowed from popular culture when, for example, clerical heretics were dressed up as fools and paraded through the streets before their execution.

From 1560 onwards, Protestants were no longer burned for heresy but hanged for sedition. This shift from religious to political crime was the direct result of Catherine de Medici's policy of conciliation, but it sparked spontaneous outbreaks of popular violence.[21] David Nicholls noted that, from about 1557 onwards, heresy trials were more likely to be the occasion of disorder as 'the audience at executions were no longer content to be mere spectators, but wanted to be executioners themselves'.[22] The fate of Huguenot prisoners was a cause of friction between the crowd and the authorities who often rescued the prisoner from being summarily executed.[23]

This would have been a major concern for the authorities who strove to prevent spontaneous outbreaks of violence at public executions. Hanging, the fate reserved for political crimes, was less spectacular than burning, which was reserved for heretics and part of the elaborate theatre of execution. Whereas the burning of heretics during the Middle Ages served a didactic function in which the spectators accepted their role passively, it is clear that, as religious tensions increased between 1557 and 1560, the theatre of execution was more likely to provoke

---

[21] Monter, *Judging the French Reformation*, pp. 177, 213–25.

[22] David Nicholls, 'The theatre of martyrdom in the French Reformation', *P&P*, CXXI (1988), pp. 49–73 (pp. 54, 56, 69).

[23] Barbara B. Diefendorf, *Beneath the Cross: Catholics and Huguenots in Sixteenth-Century Paris* (Oxford, 1991), p. 53.

rather than appease the population's lust for blood. Another argument for the abandonment of the theatre of execution was that these elaborately staged trials gave ammunition for the emerging French culture of martyrdom.[24] Orchestrated show-trials were no longer sufficient to appease the audience, and they increasingly turned into spontaneous and uncontrolled massacre. It seems that the violence of the urban massacre borrowed from both Nicholls's theatre of execution and Davis's rites of violence.

Ironically, the transition from burning to hanging gave no less occasion for disorder, as the bodies of the Protestants were taken from the places of execution to be the object of a number of desecrating rituals. This desecration of the bodies, which had been prevented before 1560 by the annihilation of the body by fire, was also carried out vicariously on effigies in the absence of the heretic, as was the case for Coligny in 1569.[25] His effigy was hanged and dragged through the streets by the people of Paris – a macabre rehearsal of the mutilation to which his actual body would be subject three years later.[26] According to Nicholls, this mechanism of vicarious execution denotes the symbolic nature of public execution, 'if an accused heretic could not be found, he or she was invariably executed in effigy, thereby underlining the ritual nature of the ceremony'.[27]

This view is compatible with the assertion by Natalie Davis that the ritual elements of religious riots were inspired by the rites of violence of official executions. Retributory justice, such as the execution of Poltrot de Méré who was drawn and quartered on the place de Grève in March 1563, probably had more to do with the violence of the French Wars of Religion than 'a collective memory of prophetic writings'.[28] William Monter has shown that in the closing years of the 1550s heresy prosecution decreased while Protestant numbers increased; which would suggest that people were taking the law into their own hands in order to make up for a failing judicial system.[29]

Crouzet directly challenges the school of thought, inaugurated by Emile Durkheim, which suggests that religion is ultimately a social phenomenon and that religious rituals are ultimately concerned with this world. According to this school, religion is inseparable from the community of believers and violence emerged in defence of its boundaries

---

[24] Nicholls, 'Theatre of Martyrdom', p. 71.
[25] Crouzet, *Guerriers de Dieu*, I, p. 234.
[26] Diefendorf, *Beneath the Cross*, pp. 76, 84.
[27] Nicholls, 'Theatre of Martyrdom', pp. 54, 56.
[28] Diefendorf, *Beneath the Cross*, p. 71.
[29] Monter, *Judging the French Reformation*, p. 157.

from the pollution of heresy.[30] Crouzet specifically rejects this utilitarianism and functionalism, as negating the specificity of religious violence which is conferred by its otherworldliness.[31] Indeed, he places himself in opposition to any cultural interpretation of religious violence when, for example, he denies the role of derision in the ritual murders of Huguenots. Whereas derision is central to Davis's parallel between popular festivity and collective violence, Crouzet stresses the earnestness of the fear of the perpetrators of such atrocities.[32]

The portrayal of Protestants in Catholic polemic, however, strengthens the cultural and social approaches to the problem of violence. A case in point is the debasement of Huguenots – through implications of 'sexual promiscuity', 'women on top' and the 'world upside down' – described in the following chapters. These echo the popular custom of derisively portraying one's enemy as a lecher or a cuckold. Such was the sole purpose of the Charivari, well represented in all parts of Christendom, which featured the cuckold riding backwards accompanied by the clatter of various implements, to the great rejoicing of onlookers.[33] The dialectic between social order and rebellion, as expressed in seasonal misrule and religious festivals, has been described often enough to avoid the need for recapitulation here.[34] The theme of inversion and the world upside down, familiar to scholars of popular culture, also features prominently in the polemic of the French Wars of Religion.[35]

This familiar appeal to the cohesion of the 'great chain of being' appeared whenever order was threatened. In this case the threat came from the Reformed faith which questioned the foundations of the social fabric. The cohesion of the social fabric, even symbolic or imaginary, was at the heart of the procession of Corpus Christi. One is familiar with the importance of the eucharistic symbolism of the procession, reflecting the communion of all Christians during Easter. After the

---

[30] N. Z. Davis, 'The sacred and the body social in Sixteenth-Century Lyon', *P&P*, XC (1981), pp. 40–70 (p. 63) and *Society and Culture*, p. 157; Emile Durkheim, *Les Formes élémentaires de la vie religieuse* (Paris, 1994); John Bossy, 'The Mass as a Social Institution 1200–1700', *P&P*, C (1983), pp. 29–61; John Bossy, 'Some elementary forms of Durkheim', *P&P*, XCV (1982), pp. 3–18.

[31] Crouzet, *Guerriers de Dieu*, I, p. 235.

[32] Ibid., I, pp. 233, 248, 255.

[33] Martin Ingram, 'Ridings, Rough Music and the "Reform of Popular Culture" in Early Modern England', *P&P*, CV (1984), pp. 79–113.

[34] Yves-Marie Bercé, *Fête et révolte: Des mentalités populaires du XVIe au XVIIIe siècle* (Paris, 1994); and *Revolt and revolution in early modern Europe: An essay on the history of political violence* (Manchester, 1987).

[35] Du Val, *Mirouer des Calvinistes*, fol. 28ᵛ.

fourth Lateran Council (1215), each Christian was bound to confess his sins before he could receive the body of Christ and be reunited to the great family of Christendom. The importance of this process has been outlined by Barbara Diefendorf, who established the synchronicity of the Corpus Christi processions held in Paris and religious violence on the eve of the first religious wars. In May 1562, the Corpus Christi sermon of the cardinal de Lorraine was a combination of devotion to the real presence of Christ and encouragement to the people's resistance while Condé's army threatened the city.[36]

Religious festivals provided both a powerful vehicle for cohesion and a means of identifying the enemies of the community. Corpus Christi, like Carnival or Charivari, could turn from the expression of social cohesion into an opportunity for rebellion and revolt. A notorious example is provided by the Peasants' Revolt of 1381 in England which took place at the time of the feast of Corpus Christi.[37] When the rioters found John of Gaunt's house empty, they held one of his jackets up in the air and set it on fire, following the pattern of vicarious execution which is frequent in the religious struggles of the sixteenth century. When Coligny was accused of *lèse-majesté* after the battle of Jarnac in 1569, he was hanged in effigy by the people of Paris on the place de Grève.[38] Both John of Gaunt and admiral Coligny were identified as enemies of the community and were executed in effigy in their absence, like straw men during Carnival.

The parallels between religious festivals, popular culture, public executions and outbreaks of violence during the French Wars of Religion are more than anecdotal. In England, for example, straw Popes were frequently burned, during the war with Spain in the 1580s, which was the occasion for public rejoicing.[39] Around the same time, an effigy of heresy in the guise of a 'great fury', was burned by the city officials in Paris, at the height of the Catholic League in June 1588.[40] The uniformity of practice points to a cultural rather than eschatological grid of interpretation for the violence of the French Wars of Religion. It was to

---

[36] Diefendorf, *Beneath the Cross*, pp. 31, 65.

[37] Margaret Aston, 'Corpus Christi and Corpus Regni: Heresy and the Peasants' Revolt', *P&P*, CXLIII (1994), pp. 3–47.

[38] Diefendorf, *Beneath the Cross*, pp. 76, 84.

[39] David Cressy, *Bonfires and Bells: National Memory and the Protestant Calendar in Elizabethan and Stuart England* (Berkeley, 1989); Emmanuel Le Roy Ladurie, *Carnival: a people's uprising at Romans, 1579–1580* (London, 1980).

[40] J.-L. Flandrin, ed., *Journal d'un bourgeois de Paris sous Henri III par Pierre de l'Estoile* (Paris, 1966), pp. 261–2: 'Le 23 Juin, au feu de la Saint-Jean, les prévôts des marchands et échevins, firent mettre sur l'arbre la représentation d'une grande furie qu'ils nommèrent Hérésie, pleine de feux artificiels dont elle fut tout brûlée.'

social cohesion that Catholic propaganda appealed in moulding popular perceptions of the Huguenot as an enemy of the community. In
doing so, they could resort to a whole repertory of stereotypes that had
been used against heretics in the past.

An example is provided by the widespread belief that Protestants
were lecherous. Although this could be construed as a blanket accusation that was used indiscriminately throughout history, it flows directly
from a tight interpretation of Scripture. Drawing on the scriptural
description of the Church as the bride of Christ, Catholics made a
parallel between heresy and adultery. This argument drawn from
Ephesians 5:22–4 was used by John Eck and by Robert Ceneau:[41]

> Wives, be subject to your husbands as you are to the Lord. For the
> husband is the head of the wife just as Christ is the head of the
> church, the body of which he is the Saviour. Just as the church is
> subject to Christ, so also wives ought to be, in everything, to their
> husbands.

The implication of this analogy is that, by breaking away from the
Church, the Protestants were committing an act akin to adultery. John
Eck pursues the analogy and argued that just as men should not have
more than one wife, they could belong to only one Church: 'Christ did
not have two wives, the Church of the Apostles and ours is one, before
Luther was born.' This argument was reproduced by Jean Talpin in his
Remonstrance a tous chrestiens arguing the analogy between fidelity in
marriage and the unity of the Church very strongly:

> We know that in true and legitimate marriage, the man is joined to
> only one bride ... We see, that in man there is but one head, also
> that there is one body ... Understand this comparison of great
> conformity, perfect communion & convenience with the things
> above said, we declare the undivided link between Jesus Christ &
> his Church.[42]

This is elaborated upon by René Benoist: 'friendship and sweetness
cannot be as great between married men and women ... as it is between
Jesus Christ and his Church in general, but in particular to each true
Christian'.[43] The flipside of the analogy between marriage and the
Church, is the association between heresy and fornication. This explains why anti-Protestant polemic often resorts to 2 Peter 2:14: 'They
have eyes full of adultery, insatiable for sin. They entice unsteady souls.

---

[41] Eck, *Les lieux communs ... contre Luther*, sigs a8r–b1r; Ceneau, *Response catholique*,
sig. E3r.

[42] Talpin, *Remonstrance a tous chrestiens*, sigs M2v, N8v.

[43] René Benoist, *La Maniere de Cognoistre Salutairement Jésus-Christ* (Paris, 1564),
sig. C1v.

They have hearts trained in greed. Accursed children!'[44] Robert Ceneau
asserted that 'Women abandon their husbands, & the husbands their
wives to run to such people' and directly accused the Protestant heresy
of breaking up marriages.[45] According to Du Preau, Catholics were
married to their Church and could not participate in the ceremonies of
the Protestants without committing something akin to adultery: 'Just as
it is forbidden for the children of God to take the daughters of men as
their wives (as found in Genesis) ... it is forbidden for Catholics to talk
to heretics or to partake in their ceremonies without offending God.'[46]

If the true Church was described as the lawful bride of Christ, heresy
was often described as a whore – in this case by the Calvinist Gui de
Brès writing against the Anabaptists: 'a whore will always defend her
virtue more vigorously than an honest woman'.[47] This is also found in
England in the work of John Proctor who translated Vincent de Lérins
and depicted heresy as a 'wanton, sensual and deceitful woman' in his
introduction.[48] Georg Witzel used the same analogy to describe the
Protestant Church as a young girl: 'our Calvinists prefer to our [Church]
a young girl who is only ten years old'.[49] The same image was used in a
Protestant source against the duc de Guise: 'He has turned ... from his
legitimate wife ... to chambermaids and whores.'[50] Martino del Rio, in
his discourse about magic published at the turn of the seventeenth
century, speaks about heresy in these terms: 'Evil spirits are accustomed
to use heretics as though they were beautiful prostitutes to draw people
into error. For it is clear that in Scripture heresy is called a prostitute.'[51]

The numerous references to adultery and incest in anti-Protestant
polemic can be explained by the theologians' conception of the Church
as the bride of Christ, and of heresy as a whore. The description of

---

[44] Antoine de Mouchy, *Responce a quelque apologie que les heretiques ces jours passés
ont mis en avant sous ce titre: Apologie ou deffence des bons Chrestiens contre les
ennemis de l'Église catholique* (Paris, 1558), sig. G5ᵛ; Gabriel du Preau, *Des faux
prophetes, seducteurs, & hypocrites, qui viennent à nous en habit de brebis: mais au
dedans sont loups ravissans* (Paris, 1563), sig. C1ʳ.

[45] Ceneau, *Response catholique*, sig. B3ʳ.

[46] Du Preau, *Des faux prophetes*, sig. C1ᵛ.

[47] Gui de Brès, *La racine, source et fondement des Anabaptistes ou rebaptisez de
nostre temps* ([Rouen], 1565), p. 68.

[48] John Proctor, *The waie home to Christ and truth leadinge from Antichrist and
errour* (1556), a translation of the fifth-century French Saint Vincent de Lérins cited in
Tom Betteridge, '"Mete Covers for such Vessels": Sexual Deviancy and the English
Reformation' (unpublished paper, Reformation Colloquium, Wadham College, Oxford,
1998), 16 pages, p. 4.

[49] Witzel, *Discours des moeurs*, p. 9.

[50] *Advertissement a la Royne Mere du Roy*, sig. b3ᵛ.

[51] Maxwell-Stuart, ed., *The Occult in Early Modern Europe*, p. 167.

Protestants as being 'soiled with all sorts of fornication and adultery',[52] accused of assembling in secret 'to conceive bastards, with poor, and well abused *femmellettes*',[53] and 'ravish & rape the sacred virgins of God, entertain & debauch the women from their husbands',[54] flow directly from this analogy.

The writings of these authors provide useful insights into the contemporary perceptions of the Protestants. The Reformed conventicles which were held in secret were thought to be the scene of sexual orgies and excuses for depravity, which contrasted with apparent virtue in daylight. This view was published in 1558 by Antoine de Mouchy and Robert Ceneau, both prominent members of the Faculty of Theology, in the aftermath of the affair of the rue St Jacques. This view in print is paralleled by the behaviour of the mob towards the women who were caught during the affair and treated like whores.[55] This is reported through various sources, both Catholic and Protestant, which suggests that it was at the origin of much prejudice. Although the majority would have been insensitive to the finer points of the analogies that were drawn by Catholic authors, all could understand their conclusions.

I should like to argue that the perception of the Huguenots held by the perpetrators of massacres is crucial to our understanding the violence of the French Wars of Religion. Natalie Davis diverged from Garrisson's interpretation of St Bartholomew as an attempt by the Catholics to exterminate the Huguenots as a race: 'There seems to me very little evidence, however, that the Catholic killers wished to exterminate "a foreign race" ... Heretics were hated for their polluting, divisive, and disorderly actions, not as a "race".'[56] For Davis, Protestants were not killed for what they were but for what they believed, whereas Garrisson posited that Protestants were killed 'because they were not as others were, because they were different'.[57] To elaborate on this view, perhaps Protestants were not killed for their faith or for what they were, but for what they were *perceived* to be. It seems evident that it was the actual

[52] Ceneau, *Response catholique*, sig. D8ʳ.

[53] [Saconay], *Discours Catholique*, sig. D7ʳ.

[54] Bontemps Legier, *Response aux objections et poincts principaux de ceux qui se disent aujourd'huy vouloir reformer l'Église, & s'appellent fideles & croyans à l'Evangile* (Paris, 1562), sig. C4ᵛ.

[55] Diefendorf, *Beneath the Cross*, p. 50; Crouzet, *Guerriers de Dieu*, I, p. 244.

[56] Davis, *Society and Culture*, p. 160.

[57] Estèbe and Davis, 'Debate: The Rites of Violence', pp. 130, 134.

physical presence of Protestants that gave rise to Catholic hatred, unlike
Protestant violence that was directed at symbols, images and figures of
authority;[58] Protestants were killed for what the Catholics believed
them to be, not for their faith – not as human beings, but as monsters. If
we accept this premise, then the demonizing of Protestants in Catholic
polemic is absolutely crucial to understanding the violence of the French
Wars of Religion.

A major characteristic of Catholic polemic is its reliance on the
authority of precedents – which were the building blocks of the legitimacy of any argument during this period. Catholics plundered the
history of the Roman Catholic Church's repeated skirmishes with heresy from the third century onward, which had peaked notably during
the central Middle Ages. The lengthy arguments which had been used
against a variety of heretical groups –Arians, Donatists, Manichees, and
so on – were quoted out of context and applied to Protestants. Theological arguments grossly misrepresented the Reformed propositions so
that they could fit the pattern of previous refutations. But, which is
more relevant to the problem of violence outlined above, Protestants
were also compared to previous heretical groups on the grounds of their
moral character.

This enabled the Catholic polemicists to use a register of ready-made
stereotypes which had been applied to heretics before and allowed them
to reduce Protestantism to a mere repetition of history. This also placed
them in a rhetorical position of superiority implying that, since these
earlier heretical groups had been defeated, Protestantism would soon
know the same fate. A particularly strong case was made in this vein for
the similarity between the Crusade against the Albigensians in the thirteenth century and taking up arms against the Protestant movement.
This analogy was first used in the wake of the tumult of Amboise in
March 1560 and then elaborated upon in the thick of the Wars of
Religion and during the League. Ironically, this kinship was embraced
by the Protestants and was at the origin of the enduring myth that
Albigensians had been forerunners of the Reformation. This alleged
connection with medieval heresy, however, enabled Catholic polemicists
to push forward a policy of persecution in spite of the conciliatory
efforts of Catherine de Medici and Michel de L'Hôpital.

This book suggests that the dissemination of these stories in print
contributed to building a mental picture of Huguenots as monsters. The
demonizing of Protestants goes towards explaining the cruelty with

---

[58] O. Christin, *Une revolution symbolique: l'iconoclasme huguenot et la reconstruction catholique* (Paris, 1991).

which they were treated by the urban mobs throughout the French Wars of Religion. This places much more responsibility on the Catholic authors, pamphleteers and preachers, as was suggested by Mark Greengrass: 'In France, the public context must surely include, at the least, the institutions, ecclesiastical and lay, which had done so much, traditionally, to influence religious discourse.'[59]

The effect that the dissemination of these ideas through print would have on the population at large were probably unforeseen by their authors. Nevertheless the use of medieval stereotypes to describe Protestants must have contributed to building a mental picture of Protestants as heretics and as such 'non human'. This would explain why Catholics had so little respect for human life during urban massacres and why they attempted to exterminate Protestants to the last man. This would be consistent with the observations of many who found that, unlike the desacralizing violence of Protestants which was directed towards objects and symbols, the mutilations perpetrated by Catholics were taken out on the bodies of their victims.[60] These mutilations would have been the enactment in the flesh of what was first found in print – that Protestants were not human beings but monsters. The study of the mechanisms of stereotyping in Catholic printed polemic should further our understanding of violence in the French Wars of Religion.

---

[59] Greengrass, 'Psychology of Religious Violence', p. 476.

[60] Crouzet, *Guerriers de Dieu*, I, pp. 625–6; Davis, *Society and Culture*, p. 179; Greengrass, 'Psychology of Religious Violence', p. 469; M. Greengrass, 'The Anatomy of a Religious Riot in Toulouse in May 1562', *Journal of Ecclesiastical History*, XXXIV: 3 (1983), pp. 367–91 (pp. 369, 385, 389).

CHAPTER THREE

Polemic, debate and opinion-forming in sixteenth-century France

Sixteenth-century media is marked by the interconnectedness between the written and the oral. Preaching constituted the greatest point of contact between clergy and laity during this period.[1] In her work on François le Picart, Larissa Taylor has shown that preaching was probably the most influential means of conveying information during this period. Celebrated preachers commanded large audiences, and theologians were better known for their ability to speak than for their writing. The predominance of the spoken word is illustrated by René Benoist in his preface to the 1566 edition of the sermons of le Picart by Nicolas Chesneau: 'It should be noted here that the most learned and greatest men have written little or nothing ... because to teach, engage and persuade men through the spoken word is much more difficult than writing at one's leisure.'[2] We should take these words seriously as they were written by someone who was himself a celebrated preacher and a prolific writer.[3] Nicolas Chesneau also published the sermons of Claude d'Espence who wrote in June 1562: 'of the five sermons that follow, the first three were preached in part, collected and transcribed by a man of great memory'.[4]

Reliance on memory is a predominant feature of oral cultures, and these lines indicate a changing relationship with the written text. Polemical authors valued the spoken word but reluctantly recognized the need to challenge the views of the Reformers in print. The overlap between the written and the oral is illustrated by the performance of

---

[1] Soman, 'Press, Pulpit, and censorship', p. 440.

[2] Taylor, *Heresy and Orthodoxy*, pp. 2–5; René Benoist, Preface to François Le Picart, *Les Sermons et instructions chrestiennes pour tous les jours de caresme et féries de Pasques* (Paris, 1566), sig. *5ʳ.

[3] René Benoist, François le Picart and Nicolas Chesneau were friends as well as linked by the same voluntary zeal to defend the Catholic faith against heresy. Nicolas Chesneau was a powerful printer, probably the most important printer in Paris, and from 1563 onwards he printed the works of René Benoist, one of the most published Catholic authors of the sixteenth century. Benoist's notoriety was such that he benefited from a royal privilege that allowed him to nominate a printer who had the exclusive rights to print his works. A copy of this privilege dated 4 December 1563 names Chesneau as the beneficiary.

[4] Claude d'Espence, *Cinq sermons ou traictez de maistre Claude d'Espence* (Paris, 1562), sig. *2ʳ.

Antoine de Mouchy at the Council of Trent. This significant insight in the rhetorical conventions of the time is provided by the diary of an Italian cardinal who admired de Mouchy's ability to speak continuously for two hours 'as if he had learned by heart something that he had written'.[5] Antoine de Mouchy was a virulent polemicist who disseminated his views in print, as did Robert Ceneau, also noted at Trent. Another celebrated preacher was Simon Vigor who ran into trouble with the Crown on several occasions for speaking his mind in public.[6] Vigor also published his sermons in which the Crown was criticized for not taking a strong enough stance against heresy.[7] Another preacher who published his sermons, Claude d'Espence, offers another insight in the relationship between writing and preaching: 'But I forget myself and instead of writing a preface I catch myself delivering a sermon.'[8]

What can be found in print was probably a pale reflection of what was heard in sermons. Although few printed sermons survive, we know that many preachers got into trouble for the views they expressed in public. A notorious example is provided by Jean de Hans whose sermon provoked the disturbance at the Church of St Médard in 1561, and who was subsequently arrested.[9] In 1564, Artus Désiré encouraged the population of Paris to resist the royal order to disarm from the pulpit and was banished for his pains.[10] Simon Vigor ran foul of the Crown on at least two occasions, in 1568 and 1571, for criticizing the royal policy of conciliation.[11] René Benoist was also asked to withdraw one of his books which dealt with the incendiary topic of the Cross of Gastines in 1571.[12] Popular preachers were hugely influential in disseminating specific religious or polemical messages and vigorous preaching during this period often resulted in outbreaks of popular violence on both sides of the confessional divide. Prophetically, Jean Bodin asserted in 1583: 'The eloquent tongue of a mutinous orator is like a dangerous knife in the hands of a madman.'[13] Nicolas Pasquier very much makes the same point after the assassination of Henri IV:

---

[5] Tallon, *La France et le Concile de Trente*, pp. 735, 741–2.

[6] Diefendorf, *Beneath the Cross*, pp. 153, 157; Tallon, *La France et le Concile de Trente*, p. 735.

[7] Vigor, *Oraison funebre prononcee aux obseques ... de ma Dame Elizabeth de France*, sig. H4[r].

[8] D'Espence, *Cinq sermons*, sig. **1[r].

[9] Ruble, 'L'arrestation de Jean de Hans'.

[10] Giese, *Artus Désiré*, p. 30.

[11] Diefendorf, *Beneath the Cross*, pp. 147–58.

[12] Barthélemy, ed., *Journal d'un curé Ligueur*, p. 134.

[13] Jean Bodin, *Les six livres de la république*, 7 vols (Paris, 1583), IV, pp. 661–2; quoted in Soman, 'Press, Pulpit, and censorship', p. 441.

> The ability of a preacher to speak well is an attractive and valuable
> gift ... But, if he decides to abuse the sweetness of his language,
> there is no more terrible plague on a Kingdom than this well-
> spoken preacher ... his tongue becomes a weapon of violence on
> which depends the life or death of those for whom and against
> whom he uses it.[14]

In our age of information technology, dominated as it is by the
printed word, it is difficult to think back to a time where the bulk of
information was transmitted through the spoken word. The early
modern information networks were predominantly oral, and news
was passed on by word of mouth. The sermon was probably to the
sixteenth century what television is to us today: it provided information as well as entertainment, and enjoyed considerable popularity.[15]
Although the surviving printed sources provide only a fraction of
what was said, indirect evidence points to a language made up of
symbols – iconic representations drawing on popular imagery, familiar stories and fears. For example, the representation of heresy as a
hysterical woman turning scripture on its head can be found in print
in the work of Robert Ceneau in 1562.[16] Pierre de l'Estoile reports
that on 23 June 1588 (on St John's Day) 'the representation of a great
fury named heresy was burned on the fire of St John'.[17] This representation finally emerged in visual form at the turn of the seventeenth
century in Cesare Ripa's *Iconologia* (reproduced on the jacket of this
book) and was used in a German anti-Calvinist pamphlet.[18] This
example gives us an insight into the power of symbolism and the
cohesion between different media in representations of heresy.

Historians of the Lutheran Reformation have also pointed out the
role of the visual and the oral in relations to print in what McLuhan
called 'hybridisation of media'.[19] For visual material, one needs look no
further than processions, public trials and executions (in effigy and in
the flesh), which punctuated the French Wars of Religion. The combined effect of processions, preaching, singing and printing participated

---

[14] Sawyer, *Printed Poison*, p. 18.

[15] Taylor, *Soldiers of Christ*, p. 229.

[16] Robert Ceneau, *Response catholique contre les heretiques de ce temps* (Paris, 1562),
sig. D5r.

[17] Flandrin, ed., *Journal d'un bourgeois de Paris*, pp. 261–2.

[18] Cesare Ripa, *Nova Iconologia* (Padua, 1618), p. 244; C. S. Clifton, *Encyclopedia of
Heresies and Heretics* (Oxford, 1992), p. 123; Nischan, *Prince, People, and Confession*,
p. 53 (the woodcut represents Calvinism as a medusa flailing Luther with snakes,
preventing him from arguing with a Catholic bishop).

[19] Matheson, *Rhetoric of the Reformation*, p. 37; Robert W. Scribner, *For the Sake of
Simple Folk: Popular Propaganda for the German Reformation* (Cambridge, 1981), p. 3;
Marshall McLuhan, *Understanding Media: The Extensions of Man* (New York, 1964).

to the emergence of public opinion which can be traced in printed sources.[20] Orality, however, pervaded the written word and it is possible to find its traces in the printed texts. The style of Catholic polemic is often marked by orality following the criteria that have been identified by Peter Matheson in *The Rhetoric of the Reformation*: rhythm, repetition, alliteration, antithesis, and parallel. The extent to which this material spread through the illiterate population orally would determine the success of a given idea, opinion or rumour expressed in print. This is not simply a one-way phenomenon – the flowing of ideas from printed page to oral discourse – but a reciprocal relationship. The ideas found in print probably owed as much to the welling-up of oral discourse into the literate world as the reverse.[21]

Clearly, the material found in print flowed into the oral discourse of everyday life through various means. Estimates of literacy and population given by Sawyer indicate that, by 1615, 'the most popular pamphlets might have reached the hands of 1% of France's urban population'.[22] This does not mean, however, that the ideas contained in those books circulated only within these circles. What Robert Scribner has written about early modern Germany is here particularly relevant: 'Printing was, in fact, an addition to, not a replacement for, oral communication. Indeed, it was as likely as not that most people would have experienced the printed word only indirectly, by having it read aloud to them.'[23] This has been observed for both Reformation Germany and early seventeenth-century France, and was also true of France in the second half of the sixteenth century.[24] There is, of course, an evolution between 1520s Germany and early seventeenth-century France as print entered into a symbiotic relationship with its readership. For example, the conspicuous absence of woodcuts in this period in France has theological reasons, the Calvinist distrust of images.[25] But Robert Scribner also indicates

---

[20] Sawyer, *Printed Poison*, p. 13; Matheson, *Rhetoric of the Reformation*, p. 34.

[21] Ibid., pp. 20–21, 37; Sawyer, *Printed Poison*, p. 69.

[22] Ibid., p. 48.

[23] Scribner, *For the Sake of Simple Folk* (1981), pp. 2–3.

[24] Matheson, *Rhetoric of the Reformation*, pp. 20–21, 37, Sawyer, *Printed Poison*, p. 69.

[25] French exceptions include Luther and Melanchthon, *De Deux monstres prodigieux, a savoir, d'un Asne-Pape, qui fut trouvé à Rome en la riviere du Tibre, l'an 1496. Et d'un veau-moine nay à Friberg en Misne, l'an 1528* (Geneva, 1557), printed in Gothic font which is extremely unusual in itself as the great majority of French printing was in Garamond font; another exception is reported by Philip Benedict, 'Of Marmites and Martyrs: Images and Polemics in the Wars of Religion', in *The French Renaissance in Prints from the Bibliothèque Nationale de France* (exhibition catalogue of the Grunwald Centre for the Graphic Arts, Los Angeles, 1995), pp. 108–37; Scribner, *For the Sake of Simple Folk* (1981), p. 249.

that woodcuts were gradually superseded by print by the middle of the sixteenth century in Germany as well:

> The second half of the sixteenth century saw a noticeable deterioration in technique, which robbed the woodcut of much of its simplicity of line and so of its effectiveness. ... This points unequivocably to the long-term triumph of printing over the print as a major form of mass communication, a fact of which there could be no doubt by the middle of the sixteenth century.[26]

Andrew Pettegree suggested that the psalm replaced the woodcut in France as a way of conveying the Protestant message to the illiterate. Songs were also expressions of militancy, sung in defiance of the Catholic majority in cities, and later on the battlefield of the Wars of Religion.[27] Catholics also wrote many songs that were reported by Pierre de l'Estoile during the League and collected in modern editions.[28]

This example shows that the readership had an impact on printing as well as the reverse. The symbiotic and interactive relationship between printing and its readership created a new phenomenon in the sixteenth century, which can be called 'public opinion'. As Jeffrey Sawyer has said: 'There was a public, and it had opinions. But what did it matter? The history of pamphleteering helps explain at least part of the story. For roughly three hundred years pamphlets were a principal vehicle for public political discourse in Old Regime France.'[29] Public opinion played an increasing role in determining the content of books. To make an analogy with the laws of supply and demand: the creation of a new product created a new market. As this market evolved, the relationship between supply and demand became fluid, as a one-way relationship became interactive. 'Public opinion' is the product of this interaction between media and public.[30]

The intentions of the polemical writers are difficult to establish, but can be pieced together from the texts themselves. The avowed aim of Antoine du Val's *Mirouer des Calvinistes*, for example, is unambiguous: 'We have collected this little book, to guard and arm you against them [the protestants]. By reading it, you will learn their false doctrine, their life

---

[26] Scribner, *For the Sake of Simple Folk* (1981), pp. 7, 249.

[27] Andrew Pettegree, *Huguenot Voices: The Book and the Communication Process During the Protestant Reformation* (Greenville, NC, 1999).

[28] Flandrin, ed., *Journal d'un bourgeois de Paris*; H. L. Bordier, ed., *Le Chansonnier Huguenot du XVIe siècle* (Geneva, 1969).

[29] Sawyer, *Printed Poison*, p. 13.

[30] Matheson, *Rhetoric of the Reformation*, p. 34.

and diabolical jargon, to be contrary to their pretence and false discourse.'[31] The use of the rhetorical convention of the mirror in the title is itself significant; upholder of the truth, the mirror represents things as there are, without deformation. Years later, Arnaud Sorbin would make good on the play on words between 'Reformation' and 'deformation' by calling the Calvinists 'our modern deformed'.[32] On the whole, pamphlets were designed to influence public opinion, to spread or deny rumours about the character of Protestants and defend the basic tenets of Catholic orthodoxy against the Calvinists' attacks.[33]

Is it legitimate to speak of 'propaganda'? Historians of early modern print disagree on this question. Robert Scribner, for instance, does not hesitate to use the word 'propaganda' to describe the material analysed in *For the Sake of Simple Folk*, whereas Peter Matheson is unhappy with the term: 'There are strong arguments for avoiding the term "propaganda" altogether in relation to the pamphlet, in view of its modern associations with massive media penetration and a manipulative ethos ... The aim is simply to influence public opinion, to "sell" ideas.' But Matheson argues that the polemic of the German Reformation hardened into propaganda by the mid-sixteenth century through a process of 'gradual declension of Reformation rhetoric' where 'opponents were bestialised, Jews transmuted into well-poisoners, the Papacy depicted as the gaping arse of Hell'.[34] In France in the seventeenth century there is no doubt that the material we are dealing with is propaganda. All agree that this material was designed to achieve the specific aim of influencing the thoughts and actions of its audience.[35]

The boundary between avowed aims and hidden agendas is sometimes thin. A great deal of this material is unsophisticated and unsubtle in its techniques; yet it is unlikely that the contemporary reader had the sophistication to discern the highly polemical content of works which purported to be theology for the layman.[36] Calling this material 'propaganda' does not necessarily imply that the authors were willingly manipulating people's

---

[31] Du Val, *Mirouer des Calvinistes*, fol. 3ʳ.

[32] Arnaud Sorbin, *Histoire des albigeois, et gestes de noble simon de monfort. Descrite par F. Pierre des Vallées Sernay, Moine de l'Ordre de Cisteaux* (Paris, 1569), sig. a4ᵛ.

[33] Maurice Prestat, 'De la Guerre Psychologique à la Guerre Médiatique', in G. Chaliand, ed., *La Persuasion de Masse: Ses origines contemporaines* (Paris, 1992), pp. 23–81 (p. 27).

[34] Matheson, *Rhetoric of the Reformation*, pp. 26, 44–5, 249.

[35] Scribner, *For the Sake of Simple Folk* (1981), p. 8; Sawyer, *Printed Poison*, pp. 9, 16; Matheson, *Rhetoric of the Reformation*, p. 6.

[36] F. Higman, 'Les genres de la littérature polémique calviniste au XVIe siècle', *THR*, CCCXXVI (1998), pp. 437–48.

perceptions, by telling them lies,[37] for this calls for a judgement on the
authors of these tracts that is difficult to make. It is clear, in many
instances, that the authors were sincere, however misguided, and were
convinced that what they were putting forward was true. If the intentions
of the authors are difficult to discern, it is undeniable that they were
following rules that have been recently associated with propaganda:

1. The rule of 'simplification': reducing all data to a simple con-
    frontation between 'Good and Bad', 'Friend and Foe'.
2. The rule of disfiguration: discrediting the opposition by crude
    smears and parodies.
3. The rule of transfusion: manipulating the consensus values of
    the target audience for one's own ends.
4. The rule of unanimity: presenting one's viewpoint as if it were
    the unanimous opinion of all right-thinking people: drawing
    the doubting individual into agreement by the appeal of star-
    performers, by social pressure, and by 'psychological contagion'.
5. The rule of orchestration: endlessly repeating the same mes-
    sages in different variations and combinations.[38]

Although all these rules are not followed unanimously, a given pamphlet will at least conform to two or three of these principles. Rule one,
the polarization and over-simplification of complex and ambiguous
issues, pervades the material published by Catholic authors. As one of
these authors, Robert Ceneau, put it, it is necessary to be 'either all
calvinist or totally faithful, in short either totally white or totally black'.[39]
Inversion was used by Catholic polemicists who turned the table on the
first generation of Reformers to show that the Reformation was a
manifestation that 'time was out of joint'. The words of Isaiah 5:20:
'Woe unto them that call evil good, and good evil: that put darkness for
light, and light for darkness; that put bitter for sweet, and sweet for
bitter!' were used often against Protestants, notably by Antoine de
Mouchy, Claude d'Espence, and Artus Désiré.[40] It was also used by

---

[37] Bertrand Taithe and Tim Thornton, 'Propaganda: a misnomer of rhetoric and
persuasion?', in B. Taithe and T. Thornton, eds, *Propaganda: Political Rhetoric and
Identity 1300–2000* (Sutton, 2000), pp. 1–16 (p. 2): 'propaganda is a social phenomenon and therefore operates in several directions, that is not simply a message
communicated from the powers to the public but also a reciprocal message, self-reinforc-
ing and flexible, which must contain the logic and elements of truth, which must explain
and make sense of political and social reality to the point that the propaganda message
will become significant of a whole political cosmology'.

[38] Norman Davies, *Europe: A History* (London, 1997), p. 500.

[39] Ceneau, *Response catholique*, sig. A7ʳ.

[40] Mouchy, *Responce a quelque apologie*, sig. A4ᵛ; d'Espence, *Cinq sermons*, sig. C8ᵛ;
Artus Désiré, *L'origine et source de tous les maux de ce monde, par l'incorrection des
peres & meres envers leurs enfans, & de l'inobedience d'iceux, Ensemble de la trop
grande familiarité & liberté donnée aux servans & servantes* (Paris, 1571), sig. E4ᵛ.

Protestants against their arch-enemy, the duc de Guise: 'This one has changed God into Satan: Christ into Bel, peace into war, the blessing into the wrath of God, a legitimate government into a tyranny.'[41]

The second rule, crude smears and parodies, was probably the most consistently observed and produced much of the material analysed in the following chapter (notably the 'blood libel'). The third rule is observed in many works that appealed to the consensus value of gender roles and the 'great chain of being' to show that Protestants were turning 'the world upside down' (discussed in Chapter 6 below). The fourth rule is illustrated by the Catholics' ability to argue that theirs was the view that was universally held before the advent of the Reformation. Finally, the fifth rule is illustrated by the recurrence – in many different editions, by many different authors in the course of at least half a century – of the themes analysed in the following chapters.

The work of historians of early modern polemic suggests that there was an evolution between the literature of persuasion at the beginning of the Reformation and the emergence of modern 'propaganda' towards the end of the sixteenth century. The Catholic tracts examined here probably belong to an interim hybrid category. Although it is clear that this material had abandoned all idea of dialogue with the Protestant faith, it cannot be described as pure 'propaganda' even though it shares some of its traits. It is undeniable that the authors of polemic were themselves convinced of what they put forward; which cannot be said of the propaganda that was produced in the course of the twentieth century.

In France, in the second half of the sixteenth century, polemical authors were certainly aware of the impact of their opponents' writing and were themselves writing to add credit or deny a given rumour. This concern can be found among Protestant authors who wrote 'to universally serve the people' to dispel the false image that Catholics were disseminating.[42] Thus Nicolas des Gallars accused the Catholics of rousing the 'common rabble' against the Protestants: 'These imps of the devil seek the ear of kings, bishops, doctors, and the common people, raising the alarm, calling to arms, in order to move all to rage, to encourage the shedding of innocents' blood.'[43]

---

[41] *Advertissement a la Royne Mere du Roy*, sig. b3^v.

[42] Antoine de la Roche Chandieu, *Histoire des persecutions, et martyrs de l'Eglise de Paris, depuis l'an 1557. Jusques au temps du Roy Charles neufviesme* (Lyon, 1563), sig. b1^r.

[43] [Nicolas des Gallars], *Seconde apologie ou defense des vrais chrestiens, contre les calomnies impudentes des ennemis de l'Eglise catholique. Ou il est respondu aux diffames redoublez par un nommé Demochares docteur de la Sorbonne* (1559), sigs A2^v, D6^v-D7^r. (Demochares is Greek for 'pleasing to the people'.)

Antoine de la Roche Chandieu, for his part, denounced the false accusations spread by the Catholics as responsible for the turning of the lower orders against well-born Protestant women:

> The cruelty with which great and small have treated the children of God ... speaks for itself ... but this rage is getting stronger every day as the fury with which the rabble have treated the god-fearing men and women demonstrates, even against ladies and maidens of quality, whom they would otherwise respect and fear.[44]

Chandieu is clearly accusing the Catholics of demagogy, of spreading false accusations among the 'rabble' and thus encouraging outbreaks of violence. The allegation that it is the 'vulgar' whose opinion was manipulated is made by the anonymous chronicler of the massacre of Cabrières and Mérindol, writing in 1555:

> They have had the reputation among common folk of practising incest, sorcery and enchantment and of being completely devoted to the Devil, meeting in conventicles as much to indulge in lewd behaviour and do other execrable things as to conduct their 'Sabbat' (I use their terminology) with the Devil who is present on that occasion.[45]

The concern of Protestant authors over the dissemination of rumours among 'common folk' is an interesting reversal of the situation in Germany described by Robert Scribner. It seems that, in France, it was the Catholics who had the ear of the common folk.

Robert Ceneau and others abhorred the 'middle ground', specifically because it allowed for the development of self-determination and choice. By polarizing the issues in this way, these authors were hoping that their audience would stay in the bosom of the Roman and apostolic Church and close the dangerous debate initiated by the Reformers. This standpoint has the unfortunate consequence of cutting out completely those who had already been converted. The works studied here addressed themselves to Catholics. They did not seek to convince the heretics of their errors, and it can be argued that it was not until after the Edict of Nantes that any such efforts were made. The aim of the authors of Catholic polemic was 'containment' rather than 'roll-back', to use Cold War rhetoric.

Unlike the Reformers, the authors studied here did not seek to convince their audience of the validity of change but, on the contrary, of the dangers of straying from tradition. While the Reformers sought to

---

[44] Chandieu, *Histoire des persecutions*, sig. b2ᵛ.

[45] Anon., *Histoire memorable de la persecution & saccagement du peuple de Merindol & Cabrieres & autres circonvoisins, appelez Vaudois* (1555), sig. *4ᵛ; translated by Maxwell-Stuart, ed., *The Occult in Early Modern Europe*, p. 168.

motivate their audience towards change, these authors appealed to the wisdom of remaining faithful to the old religion. The argument, used in the Empire and in England, that the Reformation allowed secular rulers to establish a state religion, was detrimental to the progress of the Reformation in France, where Gallicanism was already a state religion of sorts. The close association between the ruler and the Catholic Church in France allowed Catholic authors to argue that heretics were betraying the Crown as well as the Church and were by definition seditious. It can be argued that Catholic polemic of the kind described here was relatively successful in convincing the Catholic majority to remain in the bosom of the Church. On the other hand, it could do little to prevent the establishment of confessional pluralism in France (sanctioned by the Edict of Nantes), the one thing that its authors abhorred the most. It was not until the Counter-Reformation took hold in France, at the turn of the seventeenth century, that Catholic writers pursued a more positive policy of conversion and Catholic regeneration.

Insofar as one can make out the aims of the Catholic printed polemic, to what extent was it successful in influencing the thoughts and actions of its intended audience? What did common perceptions of Protestants owe to the writings and sermons of Catholic authors? The interactivity between printed material and its readership outlined above suggests that it might be more productive to turn the question on its head: to what extent did the perceptions and portrayal of Protestants found in printed polemic reflect the concerns and fears of the intended readership? Robert Scribner and others have argued that the relationship between pamphlets and their audience was a two-way process.[46] Not only did pamphlets have an impact on their audience but they also reflect its views.[47]

Oral discourse, which, unless it leaves a written trace, is inaccessible to the historian, can thus be grasped through written material which, allegedly, had such an interactive relationship with its intended audience. Matheson has argued that the success of pamphlets depended on how well they addressed the concerns of their audience and thus reflected their views:

> Perhaps the pamphlet, however, is the most reliable evidence, like a periscope sticking out of the ocean, of that vast, submarine force of discussion and dissent, which we call public opinion. ... Successful

---

[46] Scribner, *For the Sake of Simple Folk* (1981), p. 8.

[47] Miriam Yardeni, *La conscience nationale en France pendant les guerres de religion 1559–1598* (Louvain and Paris, 1971), p. 5.

> pamphlets are those which reflect and at the same time spread and
> modify the 'pulsations' of oral discourse.[48]

Unfortunately, there is still insufficient data to carry out a systematic
study of the relative success of certain books as opposed to others, but
some trends can already be discerned from the sample collected here.[49]
Although there are limits to what one can deduce from simply looking
at book production, the relative success of certain topoi might reflect
the concerns of the readership. The violent polemic which has been
outlined here responded to a certain 'demand' and the recurrence of
certain ideas suggests that they enjoyed a relative success. It this way,
polemical pamphlets can be construed as a gauge of 'public opinion', a
recipient of influences coming from below, rather than as a purely 'top-
down' phenomenon.

In France, 'public opinion' emerged during the Wars of Religion as a
political force to be reckoned with, and it can be argued that the failure
to recognize its political significance contributed to the downfall of the
Valois. The League, for instance, was remarkably successful in imposing
its own vision of Henri III on the public – to the extent that this still
remains in the French collective memory.[50] Sawyer suggests that this
phenomenon was understood to a certain extent by Henri IV (whose
popular legend is even more notorious) but that all its lessons were not
drawn until the reign of Louis XIII:

> Pamphlet authors and political leaders ... worked hard to influence
> the general public's perceptions of the conflict. ... Experienced
> tacticians ... realized that the confrontation would actually be won
> in the sphere of public opinion before it was won on the battlefield.
> ... Governments sought to control the printing press from the
> beginning. It is well known that this effort broke down in the
> sixteenth century, once pamphlets began to be used systematically
> as weapons in the arsenal of Protestant [one should add 'and
> Catholic'] reformers. ... Effective control of the printing industry
> did not begin until the 1620s, when Richelieu was finally able to
> enforce the law.[51]

At the beginning of the French Wars of Religion, however, 'public
opinion' was not wholly recognized as either a legitimate or desirable
political force. Public opinion is known to us as the private sphere,
either individual or collective, where one makes a choice between several

---

[48] Matheson, *Rhetoric of the Reformation*, pp. 27, 32.

[49] This research will be facilitated once the St Andrews French Book Project is completed.

[50] The characterization of Henri III in Dumas' *La Reine Margot* and in the film by
Patrice Chereau owes much to League propaganda.

[51] Sawyer, *Printed Poison*, pp. 5, 25, 46.

options available. Although its influence was acknowledged in passing, it was invariably described as a negative and dangerous entity; words describing 'public opinion' are pejorative. This constitutes a small paradox as the authors who wrote in the vernacular to reach as wide an audience as possible, also despised those whose opinion they were attempting to influence. 'Opinion' does not have the meaning it has now and connotes an entrenched view closer to 'belief' or 'doctrine' than 'judgement' or 'opinion' in the modern sense. For Catholic authors, 'opinion' is simply synonymous with heresy, as indeed the Greek origin of the word suggests: 'I leave out several other heretical opinions that they hold for fear of offending Christian ears.'[52] For the Protestants, 'opinion' is a false accusation, a belief which was ascribed to Protestants by the Catholics to blacken their reputation: 'I am astonished that such a respected body, the court of the Parliament of Paris, allows such detestable opinions to be published, even with a privilege.'[53] In both cases, there is no such thing as a 'good' opinion and diversity of opinion is clearly not an option. Nonetheless, there is a reluctant realization among authors that popular perceptions can be modelled and that this public voice somehow matters.

Furthermore, the material found in these pamphlets pervades the culture of sixteenth-century France. The ideas disseminated in polemic at once shape and are shaped by the emerging 'public opinion'.[54] For example, in the affair of the rue St Jacques, it is obvious that the idea that Protestants took part in orgies existed in both the oral and the written sphere. Feeding off each other, the rumours which spread by word of mouth in the streets of Paris were fuelled by written accounts disseminated by Catholic authors, and vice versa. The ideas found in these pamphlets played an active role as propaganda but also answered the expectations of a captive audience.

To use the analogy of disease, so prized among Catholic authors, ideas spread like viruses. This analogy is probably even more powerful

---

[52] Gabriel de Saconay, *De la providence de dieu sur les roys de france treschrestiens, par laquelle sa saincte religion Catholique ne defaudra en leur Royaume. Et comme les Gotz Arriens, et les Albigeois en ont esté par icelle dechassés* (Lyon, 1568), sig. F3ʳ; Gay, *Histoire des scismes et heresies des Albigeois*, p. 39; Hozius, *Des sectes et heresies de nostre temps*, p. 48.

[53] [Augustin Marlorat], *La Response aux lettres de Nicolas Durant, dict le Chevalier de Villegaignon, addressées à la Reyne mere du Roy. Ensemble la Confutation d'une heresie mise en avant par ledict Villegaignon, contre la souveraine puissance & authorité des Rois* (1561), sig. E7ᵛ; Jean Chassanion, *Histoire des Albigeois: touchant leur doctrine & religion, contre les faux bruits qui ont esté semés d'eux, & les ecris dont on les a à tort diffamés: ...* ([Geneva], 1595), p. 51; Chandieu, *Histoire des persecutions*, sig. d1ᵛ.

[54] Matheson, *Rhetoric of the Reformation*, pp. 20–21, 239.

today, deepened by our knowledge of how viruses actually work. A media analyst, Douglas Rushkoff, recently carried the analogy to its logical conclusion in *Media Virus!*. Like viruses, ideas travel in the datasphere replicating themselves in as many ways as possible. This process has given rise to a neologism, 'meme', which describes an idea which spreads through the media like a virus in an organism: 'Media viruses spread through the datasphere the same way biological ones spread through the body or a community. ... Once attached, the virus injects its more hidden agendas into the datastream in the form of ideological code-not genes, but a conceptual equivalent we now call "memes".'[55] To carry the analogy further, 'memes' affect the collective organism, society at large, or for want of a better word 'public opinion'. Peter Matheson uses a similar analogy to describe the spread of the Reformation in print: 'universal access to public media can carry the bacilli through the body politic'.[56] The themes, topoi or ideas identified in this book could be described as 'memes'. Their recurrence in so many different sources suggests they enjoyed a wide distribution not only in print, but also in the predominant medium of orality.

Indeed Catholic authors added credence to their accusations by resorting to the ubiquitous 'rumour' recently described as the oldest media in the world.[57] For example, Robert Ceneau wrote: 'I only know this by hearsay', or Simon Vigor: 'As soon as I heard that [Margaret of Spain] was horrified at hearing what was said ... '.[58] Protestant authors, such as des Gallars and Chandieu, were particularly quick to accuse Catholic writers of spreading false rumours: '... monks flock to hear the news ... spies report to our betters ... and spread false rumours and feed the population with nonsense and lies'.[59] The best example of the relationship between written polemic and the spread of rumours by word of mouth is provided by the affair of the rue St Jacques: 'it was at the origin of the commonly held belief that assemblies were excuses for orgies and that there were witnesses to that effect'.[60] The work of Robert Darnton has shown that the revolutionary movement in France was greatly facilitated by a dense network of 'news gatherers' who travelled the length of

---

[55] Douglas Rushkoff, *Media Virus! Hidden Agendas in Popular Culture* (New York, 1991), pp. 9–10.

[56] Matheson, *Rhetoric of the Reformation*, p. 28.

[57] Jean-Noël Kapferer, *Rumeurs: le plus vieux média du monde* (Paris, 1987); Gabriel-André Pérouse, 'De la rumeur à la nouvelle au XVIe siècle Français', in M. T. Jones-Davies, ed., *Rumeurs et Nouvelles au temps de la Renaissance* (Paris, 1997), pp. 93–106.

[58] Ceneau, *Response catholique*, sig. E1[r]; Vigor, *Oraison funebre prononcee aux obseques ... de ma Dame Elizabeth de France*, sig. F2[v].

[59] [Des Gallars], *Seconde apologie*, sig. D7[r].

[60] Chandieu, *Histoire des persecutions*, sig. x7[v].

the country disseminating rumours which had been heard in the 'salons' of Paris or at Court.[61] If anything, this pattern must have been even stronger at the time of the French Wars of Religion.

Catholic propaganda thus offers us an inestimable hindsight into the mentality of the first decade of the French Wars of Religion, a sensitive period which can be characterized as 'make or break' for the Reformation. In the following chapters specific themes that emerged strongly out of a range of printed sources are analysed in more detail. The overall impression, expressed perhaps for the very first time, is that the Catholic riposte to the Reformation in France was far richer than it was given credit for and had a 'universal' appeal for the Catholic population. This sometimes crude response was probably more popular than the arguments of the Reformers, however more sensible and better articulated they might seem to the modern reader.

---

[61] Robert Darnton, *The corpus of clandestine literature in France, 1769–1789* (New York, 1995).

CHAPTER FOUR

The use of 'the blood libel' on the eve of the French Wars of Religion

This chapter is concerned with the portrayal of Protestantism in the closing years of the reign of Henri II and during the ensuing period of political instability which followed his death up to the outbreak of the French Wars of Religion. Catholic authors deliberately exploited the clandestine nature of Protestant gatherings to accuse them of conducting orgies and, after the politicization of the conflict, plotting against the Crown. The aim of these authors was to justify the persecution of Protestantism during the reign of Henri II, and forestall the efforts of conciliation that were made during the regency of Catherine de Medici. These accusations were published by the most committed anti-Protestants in the ranks of the Faculty of Theology and the Parlement of Paris, with the obvious aim of swaying public opinion and policy at Court against conciliation.

This is a period when the Catholic majority became increasingly aware of the presence of a Protestant minority in its midst. It is marked by what were perceived as acts of provocation and defiance by the Protestants. On the night of 4 September 1557, students of the Collège du Plessis stumbled upon a clandestine Protestant meeting in a house in the rue St Jacques where between 300 and 400 people had gathered to celebrate the Lord's Supper. The presence of women among them inspired a rumour, which was reproduced in print by Catholic polemicists, that they had assembled there to take part in an orgy. In May 1558, between 4,000 and 6,000 Protestants met every evening of a whole week in the Pré aux Clercs to sing psalms. The French Reformed Church was becoming more aggressive and organized, and its first national synod was held in Paris in 1559. These events marked the intensification of religious divisions and the beginning of a polemical campaign to revile Protestants.[1] This campaign intensified at the beginning of the reign of Charles IX as the regent, Catherine de Medici, sought measures of conciliation towards Protestantism.

---

[1] G. Baum and E. Cunitz, eds, *Histoire Ecclésiastique des Eglises Réformées au Royaume de France*, 3 vols (Paris, 1883–87); Chandieu, *Histoire des persecutions*; Diefendorf, *Beneath the Cross*, p. 50.

The importance of the Eucharist at the heart of the contention between Catholics and Protestants cannot be overestimated. Calvinists
denied the real presence of Christ in the sacrament of the Eucharist and
emphasized the symbolic nature of the Lord's Supper. It had been a
Protestant attack on the Catholic Mass in 1534, the affair of the Plac-
ards, that turned François I against evangelism. At the colloquy of
Poissy in 1561, the ultimate attempt at conciliation before the outbreak
of the Wars, Theodore Beza declared that the body of Christ was as
distant from the wine and the bread as the sky was from the earth. The
intractability of the Catholics and the Protestants on this particular
point of doctrine rendered any attempts at conciliation ineffectual.

It was the celebration of the Lord's Supper, the Protestant answer to
the Catholic Mass, that was at the centre of the polemical campaign to
revile them. In order to avoid detection, Protestants were made to swear
an oath not to reveal the names of those who took part in their ceremonies.[2] The clandestine nature of these proceedings was the source of
much suspicion just as the ceremonies of the Manichees had roused the
suspicion of Augustine: 'I cannot know what you, the elect, do among
yourselves. I have often heard you say that you received the Eucharist,
but the moment of its reception remains hidden from me: how could I
have known what you received?'.[3] Like the early Christians, Jews and
heretics of antiquity, it was the secrecy of the Protestant's celebrations
which enabled the Catholics to spread these stories against them. Jean
de la Vacquerie, writing in 1560, addressed himself directly to the King
to make that very point: 'Now (if I understand correctly) after they
realised that your royal majesty was offended by such insolence, they
retired in caverns, forests, and hidden places, where they conduct their
Sabbath, and diabolical Eucharist, revoking from hell the superstitions
of the ancient idolaters.'[4]

In the 1550s, and especially in the wake of the affair of the rue St
Jacques in September 1557, Protestants were accused of conducting
orgies under the cover of darkness. Reference to darkness, secrecy and
enclosed spaces, are recurrent in each description of the 'diabolical
Sabbath' of the Protestants. The word 'cavern' is the most often reproduced in these accounts: 'caverns, forests, and hidden places', 'caverns,
and subterranean hidden holes', 'what characterises the heretics is to

---

[2] Ibid., p. 122.

[3] R. Jolivet and M. Jourjon, eds, 'Six traités anti-manichéens', *Oeuvres de Saint
Augustin*, (Paris, 1961), p. 137.

[4] Jean de la Vacquerie, *Catholique remonstrance aux roys et princes chrestiens, a tous
magistrats & gouverneurs de Repub. touchant l'abolition des heresies, troubles & scismes
qui regnent aujourd'huy en la Chrestienté* (Paris, 1560), sigs D2ᵛ–D4ʳ.

have pits, caverns and hideouts'.[5] These conventicles always take place at night or under the cover of darkness: 'surely when you see them, you will say that they are enemies of light as the owls are, night thieves, blind moles, when entire companies of them throw themselves in caverns to hide, in pits and remote places and any other hideout that they can find'.[6] Because Protestants gathered clandestinely at night to celebrate the Lord's Supper, Catholic propagandists were able to summon ancient nightmares of heretics conducting a parody of the Mass, drinking the blood and eating the flesh of a slain infant. This parody of the central sacrament of the Christian faith had emerged during the Christian persecutions under the Roman Empire; it had antecedents in anti-Semitic accounts of the Jewish ceremony of Passover, which were assimilated by pagan critics of the new Christian religion.

The ritual murder of children has deep roots in the collective memory of the Judaeo-Christian world. The Old Testament associates the ritual burning of children with the cult of the Canaanite fire god Moloch.[7] The Greeks and Romans were thought to sacrifice children to Kronos or Saturn, a deity which was often depicted as eating his own children. At the turn of the third century Tertullian wrote: 'children were openly sacrificed in Africa to Saturn as lately as the proconsulship of Tiberius'.[8] In both cases, the ritual killing of infants was attributed to a pagan cult, that of Moloch in the Old Testament and that of Saturn in the Classical world. The versatility of the accusation of infanticide, associated with a hostile religious cult, points to its universal appeal as a mark of infamy.

Although both the Old and New Testaments condemned it, both Jews and Christians were accused by the Romans of committing infanticide. Jews were accused of the ritual killing of infants under Emperor Caius: 'Appion spread the rumour against the Jews that they killed a Greek child in their temple and sucked his blood, after having fattened him for a year.'[9] The 'blood libel' dates back to at least the second century BC when the Syrians captured Jerusalem and heard that every seven years Jews carried out a similar ritual in the temple.[10] During the persecutions

---

[5] Ibid., sigs D4[r], E5[v], E6[v]; Eck, *Les lieux communs ... contre Luther*, sig. c4[r]; de Mouchy, *Responce a quelque apologie*, sig. K1[r]; Thomas Beauxamis, *Histoire des sectes tirées de l'armée sathanique* (Paris, 1576), p. 83.

[6] Ceneau, *Response catholique*, sig. A5[v].

[7] Leviticus 18:21, 20:2–4; 2 Kings 23:10; Jeremiah 19:5, 32:35.

[8] T. R. Glover and G. H. Rendall, eds, *Tertullian: Apology* (London, 1984), p. 184.

[9] Beauxamis, *Histoire des sectes*, p. 18.

[10] Gavin I. Langmuir, 'Thomas of Monmouth: Detector of Ritual Murder', *Speculum*, LIX (1984), pp. 820–46 (p. 823).

in Rome, Christians were accused of committing ritual murder and of eating the flesh of infants. It has been suggested that the allegation of ritual murder at the hands of Christians sprang from a misunderstanding of the Christian Eucharist; the biblical entreaty 'Whoever eats my flesh and drinks my blood has eternal life' perhaps being interpreted literally by those outside the Christian faith.[11] As we shall see, cannibalism and the burning of infants to make flour and bake a simulacrum of the wafer was also a leitmotiv of Patristic anti-heretical literature.

Indeed, having been used against pagans, Christians, and Jews, the accusation of ritual murder became the mark of the heretic. After the conversion of Constantine, when Christianity became the official religion of the Empire, the 'blood libel' was appropriated by the Church Fathers for use against the first Christian heretics. Clement of Alexandria, in the second century, had originally used the story against the Manichees, who were among the first challengers of Christian orthodoxy.[12] A contemporary of Clement, Irenaeus of Lyon, cast some doubt as to the veracity of such tales: 'Do they really commit all these crimes, impieties and abominations? For my own part I find it hard to believe.'[13] Epiphanius of Salamis (AD 315–403) used narratives of ritual murder against the Gnostics, who were among the first challengers of Christian orthodoxy:

> In the first place, they hold their wives in common ... the next thing they do is feast ... they next go crazy for each other ... . And when the wretched couple has made love ... the woman becomes pregnant. ... They extract the fetus at the stage appropriate for their enterprise, take this aborted infant, and cut it up in a trough shaped like a pestle. And they mix honey, pepper, and certain other perfumes and spices ... and then all the revellers ... assemble, and each eats a piece of the child with his fingers.[14]

Epiphanius' catalogue of heresies was followed by a similar work by St Augustine of Hippo (AD 354–430) who used a variation of the 'blood libel' against the Montanists:

> They are said to have a baleful sacrament: they make their wafer the same way they would bread, mixing flour with the blood of a one year old child, extracted from small puncture wounds from his whole body: if the boy dies, he is venerated among them as a

---

[11] John 6:54.

[12] Gentian Hervet, ed., *Clementis alexandrini viri longe doctissimi ... omnia quae quidem extant opera* (Paris, 1566), sig. H3ᵛ.

[13] Irenée de Lyon, *Contre les Hérésies: Dénonciation et réfutation de la gnose au nom menteur* (Paris, 1984), p. 116.

[14] Frank Williams, ed., *The Panarion of Epiphanius of Salamis*, 2 vols (Leiden, 1987–94), I, pp. 85–7.

martyr; if however he survives, he is held among them as a great priest.[15]

The Church Fathers provided precedents against which every subsequent heresy was compared. From the twelfth century until the sixteenth, several heretical movements were accused of the 'blood libel'. Guibert, abbot of Nogent (1055–1125) describes in his autobiography the bacchanalia of the heretics of Soissons at the beginning of the twelfth century, with a slight variation:

> In caves or other subterranean & hidden places, they hold their council ... they extinguish the lights, and ... everyone grabs the person nearest at hand and makes love. If, following from this, a woman is pregnant ... a great fire is kindled ... people ... throw [the baby] into the fire where it is consumed; when it is reduced to ashes, they use it to make bread that is divided between all of them. ... If you read Augustine's list of heresies, you will find a similar account concerning the Manichees.[16]

Different versions of this story were used throughout the Middle Ages when the Church was faced with a wave of heterodoxy.[17] It was used at regular intervals against a variety of heretical groups, including the Templars, at the turn of the thirteenth century.[18] Significantly, Jews were equally persecuted during the Middle Ages and were singled out as scapegoats in times of plague.[19] They were often accused of having kidnapped missing children to offer them in sacrifice in the ceremony of Passover.[20] The children who were thought to have been killed in this way became martyrs and sometimes saints and their graves were visited in pilgrimage and were the sites of miracles.[21]

Protestants were also compared with Jews and accused of poisoning Christendom. For example, Georg Witzel lists twelve things that both Jews and Lutherans have in common.[22] Jean Gay puts Protestants,

---

[15] L. G. Müller, ed., *The De Haeresibus of Saint Augustine: a translation with an introduction and commentary* (Washington, DC, 1956), p. 74.

[16] E. R. Labande, ed., *Guibert de Nogent: Autobiographie* (Paris, 1981), pp. 430–31.

[17] G. Mollat, ed., *Bernard Gui: Manuel de l'Inquisiteur*, 2 vols (Paris, 1964).

[18] Vacquerie, *Catholique remonstrance*, sig. E7ʳ; Beauxamis, *Histoire des sectes*, p. 83; Michel de Castelnau, *Mémoires* (Paris, 1621), p. 7.

[19] Andrew Colin Gow, *The Red Jews: antisemitism in an apocalyptic age 1200–1600* (Leiden, 1995), p. 49.

[20] Anna Sapir Abulafia, *Christians and Jews in the Twelfth-Century Renaissance* (London, 1995), pp. 134–5.

[21] Langmuir, 'Thomas of Monmouth'; Gavin Langmuir, 'The Knight's Tale of Young Hugh of Lincoln', *Speculum*, XLVII: 3 (1972), pp. 459–82; R. Po-Chia Hsia, *Trent 1475: Stories of a ritual murder trial* (New Haven, 1992).

[22] Georg Witzel, *Discours des moeurs, tant des anciens hérétiques que nouveaux Lutheriens & Calvinistes, auquel leur resemblance est clerement demonstrée* (Paris,

Albigensians and Jews in the same basket: 'They have become true Jews
... what was also done by the Albigensians ... not to mention usury that
they tolerate more than Jews.'[23] Robert Ceneau also dwelt at length on
this topic: 'Our Calvinists commit usury more than Jews ... '.[24] Finally,
leprosy was also a strong feature of anti-Protestant polemic, although
Protestants were not literally compared to lepers. Gentian Hervet made
a comparison with Jews and argued that, unlike them, Protestants were
able to mix freely among the Catholic population and spread their
heresy as they would the plague.[25] Protestantism was described as a
form of leprosy, in agreement with the medieval tradition of describing
heresy as 'spiritual leprosy', by the cardinal Hozius and Antoine de
Mouchy.[26] Protestants were also accused of poisoning Christendom
more directly, both figuratively and literally. The persecution of Jews
and lepers for poisoning wells during the reign of Philippe V is used by
de Mouchy to argue that because they were burned, so should the
Protestants be for 'poisoning the souls with false doctrine'.[27] Although
de Mouchy's accusation might have been intended figuratively, it was
interpreted literally by Claude de Ruby during the plague epidemics of
Lyon in 1564 and 1576.[28]

The recurrence of these accusations has been noted by Robert Moore
and Carlo Ginzburg who have each offered a different explanation: the
theory of a medieval persecuting society, and the pre-Christian origins
of the witches' sabbath.[29] Both theories, however, have been criticized
for being too reductive.[30] But, even if one excludes Jews and witches
from this debate, the uniformity of treatment meted out to heretics in

---

1567), p. 50; on Witzel see Ralph Keen, 'The Fathers in Counter-Reformation Theology
in the Pre-Tridentine period', in I. Backus, ed., *The Reception of the Church Fathers in
the West: From the Carolingians to the Maurists*, 2 vols (Leiden, 1997), II, pp. 701–43
(p. 725).

[23] Gay, *Histoire des scismes et heresies des Albigeois*, pp. 37, 39.

[24] Ceneau, *Response catholique*, sigs C3^r–C4^r.

[25] Gentian Hervet, *Discours sur ce que les pilleurs, voleurs, & brusleurs d'Eglises
disent qu'ilz n'en veulent qu'aux prestres* (Reims, 1562).

[26] Hozius, *Des sectes et heresies de nostre temps*, p. 78; Mouchy, *Responce a quelque
apologie*, sig. C8^v.

[27] Ibid., sigs C7^{r-v}.

[28] Claude de Ruby, *Discours sur la contagion de la peste qui a esté ceste presente
annee en la ville de Lyon* (Lyon, 1577), sigs C1^{r-v}. I am grateful to Dr W. Naphy
(University of Aberdeen) for this quote.

[29] R. I. Moore, *The Formation of a Persecuting Society: Power and Deviance in
Western Europe 950–1250* (Oxford, 1987), p. 65; Carlo Ginzburg, *Ecstasies: Deciphering the Witches' Sabbath* (London, 1991), pp. 33, 36, 38–9.

[30] David Nirenberg, *Communities of Violence: Persecution of Minorities in the Middle
Ages* (Princeton, 1996), pp. 4–16, 242–3.

the history of Christendom is still notable. There is no mystery attached
to this; each successive generation of theologians referred to the preceding wrangling with heretics to defend the Church against their current
enemies, as is shown conclusively by the continuous use of the same
accusations (with minor variations) against heretics from the third to
the sixteenth century. Whether, as both Moore and Ginzburg argue, this
tradition had an impact on the Catholic Church's dealings with Jews,
lepers and witches is still a matter of contention.[31] Further pieces of
evidence from sixteenth-century France should nonetheless be added to
the debate opened by Moore's *Persecuting Society*.

Comparison between Protestantism and the heresies of late antiquity
and the medieval period was a common staple of the anti-Protestant
polemic. These key periods of Church history were marked by two
fundamental Church Councils (Nicaea in 325 and the fourth Lateran
Council in 1215) which defined orthodoxy in the face of heresy. The
heretics condemned at these Councils became indistinguishable from
one another in the minds of theologians and were used as precedents to
condemn further heresies. To all intents and purposes all these heretical
groups were related and any new heterodox movement was added to
the family tree of heresy. Augustine had described the tree of heresy and
the great medieval summas perpetuated this image and passed it on to
the sixteenth century.[32] For example, Bernhard von Luxemburg's
Catalogus haereticorum omnium (1522) and Alonso de Castro's *Adversus Omnes Haereses* (1534) catalogue heresies along the principles laid
down by Augustine.[33]

From the outset of the Reformation, Catholic theologians compared
Protestants with what they saw as their medieval counterparts. For
example, in 1537, the Catholic controversialist Georg Witzel described
the Lutherans in these terms: 'the sects of this age have great affinity
with the old ... . The similarity in nature and behaviour is in all points
obvious.'[34] In order to fuel their arguments, Catholic theologians also
translated and borrowed heavily from Church Fathers' treatises against

[31] R. I. Moore, 'Heresy as Disease', in D. W. Lourdeaux and D. Verhelst, eds, *The
Concept of Heresy in the Middle Ages* (Louvain, 1976), pp. 1–11.

[32] M.-M. Fragonard, 'La détermination des frontières symboliques: nommer et définir
les groupes hérétiques', in R. Sauzet, ed. *Les Frontières religieuses en europe du XVe au
XVIIe siècle* (Paris, 1992), pp. 37–49.

[33] Bernhard von Luxemburg, *Catalogus haereticorum omnium* (Köln, 1522); Alonso
de Castro, *Adversus Omnes Haereses* (Paris, 1534), sigs o1ᵛ–o2ʳ.

[34] Witzel, *Discours des moeurs*, p. 5.

heretics.[35] The editor of Vincent de Lérins (a fifth-century Gallic saint), for example, thought that no modern author could be as eloquent, or brief, on the subject of heresy: 'The more learned of our contemporaries confess that they have never found elsewhere more holy sentences in so little paper.'[36] When Georg Witzel compared the doctrine of salvation by faith with the Manichees' beliefs, he was echoed by the French authors who wrote against the Calvinists.[37] This argument was used, for example, by Nicolas Durand, Chevalier de Villegagnon, who directly addressed the Queen Mother: 'If you want to know which eucharist they advise you to take in exchange for yours, it is none other than that of the raving Manichee against which St Augustine wrote.'[38] To all intents and purposes, all heretics were interchangeable and were guilty of the same crimes.

At the beginning of the sixteenth century, the 'blood libel' was influentially relayed by Desiderius Erasmus in his book on the concord of the Church (1533):

> ... within recent memory there have been discovered nightly gatherings at which, after praise has been given to God, the lights are extinguished and the men and women consort in promiscuous love. Or the ceremonies in which mothers freely hand over their infants to be butchered, and even watch serenely the horrid crime, so persuaded are they that their children will thus find a high place in heaven.[39]

Whether this passage was inspired by a rumour that circulated in Paris in 1532 about a sect that sucked the blood of infants is unclear,[40] but the use of the 'blood libel' by Erasmus gave it a degree of credibility and subsequent authors cited it as a precedent. Stanislas Hozius, a Polish cardinal, refers to Erasmus as his source in his *Des sectes et heresies de nostre temps* (1561): '... another sect (which is mentioned by Erasmus) amongst whom mothers bring their own children to be killed, & consider lightly such a horrible sacrifice'.[41] A Frenchman,

---

[35] Optat, *Histoire du schisme, blasphemes & autres impietez des Donatiens* (Paris, 1564), and Hervet, ed., *Clementis alexandrini*.

[36] Vincent de Lérins, *Petit traite de Vincent Lerineuse pour la verite et antiquite de la foy catholique* (Paris, 1563), sig. F6^v.

[37] Witzel, *Discours des moeurs*, pp. 22–5.

[38] Durand, *Lettres du Chevallier de Villegaignon*, sigs B3^{r-v}.

[39] Desiderius Erasmus, *Liber de sarcienda Ecclesiae concordia deque sedandis opinionum dissidiis* (Basel, 1533); reproduced in J. P. Dolan, *The essential Erasmus* (New York, 1964), pp. 442–3.

[40] L. Lalanne, ed., *Journal d'un bourgeois de Paris sous le règne de François Premier 1515–1536* (Paris, 1854), p. 429; [des Gallars], *Seconde apologie*, sig. B7^r.

[41] Hozius, *Des sectes et heresies de nostre temps*, pp. 166–7.

Antoine du Val, referred to Erasmus for a precedent of what he inferred
had occurred at the assembly of the rue St Jacques in September 1557:

> Our Calvinists are like those heretics: after having sung psalms &
> other songs, they put out the lights: as for what they do after that, I
> refer you to what was done in Paris, in the night of 4 September
> 1557, in the great rue St Jacques, where there were more than 500
> heretics assembled ... who after the candles were put out, mixed
> together indiscriminately, men and women, to make love. Erasmus
> adds in his book on the admirable concord of the church that far
> worse was done at these nocturnal meetings, where fathers will-
> ingly offered their own children to be sacrificed, seeing such horrible
> crime favourably, believing that their children, thus killed, became
> martyrs.[42]

By using this story, Catholic polemicists associated Protestantism
with a long list of heretics and sought to justify their persecution at a
time when Protestantism threatened to take over the body politic. The
use of the 'blood libel' against the Protestants of the rue St Jacques must
be seen in the context of centuries of characterization of heretics, which
had become ingrained in the culture of western Christendom. The story
had become an integral part of the institutionalized Church's response
to heresy and the Catholic authors were perpetuating medieval persecution mechanisms. The use of the accusation of infanticide against
Protestantism on the eve of the French Wars of Religion was not unprecedented. What is remarkable is the scale on which these accusations
were spread in print and in the vernacular, crediting rumours that had
previously been given only restricted circulation.

It is difficult to gauge the impact that the 'blood libel' had on contemporaries. There is evidence that one of its pedlars, Antoine de Mouchy,
attempted to substantiate his claims with first-hand accounts of the
clandestine meetings. The controversy that had been roused by the
affair of the rue St Jacques in 1557 was intensified during the short
and controversial reign of François II, marked as it was by the rivalry
between the Guises and the Bourbons. This period coincides with an
unprecedented wave of persecution that lasted from August 1559 to
March 1560 and culminated in the purge of royal officials and high-
ranking civil servants. In addition to accusations in print, it was
suggested that the cardinal de Lorraine, the duc de Guise's brother,
conspired with de Mouchy to add credibility to these stories at Court.[43]

---

[42] Du Val, *Mirouer des Calvinistes*, fol. 9r.
[43] Diefendorf, *Beneath the Cross*, pp. 55, 135.

According to Protestant sources, de Mouchy received the testimony of two young apprentices who claimed to have been taken to a Protestant meeting by their master. They were coaxed into revealing the names of those who had taken part and testifying that an orgy, such as was described in the polemic, had indeed taken place. Antoine de la Roche Chandieu provides a detailed account of the testimony of one of the apprentices:

> The apprentice told the judges that it was his master who had led him to the assembly. As he was so prompt to denounce his master, great promises were made to him in exchange for the names of those he saw there, and he enumerated everyone without exception, adding that the rumours about the assemblies were true, that people copulated freely once the candles were put out.[44]

According to another account, one of the apprentices even claimed to have had sex two or three times with one of the daughters of the lawyer in whose house this orgy had taken place.[45] The cardinal de Lorraine brought the two apprentices to Catherine de Medici in an attempt to convince her that the stories disseminated in print by de Mouchy and others were true.[46] Theodore Beza's *Histoire Ecclésiastique* adds that the cardinal de Lorraine made a parallel with a number of medieval heresies, which suggests that he was drawing from printed polemic:

> The Cardinal, for his own part, did not miss an opportunity to use their testimony. With their written confession in hand and the two apprentices at his tail, he went to the Queen Mother, to describe to her at length the content of their confession with great exclamations, leaving nothing out so that those of the religion were portrayed as the most odious & abominable creatures that had ever lived. So that nothing would be missed, he embellished his account with all the things that various heretics had done in the past, accusations which had been suggested by the devil to cast a shadow on the light of the Gospel, from the time when it had started being preached in secret, because of the persecutions of the pagan and idolatrous emperors.[47]

The long list of heretics provided by the cardinal de Lorraine was also used as precedent in Catholic polemic, notably in Antoine de Mouchy's work. According to Protestant sources, there is no doubt that the agenda of the Guises and the productions of the Catholic polemicists

---

[44] Chandieu, *Histoire des persecutions*, sigs x7r–x8r.

[45] Baum and Cunitz, eds, *Histoire Ecclésiastique*, p. 234.

[46] Anon., *La Maniere d'appaiser les troubles, qui sont maintenant en France, & y pourront estre cy apres: A la Royne mere du Roy* ([Lyon], 1561), sig. B2r.

[47] Baum and Cunitz, eds, *Histoire Ecclésiastique*, I, p. 236.

converged.[48] According to the *Histoire Ecclésiastique*, Catherine de Medici would have been swayed by the testimony of the two apprentices but was advised to have them cross-examined.[49] This cross-examination revealed that they had been lying, and the whole matter was dropped.

Despite the exposure of the false witnesses, the belief that Protestants took part in orgies survived. Penny Roberts has uncovered the case of a city councillor of Troyes who escaped prosecution in 1562 by arguing that his only reason for attending a Protestant meeting was the hope of taking part in such an orgy:

> A few were imprisoned in the goal of the palace where they stayed
> awhile. The conseiller de Pleurre was one of them. Being brought
> before those gentlemen of the court of the Parlement to be interro-
> gated, he confessed so that he could be let out of prison. He had
> attended a Protestant assembly and sermon to fulfil his carnal
> desire and have sex with the woman of his choice, thinking that the
> rumour was true, that women gave themselves freely at those
> assemblies. But having seen and understood that this was false, and
> not having found what he was looking for, he had resolved not to
> go there again. The court, trying hard not to laugh, released de
> Pleurre.[50]

Furthermore, the myth of the orgiastic Protestants was mixed with the horrible reality of the Parisian persecutions during which children were left abandoned on the streets of Paris. Lancelot du Voisin de la Popelinière's *Histoire de France* recounts how preachers on street corners rekindled the accusations of infanticide and cannibalism by pointing at these children as those the Protestants had intended to eat during their orgies:

> One could not walk through the streets without coming across
> soldiers armed with swords who roughly led all kinds of male and
> female prisoners. Poor little children were left in the streets, crying

---

[48] Anon., *Advertissement a la Royne Mere du Roy, Touchant les miseres du Royaume au temps present, & de la conspiration des ennemis de sa Majesté* (Orleans, 1562), sigs c3ᵛ–c4ʳ; *La Maniere d'appaiser les troubles*, sig. C1ᵛ; Tallon, *La France et le Concile de Trente*, p. 735; Denis Pallier, 'Les impressions de la Contre-Réforme en France et l'apparition des grandes companies de libraires parisiens', *Revue Française d'Histoire du Livre*, XXXI (1981), pp. 215–73 (pp. 250, 269, 272); Pallier, 'Les réponses catholiques', p. 337; Stuart Carroll, 'The Guise affinity and popular protest during the Wars of Religion', *FH*, IX (1995), pp. 125–52; K. Cameron, 'La polémique, la mort de Marie Stuart et l'assassinat de Henri III', in Robert Sauzet, ed., *Henri III et son temps* (Paris, 1992), pp. 185–94.

[49] Baum and Cunitz, eds, *Histoire Ecclésiastique*, I, p. 237.

[50] Penny Roberts, *A City in Conflict: Troyes during the French Wars of Religion* (Manchester, 1996), p. 84, n. 64; BN Dupuy MS 698 (Pithou), fol. 243ᵛ. I have to thank Penny Roberts (University of Warwick) for the transcript of this document.

of hunger, and no one rescued them for fear of being arrested himself. People paid less attention to them than they would to dogs, such was the Parisians' contempt for the Protestant faith. To encourage the hatred of the Parisians, there were people at street corners who told them that the heretics gathered at night to eat those little children and copulate with one another when the candles were put out, after having eaten a pig instead of the Paschal lamb and committed together an infinity of incest and infamous deeds: and people believed it as if it was true.[51]

The use of the 'blood libel' provoked a vigorous response from the Protestants and fuelled a flurry of polemic which contributed to the definition of Protestant identity. Because the 'blood libel' had been used against early Christians, Protestants argued that their current persecution was as unjust as that of the early Church martyrs. This enabled them to make a case for the martyrdom of the victims of the persecutions during the reign of Henri II. Martyrdom was a keystone of Protestant identity, and, from 1554 onwards, it was propagated from Geneva through the numerous editions of Jean Crespin's *Histoire des Martyrs*.

Crespin's *Histoire des Martyrs*, which is perhaps the single most important text for the elaboration of a distinct Huguenot identity, celebrates the exemplary deaths of French-speaking men and women who suffered persecution under the Valois monarchy. It relied on the testimony of individuals who flocked to Geneva to flee from persecution, a phenomenon which has been well studied. What is perhaps less well understood is the debt the *Histoire des Martyrs* owes to the Catholic adversary. The elaboration of Huguenot self-perception and identity did not take place in a vacuum; it resulted from a dialectic, often hostile, between Catholic polemic and Huguenot response. Catholic contributions to the Reformation debate in France have long suffered from historiographical oversight.

Before the outbreak of the French Wars of Religion, the persecutions of the reign of Henri II gave Huguenots the occasion to draw on a comparison with the early Church. To die for one's faith was not in itself a sign of election and to call those burned at the stake 'martyrs' reflects a certain ideological standpoint. At their trial, Huguenots were asked to recant their 'heresy' and return to the bosom of the Roman and Apostolic Church. It was obstinacy, and not heresy as such, that was punishable by death. For Huguenots, obstinacy was a sign that one was unwilling to compromise one's faith, and to be killed was to be

---

[51] Lancelot du Voisin de la Popelinière, *L'Histoire de France enrichie des plus notables occurances survenues ez Provinces de l'Europe & pays voisins*, 2 vols (1581), I, fol. 148ᵛ.

martyred. As Brad Gregory pointed out in *Salvation at Stake*, martyrdom was a cultural representation which depended on one's interpretation
of execution.[52]

The Genevan reformer Guillaume Farel was one of the first to write
about martyrdom in the French-speaking world,[53] but it was Calvin
who, by giving it pride of place in his work, contributed most to the
dissemination of the culture of martyrdom. For Calvin, it was prefer-
able to suffer death than to participate in Catholic worship. In his 1543
pamphlet against Nicodemites, Calvin called upon the example of St
Cyprian who suffered martyrdom rather than worship idols.[54] Calvin's
approach to martyrdom is revealed in his letters written to French
prisoners at the height of the persecutions under Henri II, in which he
urged his co-religionists to remain firm in their faith and maintained
that their death was a proof of their election:

> Persecutions are the true combats of Christians to try the con-
> stancy and firmness of their faith ... . It has been said of old that
> the blood of the martyrs is the seed of the Church. If it is a seed
> from which we derive our origin in Jesus Christ, it should also be a
> shower to water us that we may grow and make progress, even so
> as to die well.[55]

The dissemination of the culture of martyrdom did not go unchal-
lenged. Catholics resorted to the dictum found in Augustine that it is
not the punishment that makes a martyr but the cause for which he
dies.[56] The fact that heretics such as Arians and Donatists had also
claimed to be martyrs, was used to disprove the validity of the Calvinist
cause. This case was difficult to answer since Calvinists themselves,
such as the Walloon Gui de Brès, used the very same arguments against
the Anabaptists.[57] The Polish cardinal Stanislas Hozius, for example,
made the most of this apparent contradiction, and described with a
certain irony the 'lust for death' of the Calvinists: 'They have begun to
glorify themselves of the number and constancy of their martyrs ...
Calvin must not boast ... that his followers are poor lambs destined to
be slaughtered: because the Anabaptists ... have done so for many

---

[52] Brad S. Gregory, *Salvation at Stake: Christian Martyrdom in Early Modern Europe*
(Harvard, 1999), p. 76.

[53] David El Kenz, *Les Bûchers du Roi: la Culture Protestante des Martyrs 1523–1572*
(Paris, 1997), p. 72.

[54] Jean Calvin, 'Petit traité montrant que c'est que doit faire un homme fidèle connaissant
la verité de l'Evangile quand il est entre les papistes', in O. Millet, ed., *Oeuvres choisies*
(Paris, 1995), pp. 136–7.

[55] Jules Bonnet, ed., *Letters of John Calvin* (Edinburgh, 1980), pp. 219, 223–4.

[56] Witzel, *Discours des moeurs*, p. 11.

[57] Brès, *La racine, source et fondement des Anabaptistes*, p. 62.

centuries before anyone had even heard of the Sacramentarians.'[58] These arguments carried a certain weight given the emphasis placed in martyrologies on the patience with which martyrs suffered death. In place of the Huguenot martyr, the Catholics offered the image of the obstinate heretic. But resort to the stereotypes of heresy fuelled rather than hindered the Huguenot representation of martyrdom. This is nowhere better illustrated than in the polemical exchange which surrounded the affair of the rue St Jacques.

The period which followed the Edict of Compiègnes (1557) marked the crystallization of the Huguenot conception of martyrdom. The discovery of a secret meeting in the rue St Jacques in September 1557, was the occasion for the Huguenots to further elaborate on the culture of martyrdom and provoked a lengthy polemical exchange between theologians of the University of Paris and ministers who had witnessed the persecutions in Paris. The most important exchange was between Antoine de Mouchy, a key Catholic figure, and Nicolas des Gallars, a minister in Paris at the time of the affair. Des Gallars had been a member of the Geneva Company of Pastors between 1544 and 1554 and volunteered to be a minister in Paris between July and September 1557.[59] Following the imprisonment of numerous Huguenots, his *Apologie ou defense des vrais chrestiens* was published anonymously. Des Gallars made the point of indicating the pagan origins of the anti-Protestant allegations: 'Is it not the same accusation that was used against Christians in the past, saying that they killed little children to eat them?'[60] The parallel between Protestants and the early Church martyrs became the official Protestant response and is reproduced in the *Histoire Ecclésiastique*: 'even saying that we killed small children, and other such things that Satan used against the primitive Church'.[61]

Des Gallars pointed out the similarity with the accusations against which Tertullian wrote his apology during the persecutions of Emperor Trajan in the second century: 'We are called abominable from the sacrament of infanticide and the feeding thereon, as well as the incestuous

---

[58] Hozius, *Des sectes et heresies de nostre temps*, pp. 136–7, 142.

[59] [Des Gallars], *Seconde apologie*; P. Feret, *La Faculté de Théologie de Paris et ses Docteurs les plus célèbres: Epoque Moderne XVI–XVIIIème siècle*, 6 vols (Paris, 1900–09), II, pp. 51–5; Mouchy, *Responce a quelque apologie*, sigs F2ʳ⁻ᵛ, F4ʳ⁻ᵛ, J8ᵛ, K1ᵛ; On 7 September 1557, des Gallars wrote to Calvin for instructions after the affair of the rue St Jacques; Kingdon, ed., *Registres de la compagnie des pasteurs*, II (1962), pp. 128–34; William G. Naphy, *Calvin and the consolidation of the Genevan Reformation* (Manchester, 1994), pp. 58, 73.

[60] [Des Gallars], *Seconde apologie*, sigs D8ʳ⁻ᵛ.

[61] Baum and Cunitz, eds, *Histoire Ecclésiastique*, I, pp. 143–4.

intercourse, following the banquet.'[62] Unlike any minority group against which the accusation had been used before, Protestants were able to turn it round to their advantage. By drawing attention to the use of the same accusation against the early Church martyrs, Protestants were able to legitimize their cause. Another Paris minister, Antoine de la Roche Chandieu, recounts in his *Histoire des persecutions* (1563), that des Gallars's arguments had been decisive:

> This small pamphlet ... dispelled the bad impression that many people had of our assemblies and even encouraged others to make deeper inquiries of our doctrine. Some doctors of the Sorbonne attempted to answer it: but the poor beasts, as in all things, discovered nothing but their own ignorance. One named Mouchi ... wrote an entire book on the punishment of heretics and showed that they must be burned and dealt with by fire and swords.[63]

Antoine de Mouchy had published a response to this first tract in 1558, where he accused Huguenots of taking part in orgies under the cover of darkness.[64] Des Gallars answered de Mouchy directly in a second tract entitled *Seconde apologie ou defense des vrais chrestiens*[65] which reproduced entire passages of Tertullian's apology, a key text of Christian martyrology.[66] Tertullian's dictum that 'the blood of the martyrs is seed' had been used by Protestants in general, and by Calvin in particular.[67] In addition, Tertullian reported accusations of sexual improprieties used by Romans against Christians so enabling des Gallars, and others, to strengthen the comparison with the early Church martyrs. Chandieu's *Histoire des persecutions*, which reports the exchange, was itself used in the first folio edition of Crespin's *Histoire des Martyrs* published in 1564.

Although Jean Crespin drew on such polemical material for the compilation of his *Histoire des Martyrs*, any adversarial or political comments were carefully left out for fear of being accused of encouraging sedition. At the time of the martyrdom of Cyprian, the cult of the emperors was law, and the refusal of the saint to worship 'idols' was in itself akin to political insurrection. So, in France, the culture of martyrdom based on political disobedience grew in parallel with a policy of outward conformity with the laws of the Prince. The model of martyrdom held up by Calvin was therefore associated with political disobedience, a problem

---

[62] J. E. B. Mayor, ed., *Tertullian: Apologeticus* (Cambridge, 1917), p. 27.

[63] Chandieu, *Histoire des persecutions*, sigs d1ᵛ–d2ʳ.

[64] Mouchy, *Responce a quelque apologie*.

[65] [Des Gallars], *Seconde apologie*.

[66] Mayor, ed., *Apologeticus*, pp. 7, 25, 29, 31.

[67] Gregory, *Salvation at Stake*, p. 150.

that was exacerbated with the outbreak of the French Wars of Religion when heresy was associated with rebellion.

The ability of the Protestants to respond to these accusations and turn them to their advantage by drawing on a comparison with the early Church martyrs was unexpected and unforeseen. Furthermore, the agenda of Catholic polemicists like Antoine de Mouchy had coincided with the royal policy of persecution during the reigns of Henri II and François II, but when the latter died in 1560 the ten-year-old Charles IX was put under the tutelage of Catherine de Medici who started implementing conciliatory measures. The Edict of Compiègne (1557) had made heresy into a criminal offence punishable by death in the civil courts rather than in the ecclesiastical courts and the reversal of this decision with the Edict of Romorantin in May 1560 was interpreted by Catholic theologians as a mark of favouritism towards Protestants. An anonymous Protestant pamphlet marks the transition from accusations of orgy to those of plotting against the Crown and printing inflammatory pamphlets: 'At this time, it was said that these assemblies always occurred in arms, that abominable acts were committed there ... and that libellous pamphlets were written, and that scandalous ... discourse was held against the King and the Queen Mother.'[68]

Catholics indeed moved away from the 'blood libel', which had provided the Huguenots with ammunition in their comparison with the early Church martyrs. It is clear that this shift to accusations of a political plot to take over the kingdom made the Protestants uneasy. Indeed, in March 1560, a small army led by La Renaudie attempted to kidnap the young king François II at Amboise, which provoked a second salvo of Catholic propaganda. The Huguenot response after this incident was increasingly defensive and clumsy, often resorting to petty personal attacks. After the outbreak of the French Wars of Religion in 1562, when the Protestant prince de Condé seized Orléans, the accusation of political disobedience was more credible and, one may argue, justified.[69] Significantly, the 'blood libel' appeared once more on the eve of the massacre of St Bartholomew, but was used against Italians.[70] The ability of the Protestants to turn the 'blood libel' to their advantage did not spell the end of this particular 'meme' that was turned against other victims.

---

[68] Anon., *Apologie contre certaines Calomnies mises sus, à la desfaveur & desavantage de l'Estat des affaires de ce Roiaume* (Paris, 1562), sigs D4ᵛ–D5ʳ.

[69] This was noted by Philip Benedict, *A City Divided: Rouen during the Wars of Religion* (Cambridge, 1981), pp. 65–7.

[70] Henri Heller, 'The Italian Saint Bartholomew: Assassins or Victims?' (unpublished paper, Sixteenth-Century Studies Conference, 1999), 17 pages.

CHAPTER FIVE

Accusations of insurrection and Protestant responses

In the 1560s, Catholic theologians discredited the myth of the Huguenot martyr with accusations of political insurrection. In March 1560, at Amboise, Protestant plotters attempted to rid the Court of the Guises' influence. The 'tumult of Amboise' marked the time when French Protestants started to be called 'Huguenots' and were irremediably associated with civil disobedience.[1] The politicization of the conflict after Amboise damaged the image of the Huguenots as innocent victims, although they continued to be portrayed as such throughout the Wars of Religion.[2] Resort to armed rebellion could no longer be squared with the image of the innocent martyr that was disseminated by Crespin. Furthermore, there was a shift from heresy to sedition in the prosecution of Protestantism and public executions increasingly resulted in scenes of violence and disorder.[3] Whereas the burning of heretics had provided a platform for the theatre of martyrdom, hanging (a fate reserved for common criminals) denied the Huguenots their martyrdom. This movement to turn heresy into a political crime went hand in hand with a polemical campaign to portray Huguenots as dangerous agitators and rebels.

The death of Henri II in 1559 marked the emergence of conspiracy theories on both sides of the confessional divide as Huguenot and Catholic factions vied for control at Court. In the polemical flood that followed the tumult of Amboise, each faction accused the other of wanting to usurp the throne and the theme of a Huguenot conspiracy began to emerge. François Hotman, one of the instigators of Amboise, provides us with a good example of the arguments that were used:

> Knowing that a great number of Lutherans or Evangelists, as they are called, were involved in the enterprise, the Gospel was blamed for everything. And everywhere in France the news are spread that

[1] Anon., *Complainte au peuple Francois*, in [Hotman], *L'Histoire du tumulte d'Amboyse*, sig. D2ʳ.
[2] Penny Roberts, 'Huguenot Petitioning during the Wars of Religion', in R. Mentzer and A. Spicer, eds, *Society and Culture in the Huguenot World, 1559–1665* (Cambridge, forthcoming).
[3] Nicholls, 'Theatre of Martyrdom', p. 69; Monter, *Judging the French Reformation*, pp. 212–43.

those who have risen are Lutherans: that their goal was to kill the King, the Queen, the Lords his brothers, and all the Princes: to promote their Religion with sword blows, to abolish the Monarchy of France, and to reduce it to a kind of Republic.[4]

By way of response an anonymous *Remonstrance a la royne mere du Roy*, probably written by Augustin Marlorat, attempted to dispel such accusations. Augustin Marlorat marks the transition in Catholic polemic from the 'blood libel' to more credible accusations of rebellion:

Our adversaries ... try to convince the King and yourself that our assemblies are nothing but a pretext for a dissolute licence to take part in an orgy ... . But seeing that it is a lie that cannot be proven ... . They find another, that is more easily received, that we meet to plot to kill the King and the nobility ... and it would be surprising if they could not find, among those that they cruelly put to death, one who could confirm their lies.[5]

It was answered directly by both René Benoist and Nicolas Durand, Chevalier de Villegagnon, who had the dubious honour of having martyred the first Calvinist during his expedition to Brazil.[6] This polemical exchange contributed to the further elaboration of the conspiracy theory and René Benoist used the denial of the *Remonstrance* to renew the accusations of conspiracy.[7] Nicolas Durand went even further in accusing the Protestants of wanting the total abolition not only of religion, but also of the aristocracy and, ultimately, the Crown: 'They mock Christianity and under the pretense of religion they want to convert us to atheism, to dissipate the holy status of this kingdom, founded on religion, extinguish the legitimate succession of our Kings in order to reduce us to a state of anarchy and mob rule.'[8] Although these accusations were a far cry from what was intended at Amboise, they presented a serious challenge to the representation of Huguenots as innocent martyrs. The tumult of Amboise had irreparably damaged the credibility of the Huguenots who were now on the defensive. After the death of François II in December 1560, many polemical tracts were addressed to the Regent, Catherine de Medici, on both sides of the confessional divide.

One of the most outspoken authors to use the idea of a conspiracy was Jean de la Vacquerie. Writing about the assembly of the Pré aux Clercs in May 1558 where 4,000 Protestants had assembled defiantly in

---

[4] [Hotman], *L'Histoire du tumulte d'Amboyse*, sig. C1ᵛ.

[5] [Marlorat], *Remonstrance a la royne mere du Roy*, sigs B5ᵛ–B6ᵛ.

[6] Frank Lestringant, *L'Expérience Huguenote au Nouveau Monde* (Geneva, 1996).

[7] Benoist, *Brieve Response a quelque remonstrance*, sig. A6ᵛ.

[8] Durand, *Lettres du Chevallier de Villegaignon*, sigs B1ʳ, B3ᵛ.

the open to sing psalms, he used the coincidence of the defeat of the King at the hands of the imperial army to make a causal link between the two:

> In this year 1558, at the same time armies on both sides were making ready for battle, a new assembly was called in Paris, not inside houses, or at night (as before) but in plain sight, and in daylight & with a company of armed men, & under the authority of great and powerful lords.[9]

The distinction made by Jean de la Vacquerie is a very important one. Indeed, under the new regime, practising the Reformed religion was permitted in certain designated areas. The assembly of the Pré aux Clercs served as a precedent for this period when Protestant assemblies were no longer confined to meeting surreptitiously in private houses. The 'blood libel' that had been used hitherto by Catholic polemicists now became more difficult to substantiate; on the other hand, the display of powerful notables bearing arms at these assemblies helped fuel the fear of a Protestant plot. Jean de la Vacquerie described a fully-fledged conspiracy to take over the kingdom by appointing Protestant magistrates, judges and city officials – the means, he argued, by which Swiss and German cities had been won to the Reformation:

> ... they conspire to see how they can bring the end, or deprive them of their office, of the magistrates that are contrary to them: in order to replace them with those favourable to their faction: and in this way hold the reins of power ... this is how they won Geneva, Lausanne and several other Swiss and German cities.[10]

The fear that Protestants were infiltrating the Parlement of Paris was very real and inspired the purge that culminated with the execution of Anne du Bourg in March 1560. These accusations posed a considerable problem to Protestant writers who, once more, fell back on a comparison with the early Church martyrs.

Antoine de la Roche Chandieu, for example, used the fact that Protestants were blamed for the failure of the Franco-Habsburgh war: 'our adversaries were so enraged that they blamed all these miseries on the Christians ... many complain and think that the wars ... plagues, famines, floods happen because of us'.[11] This mirrors the writing of other Protestant authors who referred to earlier persecutions – for example, the Walloon Gui de Brès writing in 1555: 'If the Tiber rises to the walls. If the Nile descends on the fields. If the sky stops. If the earth trembles.

---

[9] Vacquerie, *Catholique remonstrance*, sigs D2^v–D4^r.

[10] Ibid., sigs F1^{r-v}.

[11] Chandieu, *Histoire des persecutions*, sigs a1^v, b8^v.

If there is famine or pestilence: without delay they blame the Christians who are led to the lions.'[12] This argument was used by des Gallars with an added edge after the affair of the rue St Jacques: 'It will be said that we are the cause of wars, defeats and losses, famines and pestilence ... the same was said in the past about the Christians.'[13] According to this interpretation of events, Protestants, like the early Christians, were the scapegoats of a society that blamed them for natural disasters, war, famine and disease. This is what the Protestant Jean de Serres concluded in 1595 about the persecutions which followed the affair of the rue St Jacques: 'in many other places, others were seized and sentenced to death, the people blaming them for the misfortunes of France'.[14] It was very much in the interest of the Protestant authors to draw a parallel with the early Church, and hence portray the Protestants as innocent martyrs.

But the myth of the Protestant as an innocent martyr could not withstand the increasing politicization of the conflict. The onus of the Protestant response to Catholic arguments fell on the shoulders of authors who could no longer deny that Protestants were involved in acts of rebellion. This contrasts markedly with the Protestant response before the conspiracy of Amboise and reflects a shift of emphasis in Catholic polemic from the 'blood libel' to accusations of conspiracy. Whereas the 'blood libel' enabled the Protestants to draw a parallel with the Christian persecutions, the shift towards a Protestant conspiracy was much more difficult to address. From this point onwards, the Protestant response within France is characterized by its defensive nature; accusations were turned round and personal attacks on the characters of Catholic writers were frequently made. The Protestant response after Amboise set the tone for the whole period of the wars during which the University of Paris and the Guises were consistently attacked.[15] The personal nature of these attacks shows that the Protestants held specific individuals responsible for the persecutions rather than the King. On the one hand, they attacked these individuals while, on the other, they appealed to the clemency of the Crown. By blaming the University of Paris and the Guises for the situation, Protestants allowed for the possibility of reconciliation with the Crown. This is

---

[12] [Gui de Brès], Le Baston de la foy chrestienne, Livre tresutile a tous Chrestiens, pour s'armer contre les ennemys de l'Evangile: & pour aussi cognoistre l'ancienneté de nostre saincte foy, & de la vraye Eglise (Lyon, 1555), sigs Z4[r-v].

[13] [Des Gallars], Seconde apologie, sig. E6[r].

[14] Jean de Serres, Recueil des choses memorables avenues en France (1595), sig. D1[r].

[15] Examples can be found in Shaw, ed., Comedie du Pape Malade; and Bordier, ed., Chansonnier Huguenot.

reflected in the *Histoire Ecclésiastique* (1580) where Antoine de Mouchy and the cardinal de Lorraine are described as the chief instigators of the persecutions.[16]

The Guise brothers were the favourite targets of Protestant adversarial polemic. An anonymous pamphlet even used the defeat of St Quentin to denigrate the Guises in the eyes of the King: 'It is him who put your enemy in St Quentin, withdrawing, under pretence of protection, the forces of your kingdom: thinking ... that it would make you prey to the Spanish.'[17] Another anonymous pamphlet also accused the cardinal de Lorraine of being behind the conspiracy accusations: 'The adversaries of the Reformation ... proclaim that the purpose of our assemblies is to rise against the King. To that effect, the cardinal de Lorraine uses the royal edicts to disseminate treacherous lies.' The same pamphlet attributed the defeat of St Quentin and the death of Henri II to divine providence:

> If we consider the loss of St Quentin ... did it not occur when ... the decision was made to persecute as many faithful as could be found? ... and when king Henri inflamed by the cardinal de Lorraine ... vowed that he would see with his own eyes the councillor du Bourg burn ... was he not struck by the very hand of God so that he lost the use of his eyes, and thereafter his life ...?[18]

Ironically, this is just the kind of material that was used to incriminate the Protestants and to justify the persecutions which followed the death of Henri II: 'Certain pamphlets ... where the just death of king Henri by the judgement of God was mentioned ... were sent to the Queen ... who ... was extremely angry and surprised.'[19] The death of François II, which tempered the influence of the Guises at Court, was welcomed by Calvin himself: 'has the death of a king ever been more providential?'.[20] The belief that the enemies of the true religion would die a horrible death was an important part of Protestant culture but it also provided the Catholics with damaging arguments.[21]

The duc de Guise had stopped the conspiracy of Amboise in its tracks and was personally responsible for the death of the conspirators, who

[16] Baum and Cunitz, eds, *Histoire Ecclésiastique*, I, pp. 228–39.

[17] Anon., *Complainte apologique des eglises de France, au roy, royne-mere, roy de Navarre, & autres du conseil* (Jaques des Hayes, 1561), sig. E1ᵛ.

[18] *La Maniere d'appaiser les troubles*, sigs B2ʳ–C1ᵛ.

[19] Baum and Cunitz, eds, *Histoire Ecclésiastique*, I, pp. 234, 236; a similar account is given in Popelinière, *L'Histoire de France*, I, fol. 148ᵛ.

[20] A. Pettegree, A. Duke and G. Lewis, eds, *Calvinism in Europe 1540–1610: A Collection of Documents* (Manchester, 1992), p. 80.

[21] Gregory, *Salvation at Stake*, p. 326.

were summarily executed. François Hotman had been Calvin's envoy in Strasbourg until he left for the Court of the King of Navarre in the wake of the conspiracy of Amboise without knowledge or authorization of the city magistrates.[22] Hotman was probably the representative that the Company of Pastors had sent to Nantes a few months before, where the conspirators had met.[23] Like des Gallars with respect to the rue St Jacques, Hotman had had a personal stake in the conspiracy of Amboise and its destruction at the hands of the duc de Guise left him with an axe to grind. He had already attacked the duc de Guise in his *Lettre ad-dressee au Tigre de la France* and accused him of taking advantage of the weakness of François II:

> Rabid tiger! Venomous asp! Sepulchre of abomination! Spectacle of misfortune! How far will you go in abusing our King's youth? Will you never put an end to your immoderate ambition, to your impostures, to your misdeeds? Can't you see that the whole world knows them, hears them, sees them? Who do you think ignores your hateful design, cannot read in your face the misfortune of all our days, the ruin of this kingdom, and the death of our King?[24]

After the failure of Amboise, Hotman attacked the Guises again in the anonymously published *Histoire du Tumulte d'Amboise*, in which he accused them of conspiracy:

> The enterprise is discovered: the conspiracy is known: the machinations of the house of Guise are revealed. Here are the strangers at our doors, that they have invited despite the King, to be the ministers and instruments of their evil enterprise ... . To this cause do they now have eight thousand Italians ready to make the poor French people prey to pillage.[25]

The Guises were consistently attacked throughout the Wars of Religion in short satirical songs and poems which escaped the censorship of both Paris and Geneva. The most pointed attacks were published after the failed conspiracy of Amboise:

> These two tyrants the Cardinal and his brother, use the king as a man on a stage, making him do, say and ordain all that they see fit. ... This Epicurean Cardinal ... is in France like a Pope, and his brother is like a King ... . In the hands of these two tyrants are the two swords of France, the spiritual in the hands of the Cardinal, and the secular in the hands of his brother.[26]

---

[22] Bonnet, ed., *Letters of Calvin*, IV, p. 147.

[23] Kingdon, *Geneva and the coming of the Wars*, pp. 68–9.

[24] Read, ed., *Le Tigre de 1560*, pp. 37–8.

[25] *Complainte au peuple Francois*, sigs D1^r, D2^r.

[26] Anon., *Juste Complainte des fideles de France. contre leurs adversaires Papistes, & autres. sur l'affliction & faux crimes, dont on les charge à grand tort. Ensemble les*

The accusation that the duc de Guise and the cardinal de Lorraine were wielding the swords of temporal and spiritual power were repeated several times in anonymous poems and songs.[27] The attacks increased in intensity after the massacre of Vassy in March 1562 up to the point of the duke's assassination in 1563 when he became a martyr of the Catholic cause. A particularly resourceful poem is reproduced below. If read from left to right, it is a panegyric, but if the first column is read alone, it is a satire:

By the alliance	And eternal love
Of the cardinal,	With the king,
All evils	Can no longer
Afflict France,	And its immortal flower.
Who despises God, [?]	He chastises.
He does [.]	Love and sustain the faith.
Who pillages [?]	And wants to live without rule,
His brother Guise [.]	Afflicts with good zeal.
These two	Being of one mind,
Make sure that nothing,	Remaining unpunished
Escapes them.	O fortunate France!
One for himself	Is so fearful of whoever
Wants to be king,	That he takes up his justice,
And the other the Pope	He imitates, being so devout.[28]

After the outbreak of the first War of Religion, numerous Catholic pamphlets were written on the theme of Protestant violence and particularly iconoclasm. Again, the Protestants turned the accusation around and charged the Guises of encouraging the sacking of houses and the killing of innocents: 'If there is a gathering at the sack of some house, the ministers of the Guises are there present to animate the people and shout "kill them all, break everything".'[29] The consistently bad press that the Guises had during the French Wars of Religion is still, to an extent, perpetuated by some historians. One such is Jean-Louis Bourgeon who described the Guises as 'foot servants of foreign powers' and went so far as to imply a comparison with French collaboration with the Nazis during the Second World War.[30] Other works suggest that

---

inconveniens, qui en pourroyent finalement avenir à ceux, qui leur font la guerre (Avignon, 1560), sigs D1[r–v].

[27] P. Tarbé, ed., Recueil de Poésies Calvinistes, 1550–1566 (Geneva, 1968), pp. 8, 11–2, 14, 20, 22–3, 33, 40, 65; Bordier, ed., Chansonnier Huguenot, pp. 234, 253, 257; F. Charbonnier, ed., La Poésie Française et les Guerres de Religion, 1560–1574 (Geneva, 1970), pp. 127, 176.

[28] Tarbé, ed., Recueil de Poésies Calvinistes, pp. 49–50, 103–5.

[29] Advertissement a la Royne Mere du Roy, sigs c3[v]–c4[r].

[30] Jean-Louis Bourgeon, 'Les Guises valets de l'etranger, ou trente ans de collaboration avec l'ennemi (1568–1598)', in Yvonne Bellenger, ed., Le mécénat et l'influence des Guises (Paris, 1997), pp. 509–22 (pp. 509–10, 519).

the Guises, and particularly the cardinal de Lorraine, may not have been as intransigent as they were made out to be.[31] Their close connection with a number of polemical authors and printers, however, warrants further study that might shed some light on their role in the French Counter-Reformation.

The University of Paris, and particularly the Faculty of Theology, referred to as the Sorbonne, was the second favourite target of Protestant polemic. De Mouchy, for instance, was a prominent figure of the Faculty of Theology, who made a virtue of seeking out heterodoxy within the university, its client booksellers, and schoolteachers.[32] He was instrumental in the trial of Anne du Bourg and the purge of the Parlement of Paris. It made him a perfect target for Protestants' jibes and a symbol of the authority of the University of Paris. The tone of Nicolas des Gallars's response to de Mouchy is extremely violent and personal. De Mouchy was held responsible for the persecutions by des Gallars, and there was perhaps an element of vendetta.[33] Des Gallars's *Apologie* reads like a personal attack on de Mouchy, with several puns based on his name derived from *mouche* (a fly), *moucher* (to blow one's nose), and *mouchard* (a snitch).[34] The attacks against de Mouchy were taken up by a number of authors, most notably Antoine de la Roche Chandieu and Conrad Badius, as well as other anonymous writers.[35] Through de Mouchy, the Protestant polemicists were attacking the Faculty of Theology that they identified as the source of the slander and abuse to which they were subjected: 'What would the Sorbonne do without you, oh ardent Democcare, on whose powerful back lies all the hopes of this Christian faith?'.[36] Personal attacks are also found in Conrad Badius's *Comédie du Pape Malade* where de Mouchy is easily identifiable in the character of the *Zelateur* (a compound word meaning a zealot and a snitch): 'For a spy of the Sorbonne

---

[31] Thierry Wanegffelen, *Ni Rome ni Genève* (Paris, 1997), pp. 149, 161–2; A. Tallon, 'Le Cardinal de Lorraine et la Réforme Catholique' (unpublished paper, Reims, October 1999), 8 pages, personal communication.

[32] Feret, *La Faculté de Théologie*, II, pp. 51–5.

[33] Baum and Cunitz, eds, *Histoire Ecclésiastique*, I, pp. 228–39.

[34] [Des Gallars], *Seconde apologie*, sig. D7^r. Alain Tallon even suggests that the modern French word *mouchard* comes from his name: 'Antoine de Mouchy, dit Démocharès, en fait tant contre les hérétiques que la légende veut que le mot "mouchard" vienne de son nom.'; Tallon, *La France et le Concile de Trente*, p. 660.

[35] Chandieu, *Histoire des persecutions*, sigs x7^r–x8^r.

[36] Pierre Richer, *La Refutation des folles resveries, execrables blasphemes, erreurs & mensonges de Nicolas Durand, qui se nomme Villegaignon* (1561), sig. A2^v.

your reason is good and holy: ... I am the Dean of the Sorbonne ... who pronounces the sentences of the Huguenots who are thrown in the fire.'[37] As we have seen, Conrad Badius ran into trouble with the Geneva Council and this work was published without its authorization.[38]

Augustin Marlorat's *Remonstrance a la Royne Mère du Roy* was attacked from all quarters by a number of Catholic authors, notably by Pierre Ronsard and Nicolas Durand de Villegagnon. The personal attacks directed against them from the Reformed were formidable. The fact that laymen took up the defence of the Catholic Church allowed Protestants to further deride the Faculty of Theology. Conrad Badius, and especially Theodore Beza, may have had ulterior motives for attacking Ronsard with whom they had a separate quarrel.[39] Indeed, Beza saw himself as the successor of Clément Marot, whose work he completed with the immensely successful *Pseaumes de David*. Marot had been a Court poet at the time of the reign of François I and had built his literary reputation on defending biblical rather than secular inspiration for French poetry. Ronsard, on the other hand, stood in opposition to this school and became the chief proponent of secular poetry, inspired by the Italian poets, notably Petrarch.[40]

Pierre Ronsard was not an established member of the clergy, although he had been tonsured in 1543, but a member of the *Pléiade*, a group of poets who were placed under the protection of Henri II. Between 1560 and 1564, there were no fewer than 20 pamphlets exchanged between the Reformers and Ronsard alone.[41] In 1564, Ronsard was ordered by the Court to end this exchange by not answering the latest pamphlets that had been written against him. He ended his part in this pamphleteering war with a prose preface to a collection of his poetry, which summarizes the whole exchange:

> You, whoever you are, who ... wrote a thousand sonnets against me ... I advise you ... not to write any more. ... It is a great pleasure for me to see these little suitors get agitated against me ...

---

[37] Shaw, ed., *Comedie du Pape Malade*, pp. 145, 149–50.

[38] Ibid., pp. 42–3.

[39] It should be noted that, although Beza and Ronsard were on opposite sides confessionally, they agreed on the need to reform French spelling. Nina Catach, *L'Orthographe française à l'époque de la Renaissance* (Geneva, 1968), p. 114: 'Adversaires sur le plan des luttes politiques, Ronsard, catholique, se trouve dans le camp des réformateurs de l'orthographe, R. Estienne, Th. de Bèze, liés l'un et l'autre, en sympathie et en actes, à la religion réformée, dans l'autre camp.'

[40] Malcolm C. Smith, *Ronsard and Du Bellay versus Beze: Allusiveness in Renaissance Literary Texts* (Geneva, 1995), pp. 7–9.

[41] Charbonnier, ed., *La Poésie Française*, pp. 31, 41, 60, 72, 75, 94, 98.

but from now on I will be quiet in order to obey those who have power over my hand and my will.[42]

Like Ronsard, Villegagnon was attacked personally for taking up the Catholic cause when, in the opinion of the Protestant pamphleteers, it was none of his business. On one occasion, they were both included in the same polemical poem: 'It is not fortuitous, Ronsard, that such a learned scholar ... with these divine verses has confounded your writing. ... But a lesser man than he will finish the quarrel. ... by declaring you ... more stupid, mad and twisted than even Villegagnon.'[43] The personal attacks against Nicolas Durand de Villegagnon were just as fierce as those against Ronsard, but for different reasons. Villegagnon had led a French expedition to Brazil, which had been established by Coligny in 1555, and had asked Calvin in 1557 to supply Protestant colonists to add to his numbers. Among the 14 sent from Geneva were three pastors, Pierre Richer, Guillaume Chartier and Jean de Léry, who came into conflict with Villegagnon over the sacraments.[44] On his return from Brazil, Villegagnon took up the fight against the Reformation, partly to clear his name of the suspicion of heresy and partly out of spite against the Genevans, whom he blamed for the failure of his expedition. He responded directly to Marlorat's *Remonstrance* in his *Lettres du Chevallier de Villegaignon* (1561) where he reiterated the accusations of rebellion.[45] The unprecedented response that Villegagnon provoked among the Reformed (including Augustin Marlorat) testifies to the personal nature of the controversy.[46] Pierre Richer, who had been one of Villegagnon's Genevan colonists, was particularly fierce for obvious personal reasons. His response was printed clandestinely by Conrad Badius who joined Richer in attacking Villegagnon personally in his *Comédie du Pape Malade* where the latter was given the part of *Outrecuidé*.[47] It is clear that the pieces directed at Villegagnon, like those against Ronsard, were also targeted at the University of Paris which was mocked for resorting to the services of a soldier:[48]

[42] P. de Ronsard, *Epistre au Lecteur, par laquelle succinctement l'autheur respond à ses calomniateurs*, in Charbonnier, ed., *La Poésie Française*, pp. 106, 109.

[43] Anon., *Remonstrance a la Roine Mere du Roy sur le discours de Pierre de Ronsard des miseres de ce temps* (Lyon, 1563), sig. A2r.

[44] Lestringant, *L'Expérience Huguenote*, pp. 55, 119, 125–6.

[45] Durand, *Lettres du Chevallier de Villegaignon*, sigs B3r v.

[46] Richer, *La Refutation des folles resveries*, sigs A4v–B1r; [Marlorat], *Response aux lettres de Nicolas Durand*, sig. E3r.

[47] Shaw, ed., *Comedie du Pape Malade*, pp. 135, 151–2.

[48] Anon., *La Suffisance de maistre Colas Durand, dit Chevalier de Villegaignon, pour sa retenue en l'estat du Roy. Item, Espoussette des armoiries de Villegaignon, pour bien faire luire la fleur de Lis, que l'estrille n'a point touchee* (1561), sigs B2r, C5r; Richer, *La*

How much do you think we laugh, when we see that you, a soldier, serves as a doctor to the doctors of the Sorbonne, and that they serve you as soldiers to go with sergeants, dig here and there among printers to see if they can find something printed against you.[49]

Turning the table on their adversary was a characteristic of the Protestant polemic of this period, where each accusation was turned around. A good example of this phenomenon is des Gallars's answer to de Mouchy, where he followed the original point by point, and systematically turned the argument around. In response to accusations of conducting orgies and sexual improprieties, des Gallars accused the Catholics of the same crimes: 'It is true that most of you judge according to your own criteria ... and you do not fail to seduce the most beautiful women ... and if you can attract them to your company, they will have to be virtuous indeed if they are to come back unsullied.'[50] The same tactic was used to respond to accusations of sorcery and magic, which de Mouchy had also accused the Protestants of practising:

As for witchcraft, I don't know what motive has impelled this fine defender to bring this up at the wrong moment, unless God is forcing him to stir up the dreadful crimes which hold sway under the cover of Papal darkness. For where are magicians, sorcerers, charmers, necromancers and diviners more tolerated and shown greater favour than among you?[51]

The personal nature of the Protestant polemic after the failure of the conspiracy of Amboise and the outbreak of the first War of Religion contrasts with the earlier response which had centred on the comparison with the early Church. In fact, the personal tone of these attacks was discouraged in Geneva, the bulk of the most adversarial Protestant polemic being printed from within France or clandestinely in Geneva, without the approbation of the city council. The official Genevan response, which was articulated around the idea of martyrdom, ran parallel with the polemic generated from within France. Although Jean Crespin relied on the testimony of French exiles for the compilation of his *Histoire des Martyrs*, any adversarial or political comments were carefully avoided.[52] The testimony of Nicolas des Gallars and Antoine de la

---

Refutation des folles resveries, sigs D7ᵛ, L5ʳ, N7ʳ, Q6ᵛ; [Marlorat], *Response aux lettres de Nicolas Durant*, sigs E3ʳ, C5ᵛ; Tarbé, ed., *Recueil de Poésies Calvinistes*, pp. 15–16.

[49] [Marlorat], *Response aux lettres de Nicolas Durant*, sig. C4ᵛ.

[50] [Des Gallars], *Seconde apologie*, sigs C6ʳ–C7ᵛ.

[51] Ibid., sig. B4ʳ; translated by Peter G. Maxwell-Stuart, *The Occult in Early Modern Europe: A documentary history* (London, 1999), p. 167.

[52] For example, Crespin does not mention the anecdote related in Chandieu's *Histoire des persecutions*, sigs x7ʳ–x8ʳ, about de Mouchy and the cardinal de Lorraine recruiting false witnesses to incriminate the Protestants in the eyes of the Queen.

Roche Chandieu was essential to Theodore Beza's account of the persecution in Paris in his *Histoire Ecclésiastique* (1580). It could be argued,
however, that the inclusion of these testimonies in the official history of
the persecutions by the Genevan Fathers came too late to serve as an
adequate response to the Catholic polemic.

There is a noticeable difference between the polemic which was produced in Geneva, and that produced within France. Although the council
turned a blind eye once in a while, adversarial and personal responses
to Catholic polemic were not usually encouraged. The polemic which
was produced from within France is marked by its immediacy (it was
usually produced very quickly) and its personal and defensive adversarial
tone. Virulent Protestant defences often followed the original Catholic
texts closely, to be answered in turn by their authors, and so on. This
was the case of Artus Désiré's famous satire of the Huguenot Psalter,
which was answered by a Protestant version and with poems written
against specific individuals.[53] The same applies to the polemical exchange between Nicolas des Gallars and Antoine de Mouchy and the
polemic which was produced on both sides of the confessional divide
around key events.

After 1562 the myth of the innocent Huguenot martyr was losing
credibility as the Catholic accusations of civil disobedience took flesh
with the revolt of the Prince de Condé. Huguenot polemicists understood this well and turned to writing vindictive pamphlets against the
Catholic adversary, notably theologians of the University of Paris and
the Guises. The massacre of St Bartholomew's Day increased this trend
as the Huguenot movement shed any remaining pretence of political
obedience to the monarch; in their eyes, the King had turned into a
tyrant who could legitimately be removed by force. It has been argued
that the emergence of the Monarchomachs removed all the remaining
credit that Huguenot martyrdom might have had.[54] I should prefer to
argue, however, that the massacre of St Bartholomew's Day gave a new
lease of life to the theme of Huguenot martyrdom.[55]

The strength of the official Protestant response built on the Catholics'
determination to draw a comparison between the Reformation and
medieval heresy – an area in which the adversarial polemic generated
within France was quite weak, and where the full array of scholarship
available in Geneva could be used most effectively. This went hand in
hand with a continued effort from the Genevan presses to fuel the

---

[53] Pettegree, 'Huguenot Voices'; Tarbé ed., *Recueil de Poésies Calvinistes*, pp. 103–5;
Du Val, *Les contrarietez & contredictz.*

[54] El Kenz, *Les Bûchers du Roi*, pp. 69, 188, 237.

[55] See Chapter 8 below.

Reformation in France with bibles and works of systematic theology. The argument which had been used at the outset of the persecutions by Nicolas des Gallars would be systematized and enlarged to include the medieval heretics. The idea that medieval heretics had been martyrs of the true Church, just as the early Christians had been, was an original and specifically Protestant innovation. Unfortunately, this idea was not put into practice until after the death of Jean Crespin in 1572, when the *Histoire des Martyrs* was taken over by Simon Goulard. By this time, the period when an articulate official Protestant response from Geneva was most needed had passed, and the unofficial adversarial Protestant response from within France had failed.

CHAPTER SIX

The 'world turned upside down', the *femmelettes* and the French Wars of Religion

This chapter explores two salient features of sixteenth-century society – inversion and misogyny – in the context of the French Wars of Religion. The use of the word *femmelette* and the theme of the 'world upside down' were rhetorical tools in the hands of the Catholic polemicists to discredit their Huguenot adversary. The use of these 'memes' (self-replicating media viruses) followed strict rules dictated by theology and tradition. The uniformity with which they were used in France (but also in England, Germany and Spain) against Protestants suggests that they were rhetorical conventions.

Catholic theologians argued that Protestantism was giving more freedom to women. Their reaction, which has been used as a gauge of the improvement of the condition of women by some, is indeed very strong. To allow women to take a greater part in the spiritual affairs of the community was akin, these theologians argued, to turning the world upside down. For example, Simon Vigor accuses the Protestants of turning justice on its head, to oppress the people and to turn all order 'topsy-turvy'.[1] The topos of the 'world turned upside down' had universal appeal and is still used today by reactionary politicians to curtail change.[2] Catholics accused the Protestants of turning the world upside down, and pandering to women (referred to as *femmelettes*) was one of its many manifestations. The role of inversion and misrule in popular culture was first brought to our attention by Mikhail Bakhtin in a pioneering book on François Rabelais.[3] His work was applied by others who showed the relevance of inversion to phenomena as varied as witchcraft, the reformation of manners and grain riots.[4] Prominently,

---

[1] Vigor, *Oraison funebre prononcee aux obseques … de ma Dame Elizabeth de France*, sig. F2ᵛ.

[2] The expression *on marche sur la tête* (we walk on our heads) was used repeatedly by Philippe de Villiers, the royalist candidate for the presidential election in France in 1995.

[3] Mikhail Bakhtine, *L'oeuvre de François Rabelais et la culture populaire au moyen âge et sous la renaissance* (Paris, 1970).

[4] S. Clark, 'Inversion, Misrule and the Meaning of Witchcraft', *P&P*, LXXXVII (1980), pp. 98–127; Ingram, 'Ridings, Rough Music and Popular Culture'; Christopher Hill, *The*

Nathalie Davis has shown parallels between popular culture and the
urban massacres of the French Wars of Religion.[5] The pamphlets published by French Catholic theologians during this period offer an
opportunity to explore this world of contradiction and analogy a little
further. Many aspects of contemporary culture were diverted for the use
of religious polemic, and the 'world turned upside down' was no exception.

It is the versatility of these symbols which allowed them to be harnessed by Reformers and defenders of the Catholic Church alike
throughout the Reformation. The polemical use of inversion in the
German Reformation has been well studied by Robert Scribner, who
provides numerous examples of satirical woodcuts depicting the overturning of the Papacy, the monastic orders and the ecclesiastical
hierarchy.[6] The idea of the 'world turned upside down', rather than
being the vehicle of seasonal merriment, turned into a polemical weapon
reflecting a genuine crisis. But, unlike peasants' riots where these symbols were used in the context of a 'class war', they were used by an
entire cross-section of society against another, by Protestants against
Catholics and in turn by Catholics against Protestants.

Analogies which reflect social, political and religious order were used
throughout the French Wars of Religion. The 'analogy of the body'
pervaded early modern society where everything and everyone had its
proper place in the 'great chain of being'.[7] John Knox provides us with
a very eloquent description of the analogy in his *First blast of the
trumpet against the monstruous regiment of women*:

> Besides these, he hath set before our eyes, two other mirrors and
> glasses, in whiche he will, that we shulde behold the ordre, which
> he hath apointed and established in nature: the one is, the naturall
> bodie of man: the other is the politik or civile body of that com-
> mon welth, in which God by his own word hath apointed an ordre.
> In the natural body of man God hath apointed an ordre, that the
> head shall occupie the uppermost place. And the head hath he
> joyned with the bodie, that frome it, doth life and motion flowe to

---

World Turned Upside Down: Radical Ideas during the English Revolution (London,
1972).

[5] Davis, 'Rites of Violence'.

[6] Scribner, *For the Sake of Simple Folk* (1994).

[7] Paul Archambault, 'The Analogy of the "Body" in Renaissance Political Literature',
BHR, XXIX (1967), pp. 21–53; E. M. Tillyard, *The Elizabethan world picture* (London,
1972); D. G. Hale, *The body politic: a political metaphor in Renaissance English
literature* (The Hague, 1971).

the rest of the membres. In it hath he placed the eye to see, the eare to hear, and the tonge to speake, which offices are apointed to none other membre of the bodie. The rest of the membres, have every one their own place and office apointed: but none may have nether the place nor office of the heade.[8]

This mirrors the biblical analogy between the body of Christ and the community of all believers which is found in 1 Corinthians 12: 'for Christ is like a single body with its many limbs and organs, which, many as they are, together make up one body ... . Now you are Christ's body, and each of you a limb or organ of it.'[9] This passage from Paul's first epistle to the Corinthians was used by the medieval Church to express in anthropomorphic language the cohesion of the community of believers. This conception of a well-ordered society was enacted in ritual processions where the social and spiritual hierarchy was duly represented, notably on Corpus Christi Day when the procession was led by the political and spiritual élite of the town and symbolized the unity of the community in the body of Christ. As Miri Rubin has written: 'In the medieval context the body was a metaphor of metaphors, embedded in the sacramental cosmology as well as in personal experience.'[10] Corpus Christi was celebrated in Paris at the very beginning of the troubles to express the unity of the Catholic community in the face of the threat represented by the Reformation.[11] Protestants, with their different set of practices, their refusal to partake of the host during Mass or to participate in Corpus Christi processions, set themselves apart from the rest of the community and were consequently branded as 'enemies of the community'.

Catholic polemic published in the 1560s described Protestantism as a source of divisiveness and chaos, breaking up the body social and the body politic into as many parts as a body has limbs. Cardinal Hozius's *Des sectes et hérésies* followed the anthropomorphic symbolism expressed in Corpus Christi when describing Luther as 'tearing apart the body of Christ'.[12] This analogy was used by René Benoist in a treatise defending transubstantiation against the Reformers: 'When he is eaten he is not divided into parts, and he is not torn in the sacrament in the way that meat is when sold in a butcher shop: he is

---

[8] John Knox, *The First blast of the trumpet against the monstruous regiment of women* (Geneva, 1558), sig. D3ʳ.

[9] 1 Corinthians 12:12–27.

[10] Miri Rubin, *Corpus Christi: the Eucharist in Late Medieval Culture* (Cambridge, 1991), pp. 269–70.

[11] Diefendorf, *Beneath the Cross*, p. 48.

[12] Hozius, *Des sectes et hérésies de nostre temps*, p. 32.

received without wounds, and is eaten whole.'[13] The same imagery
was used in Germany in a woodcut depicting Protestant Reformers
(Melanchthon, Zwingli and Calvin among them) dissecting the body
of Luther into as many pieces.[14] Eucharistic symbolism permeates the
discourse of Catholic polemicists, who pitched the unity of the Catholic Church against the multiplicity of the heresies. Hozius harked back
to a time when Christendom was one as in Genesis 11:1, 6: 'and the
whole earth was of one language, and of one speech ... the people is
one, and they have all one language', comparing the Reformation to
the Tower of Babel.

Hozius pitched the multiplicity of Protestant sects against a very
Erasmian picture of 'universal Christendom',[15] drawing attention to the
names of the different Protestant sects as a sign of the divisiveness of the
Reformation as opposed to the simplicity and unity of Christendom in
the bosom of the Roman Catholic Church. In the same vein Jean Gay, a
member of the Parlement of Toulouse, described Protestantism as a
synonym for disunity and divisiveness.[16] The image of the Church
divided against itself was fuelled by the diversity of Protestant 'sects' –
which is emphasized to strengthen the comparison with earlier heresies.
The same argument was used by Georg Witzel who compared the
fragmentation of the Reformed movement to that of Arianism, in the
fourth century: 'The sect of Arius became powerful and split into three
sects ... nobody questions the fact that the sect of Martin Luther is
divided into three: namely into Lutherans, Calvinists and Anabaptists.'[17]
The same argument was used by the Frenchman Gabriel Dupuiherbault
in a treatise published in 1560.[18]

Hozius, like Witzel, insisted on calling the different strands of Protestantism after their founders, Luther and Calvin, in the same way that
medieval and early Church heresies were called after theirs.[19] The attri-
bution of names was paramount in the thought of both Witzel and
Hozius in differentiating Protestants from true (Catholic) Christians.
The naming of heresies after their founders was a convenient way to
separate the wheat from the chaff, especially since Protestants at this

---

[13] René Benoist, *Claire Probation de la necessaire manducation de la substantielle &
reale humanité de Jesus Christ, vray Dieu & vray homme, au S. Sacrement de l'autel*
(Paris, 1561), sig. H3[r].

[14] Nischan, *Lutherans and Calvinists*, p. 215.

[15] Hozius, *Des sectes et hérésies de nostre temps*, pp. 4–5.

[16] Gay, *Histoire des scismes et heresies des Albigeois*, p. 39.

[17] Witzel, *Discours des moeurs*, p. 10.

[18] Gabriel Dupuiherbault, *Consolation des catholiques, molestez par Sectaires &
schismatiques* (Paris, 1560), sig. C1[r].

[19] Hozius, *Des sectes et hérésies de nostre temps*, pp. 4–5.

time frequently called themselves 'Christians' or 'Catholics'.[20] The appellation 'Lutheran' and 'Calvinist', like the word 'Huguenot', are a legacy of the Catholic polemic and it is doubtful that the Protestants used these terms among themselves. The use of different names was a particularly difficult problem for the Calvinists at a time when all hopes of a reconciliation with Lutheranism were lost.[21] Calvin himself in 1557 deplored the fact that the Reformed were being called Sacramentarians by the Catholics, in association with the Lutherans. This distinction was exploited by cardinal Hozius: 'the Lutherans think the same way about the Sacramentarians as the Sacramentarians do about Lutherans',[22] while Witzel derided the Protestant use of the word 'Catholic': 'the same way that Arius called his followers Catholics, and the Catholics heretics, we are called the same by the Lutherans and Calvinists'.[23] This confusion of terms is set against the simplicity and unity which reigned before the Reformation where everybody was called 'Christians': 'some did not call themselves Gnostics ... and others Apostolic or Evangelic ... but everyone was called Christian.'

A body divided against itself was a common way of understanding disease and Protestantism was often described as a disease afflicting the body politic.[24] Cardinal Hozius followed in the steps of a long line of authors who described heresy as a disease thereby justifying the persecution of heretics:

> A gangrenous limb is amputated for fear of infecting the rest of the body: the bodies of leprous men are segregated for fear of infecting the healthy with their leprosy: all the more reason for segregating those who are stained in their heart with the spiritual leprosy, for fear that they might infect the flock of Jesus Christ?[25]

Hozius also wrote: 'about one hundred and forty years ago, the Waldensian leprosy infected the kingdom of Bohemia'.[26] Antoine de Mouchy used a similar analogy: 'it is necessary to amputate gangrenous flesh ... to prevent the house, the whole, the body and the flock from burning, being corrupted, rotting and perishing'.[27] For the same reason Gentian Hervet argued that Protestants should be segregated like Jews to avoid contagion: 'you are mixed in with everybody else ... so that

---

[20] [Des Gallars], *Seconde apologie.*
[21] Bonnet, ed., *Letters of Calvin*, III, p. 404.
[22] Hozius, *Des sectes et hérésies de nostre temps*, p. 175.
[23] Witzel, *Discours des moeurs*, p. 8.
[24] Moore, 'Heresy as Disease', pp. 1–11.
[25] Hozius, *Des sectes et hérésies de nostre temps*, pp. 20, 78.
[26] Ibid., p. 7.
[27] Mouchy, *Responce a quelque apologie*, sig. C8ᵛ.

one is obliged whether he likes it or not to speak with you, despite the
fact that your conversation is no less contagious than the plague'.[28]
Gabriel de Saconay, writing in 1568, wrote that medieval kings had
given a good example in 'purging their kingdom from this contagious
vermin'.[29] If disease was caused by disharmony in the body, civil war
was caused by disharmony in the body politic. Religious dissent was
often compared to a disease that could only be cured by the King. This
is consistent with his role as physician expressed in the medieval custom
of 'touching for the King's Evil'. It is to these powers that Jean du Tillet
appealed in his *Sommaire de l'histoire de la guerre faicte contre les
heretiques Albigeois*:

> It is necessary to bring remedy to it, before the disease becomes
> incurable and brings ruin. ... It seemed to me that the remedy that
> was applied then to heal the wound that was inflicting the king-
> dom ... is now particularly relevant, to heal the same disease with
> which this kindgom is afflicted.[30]

This passage demonstrates Du Tillet's belief in the curative powers of
the French monarch which were demonstrated in the custom of 'touching for the King's Evil'. Gabriel de Saconay made the connection explicit
in his *De la Providence de Dieu sur les roys de France* (1568): 'the kings
of France were elected by God ... to preserve and maintain the holy
catholic religion ... and by the same grace to heal the disease of
scrofula'.[31] This was consistent with the agenda of many of these authors who appealed to the King to 'cure' the kingdom of the affliction
of heresy. Significantly, the curative powers of Henri III were questioned
by Leaguer preachers because of his accommodating position towards
Protestantism.[32]

Another way in which Protestantism was seen to disturb the great chain
of being was by upsetting the 'natural' hierarchy between men and
women, children and parents, and subject and ruler. Luke 21:16: 'You
will be betrayed even by parents and brothers, by relatives and friends;

---

[28] Hervet, *Discours*, sig. F6^v.

[29] Saconay, *De la providence de dieu*, sig. Y4^r.

[30] Jean du Tillet, *Sommaire de l'histoire de la guerre faicte contre les heretiques
Albigeois, extraicte du Tresor des Chartres du Roy par feu Jehan du Tillet Prothenotaire
& Secretaire de la maison & Couronne de France, Greffier du Parlement de Paris, sieur
de la Bussiere* (Paris, 1590), sigs ã3^r, ã8^r.

[31] Saconay, *De la providence de dieu*, p. 155; Yardeni, *Conscience nationale*, p. 103.

[32] Mark Greengrass, *France in the Age of Henri IV: The struggle for stability* (London,
1995), p. 35.

and they will put some of you to death' and Matthew 10:21: 'Brother
will betray brother to death, and a father his child, and children will
rise against parents and have them put to death' were often used by
Catholic authors to show the disunity brought about by the Reformation.[33] This was an argument in favour of the Protestants who pointed
out that these were signs of Christ's calling found in Matthew 10:34–6:

> Do not think that I have come to bring peace to the earth; I have
> not come to bring peace, but a sword. For I have come to set a man
> against his father, and a daughter against her mother, and a daugh-
> ter-in-law against her mother-in-law; and one's foes will be members
> of one's own household.[34]

The embracing of this biblical topsy-turvydom by the Protestants
justified in part the Catholics' accusations that their ultimate aim was
to turn the world on its head.

The words of Ezechiel 5:10: 'Therefore the fathers shall eat the sons in
the midst of thee, and the sons shall eat their fathers' were used by Artus
Désiré to illustrate the chaos brought about by the Protestants.[35] The title
of his book leaves little to the imagination and Désiré argues that the
source of all evil rests in the disobedience of children and servants to their
parents and masters. This is reflected in the Pauline epistle to Timothy
3:2: 'For people will be ... disobedient to their parents.' This concern for
the respect of authority is reminiscent of moral panics in the twentieth
century, where a perceived decline in values leads to the demise of all
order.[36] For instance, Antoine du Val argued in his *Mirouer des Calvinistes*
that the disagreement within a family provoked a chain reaction which
toppled the whole hierarchy and jeopardized the kingdom:

> It will come to pass that the husband will be of one opinion and his
> wife of another, the children and the servants will be of another, so
> that there will be nothing but disagreement and rebellion. Finally it
> will follow that the son will want to kill the father, the brother his
> brother ... because heresy is such that as soon as it makes its way
> into a house, city or kingdom, it brings such division and discord
> that the husband disagrees with his own wife, the servants and
> citizens with one another, and the subjects with their lord.[37]

The disobedience of children and wives to husbands mirrored disunity in the kingdom and the time when authority was respected was

---

[33] D'Espence, *Cinq sermons*, sigs *6ʳ, *8ʳ.

[34] *La Maniere d'appaiser les troubles*, sig. B2ᵛ; *Complainte apologique des eglises de France*, sig. C3ᵛ.

[35] Désiré, *L'origine et source de tous les maux*, sig. F3ᵛ.

[36] Kenneth Thompson, *Moral Panics* (London, 1998).

[37] Du Val, *Mirouer des Calvinistes*, fol. 28ᵛ.

seen with nostalgia: 'children were afraid to offend their fathers and mothers: the women were not dissolute, brazen and immodest'.[38] This idea is also found in an anonymous pamphlet published in Lyon in 1568: 'the people will be disobedient to the shepherds, so that everyone will want to live according to their own fantasy, the children will rise against their parents, the wife against the husband, the servants against the master'.[39] In the world of analogy and correspondence outlined above, the relationship between husbands and wives reflected harmony in all the other realms (physical, spiritual, political). The orderliness of the universe on the domestic scale was represented by the obedience of the wife to the husband, the obedience of children to their parents, servants to their masters, and subjects to their ruler.

If Catholic authors were concerned with the overall chaos brought about by the Reformation, nothing seemed to concern them more than the inversion of the hierarchy between men and women. Indeed, the strong polarity between the sexes that characterized early modern society also figures prominently in the anti-Protestant polemic. The association between women exercising authority over men and universal disharmony is one of the most common features of popular culture. The popular institution of the 'Charivari', in publicly humiliating men who failed to control their wives, was a ritual enactment of the idea that strong women were a danger to society.[40] In such spontaneous popular manifestations, the husband was made to ride backwards through the town, to the sound of the banging of kitchen implements. Cacophony was a universal manifestation of disharmony and it was also used in relation to heresy by cardinal Hozius: 'like in music, once one has left the harmony of a chord, there is nothing but false notes, and the whole song is spoilt: similarly if the harmony of doctrine is troubled by heresy … one moves towards an ever increasing confusion'.[41]

The fear of strong women sprung from indifferentiation, the inability to distinguish between two distinct things, and particularly between men and women. This was exploited in expressions of popular culture

---

[38] Guillaume Lindan, *Discovrs en forme de dialogue, ou histoire tragique en laquelle est nayvement depeinte & descrite la source, origine, cause & progres des troubles* (Paris, 1566), sig. A8ᵛ.

[39] [Gabriel de Saconay], *Discours Catholique, sur les causes & remedes des Malheurs intentés au Roy, & escheus à som peuple par les rebelles Calvinistes* (Lyon, 1568), sig. B3ᵛ.

[40] Ingram, 'Ridings, Rough Music and Popular Culture'; Y.-M. Bercé, *Fête et révolte*, p. 40.

[41] Hozius, *Des sectes et hérésies de nostre temps*, p. 20.

where cross-dressing was used for fun, but also in manifestations of discontent.[42] Similarly this fear was articulated in Désiré's concern regarding dress: 'today women are mistaken for men and men for women, without any distinction of dress, and we can often see girls and women wear men's habits and coats'.[43] When women literally 'wear the trousers' as well as dominate their husbands, it is a sure sign that the world is turned upside down.[44] The figure of the shrew beating or dominating her husband was found in many woodcuts of this period.[45] It was used during the English Reformation by polemicists who argued that the Reformation feminized men and violated gender boundaries.[46] French Catholics used this argument extensively to argue that the Reformation turned the 'world upside down', and particularly appealed to women.

By associating the Reformation with women, Catholic theologians had recourse to a time-honoured tradition of misogyny and a register of associations which has been summarized by Caroline Bynum:[47]

| Men | Intellect | God | Father | Reason | Husband | Order |
| Women | Body | Soul | Child | Emotion | Wife | Disorder |

Certain authors, like Robert Ceneau and René Benoist, seemed to be particularly concerned by what they interpreted as a feminization of society and wrote at length against men who allowed women to meddle in matters of religion. These authors strongly suggest that the Reformation was allowed to develop because men were showing weakness and were attracted to novelty, two characteristics normally associated with women. Pusillanimity, inability to follow rules and foolishness were all female attributes that were associated with the Reformation. In this respect, Ceneau and Benoist were appealing to the consensus values of their audience, the widespread belief that men were superior to women, for polemical purposes. These arguments have their origins in the medieval ascetic tradition and the monastic ideals of the thirteenth century, particularly the Mendicant Orders.[48] Among men who had chosen to live in celibacy, women were the embodiment of sin, and marriage was the lesser of two evils, when it was not the road to damnation. According

---

[42] Davis, *Society and Culture*, p. 136.

[43] Désiré, *L'origine et source de tous les maux*, sig. B7ʳ.

[44] Ingram, 'Ridings, Rough Music and Popular Culture'.

[45] A selection feature in Davis, *Society and Culture*.

[46] Betteridge, 'Mete Covers for such Vessels', p. 4.

[47] This series of opposites also includes: active / passive, rational / irrational, self-control / lust, and judgement / mercy. Caroline Walker Bynum, *Fragmentation and Redemption: Essays on Gender and the human body in the Medieval Religion* (New York, 1991), p. 151.

[48] Delumeau, *La Peur en Occident*, p. 317.

to this view, women were associated with a number of negative characteristics – such as weakness, stupidity and immorality – which men were encouraged to avoid. This tradition relied heavily on a selective reading of Scriptures which described women as inferior and incapable of spiritual achievement. Following the analogies discussed above, women were subjected to men like the body to the soul, and flesh to the spirit.

Adam and Eve were the first of many couples to be used as edification in the 'battle of the sexes', as the legends of Phyllis riding Aristotle, Socrates and Xanthippe, or Solomon and the Queen of Sheba testify. The image of these grave men of wisdom being ridiculed by women illustrated the frailty of human wisdom in the face of the sexual desire represented by women, who by the same token became symbols of folly.[49] To quote but one example, a pamphlet probably authored by Gabriel de Saconay makes a parallel between the success of heresy in France and Solomon's renouncing the God of Israel for the love of women: 'Salomon, tempted through pleasures to follow the dreams and superstitions of *femmelettes*, and the teachers of their errors, was the cause of his own ruin, and of the terrible division of all the Hebrew nation.'[50]

The phrase coined by Virgil 'fickle and changeable always is woman' was much exploited by the polemicists to reduce the popularity of Protestantism to a mere feminine 'whim'.[51] For Robert Ceneau, the success of the Reformation could be explained through feminine weakness and mutability: 'What is lighter than a feather? Air. What is lighter than air? The impetuous wind. More than the wind? Women to speak truly, nothing is lighter or less virtuous.'[52] The Pauline injunction that '... women should dress themselves modestly and decently in suitable clothing, not with their hair braided, or with gold, pearls, or expensive clothes ...' (1 Timothy 2:9–12) was also frequently used by Catholic theologians. The argument that women's vanity and attraction to novelty and clothes made them prone to fall for the Reformation, was expressed thus by Bosquet:

> The mid-day spirit ... under pretense of reformation ... made several women desiring after novelty forget the old [religion] and made them quit the hours, & the rosary ... [and adopt instead] ... those blown gowns, wide dresses, & dissolute clothes; danses, worldly songs, as if they had been called by the holy spirit.[53]

---

[49] Walker Bynum, *Fragmentation and Redemption*, p. 30.

[50] [Saconay], *Discours Catholique*, sig. A3ᵛ.

[51] Virgil, *Aeneid* (London, 1956), IV.i.569.

[52] Ceneau, *Response catholique*, sigs E4ʳ⁻ᵛ.

[53] M. G. Bosquet, *Sur les troubles advenus en la ville de Tolose l'an 1562* (Toulouse, 1595), p. 50.

Other biblical injunctions against the wearing of ornaments – for example, Isaiah 3:17–24, Ezechiel 7:18–19 and 1 Peter 3 – were used by Artus Désiré and Robert Ceneau, who accused Protestant women of going to conventicles to attract men.[54] The accusation that Protestants met in secret to have sex (discussed in Chapter 4 above), went hand in hand with female association with the lower half of the body, with sexual desire and lust. Witzel, for example, described Protestants as being particularly promiscuous:

> From one wife they make three or four ... our Calvinists are all devoted to carnal desire ... they are like madmen running like horses after women as soon as they see them. They bray around them: they abandon themselves to their passion. ... Some among them are so devoted to Venus and to her service that they seek doctors to make their shameful member grow larger than they have by nature.[55]

Catholics drew on a general repertory of female stereotypes to associate Protestants with ignorance, sexual wantonness and changeability. Sometimes more hostile female attributes were used, drawing on older references describing women as hysterical. For example, Helinand of Froidmond (1170–1237) wrote about vexatious women as if possessed by a familiar spirit:

> A quarrelsome woman is either literally every woman, or the very flesh, life & common pursuit of the life of women, which has been made soft by lovers. Any of this always moves spiritual men to protest. O how suitably is that captive *muliercula* called Rixandis, as it is said, who drags you captive! For she is a devil who is called Rixoaldus, who always nourishes protestation. For this is said to be the personal name of an evil spirit.[56]

The archetype of the witch as a female agent of the Devil emerged at the end of the fifteenth century with treatises that implied that witches were women rather than men.[57] Ceneau described the archetypal heretic as a hysterical woman turning scripture on its head, a sure sign of satanism.[58] In Cesare Ripa's *Iconologia* (1618), heresy is portrayed as a dishevelled naked old woman, spitting smoke from her mouth, holding a book riddled with snakes in her left hand and snakes in her

---

[54] Ceneau, *Response catholique*, sig. E1ᵛ; Désiré, *L'origine et source de tous les maux*, sig. F6ᵛ.

[55] Witzel, *Discours des moeurs*, pp. 19, 42, 45, 47.

[56] J. P. Migne, ed., *Patrologia Latina*, 221 vols (Turnhout, 1970), CCXII (1995), p. 756; *muliercula* is the Latin for 'silly woman' (see below). I am grateful to Dr Peter Maxwell-Stuart (University of St Andrews) for the translation.

[57] Maxwell-Stuart, ed., *The Occult in Early Modern Europe*, pp. 171–86.

[58] Ceneau, *Response catholique*, sig. D5ʳ.

right.[59] The effigy of 'a great fury' representing heresy was ritually burned in Paris in 1588 and a woodcut depicting a similar figure was used in a 1598 German pamphlet to represent Calvinism.[60] During the first War of Religion in Toulouse, Bosquet described a gun-blazing Protestant fury who was 'known as la Broquiere' and was 'a great enemy of Catholics'.[61] The use of mysogynistic stereotypes in Catholic polemic draws on a rich repertory of images and texts that also include the Pauline epistles and the widespread use of the word *femmelette*.[62]

The diminutive for woman was derived from the Latin *muliercula* into the vernacular Spanish *mujercilla* and French *femmelette*.[63] The association with ignorance is tenacious and can be found in all three languages, suggesting that women and foolish men were thought to be synonymous. The phrase 'this is obvious even to a *muliercula* and the most ignorant of men' was used in the context of the quarrel between St Bernard of Clairvaux and Berengar as early as the twelfth century.[64] Alison Weber has suggested that it referred to merely ignorant women and was not necessarily pejorative, for example in the use that Erasmus makes of it in 1516.[65] Nonetheless, even if the Latin *muliercula* was not pejorative, the vernacular *femmelette* certainly was. A modern French dictionary gives the following definition for *femmelette*: 'Small woman. Weak man, lacking energy.' In its modern acceptation, *femmelette* is used to denote weak, effeminate men whose behaviour does not conform to socially defined canons of manhood. It is clear from the context in which it was used in Catholic polemic that, even then, the word was loaded with pejorative connotations, associated with ignorance and the blurring of gender roles.

The anti-Protestant authors drew extensively from the 'battle of the sexes' arguing that Protestantism encouraged women to teach and speak in churches by allowing them to read the Scriptures in the vernacular. According to this tradition, women were ignorant and if they were seduced by the new faith it was because of the novelty

---

[59] Ripa, *Nova Iconologia*, p. 244.

[60] Flandrin, ed., *Journal d'un bourgeois de Paris*, pp. 261–2; Nischan, *Prince, People, and Confession*, p. 53; Clifton, *Encyclopedia of Heresies*, p. 123.

[61] Bosquet, *Sur les troubles*, p. 150.

[62] 1 Corinthians 14:34–37; 2 Timothy 3:6–7; Ephesians 5:22–24.

[63] Alison Weber, *Teresa of Avila and the Rhetoric of Femininity* (Princeton, 1990), pp. 21, 24.

[64] Migne, ed., *Patrologia Latina*, CLXXXII (1982), p. 971.

[65] Weber, *Teresa of Avila*, p. 21.

rather than the potency of its message. From the very beginning of the Reformation, one of the main criticisms of the Lutheran efforts to publish bibles in the vernacular was that this placed the word of God in the hands of people who were unfit to receive it. The Reformation's effort to render the word of God more accessible, was ascribed in John Eck's commonplaces against Luther to a proselytizing effort targeted at the simple and vulgar people.[66] This was echoed by Robert Ceneau: 'what they do not dare or are unable to say in Latin, they distort in the vulgar tongue, so that the ignorant may better hear the ignorant'.[67]

Following the association coined in the phrase '*muliercula* and stupid men', this included women whom theologians thought were on a par with ignorant men. That women should remain untaught in the Scriptures was one of the main arguments for preventing religious debate from being conducted in the vernacular. In French polemic, *femmelette* was synonymous with the *ignoramus* which features in the polemic of John Eck. Georg Witzel, another opponent of Luther, reproduced the phrase in his *On the mores of the heretics*: 'By such novelty, Calvinists and Lutherans have easily gained the frivolous women and the people who are without knowledge ... this is something notorious to even imbeciles and silly women.'[68] Jean de la Vacquerie also used the word *femmelette* in conjunction with the word 'idiot': 'If they see some *femmelette*, or simple idiot, who has taken a liking to their words, they then do all they can to fuel and teach them in their doctrine.'[69] The association was so common that it was used by an anonymous Protestant author to defend the vernacular translations of the Scriptures: 'The books of the church fathers are full of exhortations to all, even to the artisans and simple *femmelettes*, to read the scriptures and to gather in the neighbourhood to do so.'[70] In Spain, several heterodox women, notably Saint Teresa of Avila, were called *mujercilla* by their opponents,[71] while, in England, Ann Askew was called *juvencula* (little maiden).[72] By associating Protestantism with women, who were 'by definition' unlearned, and attributing the popularity of the new faith to their ignorance and gullibility, the

---

[66] Eck, *Les lieux communs ... contre Luther*, sig. D7ʳ.

[67] Ceneau, *Response catholique*, sigs D4ᵛ–D5ʳ.

[68] Witzel, *Discours des moeurs*, pp. 12, 56.

[69] Vacquerie, *Catholique remonstrance*, sig. C5ʳ.

[70] *Complainte apologique des eglises de France*, sig. C1ʳ.

[71] Weber, *Teresa of Avila*, p. 24.

[72] J. Nichols, ed., 'Narratives of the days of the Reformation', *Camden Society*, LXXVII (1859), p. 307; T. Betteridge, 'Anne Askewe, John Bale, and Protestant history', *Journal of Medieval and Early Modern Studies*, XXVII (1997), pp. 265–84.

Catholic polemicists turned the tables on the Protestants who accused them of being ignorant.[73]

Catholic theologians accused Protestants of putting women on an equal footing with men although they lacked the intellect and the moral fibre to understand theology. The first Pauline epistle justifying this stance is 1 Corinthians 14:34:

> Women should be silent in the churches. For they are not permitted
> to speak, but should be subordinate, as the law also says. If there is
> anything they desire to know, let them ask their husbands at home.
> For it is shameful for a woman to speak in church.

In 1523 it was used by Johannes of Lanzhut, against Argula von Grumbach when she challenged the whole university of Ingolstadt.[74] The same passage was used over and over again by the French Catholics, notably by Thomas Beauxamis and René Benoist.[75] A pamphlet attributed to Gabriel de Saconay described arrogant Protestant women who regarded prelates as of no more consequence than their servants: 'Women make no more of the most learned & knowledgeable of ours than their servants and chamber maids.'[76] Antoine de Mouchy even accused the Protestant women of usurping the ministry: 'we know how bold the heretical women are because they dare teach, dispute, preach, dispense healing and even sometimes baptize'.[77] A satirical woodcut depicting female theologians was included in Artus Désiré's *Defense of the Christian Faith* published in 1567.[78]

The strength of the Catholic reaction suggests that Protestant women indeed took a more active part in the religious life of the community. But these passages should not be taken at face value. The Pauline injunctions were equally observed by the Protestants, as is demonstrated by the following example published in 1561:

---

[73] Witzel, *Discours des moeurs*, pp. 9, 14; Hozius, *Des sectes et hérésies de nostre temps*, p. 48; Jean Talpin, *Remonstrance a tous chrestiens qui se sont separez de l'Eglise Romaine* (Paris, 1572), sig. M8v.

[74] Peter Matheson, ed., *Argula von Grumbach: A woman's voice in the Reformation* (Edinburgh, 1995), p. 164; Peter Matheson, 'Breaking the Silence: Women, Censorship, and the Reformation', *SCJ*, XXVII (1996), pp. 97–109.

[75] René Benoist, *Remonstrance aux prestres, religieuses et moynes, qui sous le pretexte d'un licite mariage, ont commis abhominable inceste & sacrilege* (Paris, 1567), sig. Bb4v; Thomas Beauxamis, *Enqueste et griefz, sur le sac et pieces, et depositions des tesmoings produictz par les favoriz de la nouvelle Eglise, contre le Pape, & autres Prelatz de l'Eglise Catholique* (Paris, 1562), sig. A7r.

[76] [Saconay], *Discours Catholique*, sig. E1v.

[77] Mouchy, *Responce a quelque apologie*, sig. H4v.

[78] Artus Désiré, *Le Deffensaire de la foy chrestienne* (Paris, 1567), sig. K3r.

> Husbands, love your wives, teach them, console them, and govern
> them and keep them with care as weak vessels, keeping perfect
> loyalty to them. And you, wives, be subject to your husband in all
> obedience, and apparell yourselves with chastity and humility, and
> modesty, which are ornaments before god more precious than ru-
> bies, pearls, and diamonds. Your clothes should be modest, and
> not dissolute, your words full of honour and your manner of living
> should be sober and simple.[79]

This suggests that Protestant authors were no less stereotypical than
the Catholics. One famous example, John Knox's *First blast of the
trumpet against the monstruous regiment of women*, argues that the
authority of women over men is unnatural and contrary to God's will.
Although written in the aftermath of Mary Tudor's reign, it outraged
Elizabeth who took it personally. Knox's use of this theme shows the
potency of this symbolism which transcends confessional differences;
he reproduces all the passages of Paul mentioned above and his portrayal of women is not dissimilar from that of the French Catholic
authors:

> To promote a woman to beare rule, superioritie, dominion or
> empire above any realme, nation, or citie, is repugnant to nature,
> contumelie to God, a thing most contrarious to his reveled will and
> approved ordinance, and finalie it is the subversion of good order,
> of all equitie and justice ... . Nature I say, doth paynt them furthe
> to be weake, fraile, impacient, feble and foolishe: and experience
> hath declared them to be unconstant, variable, cruell and lacking
> the spirit of counsel and regiment ... . So, I say, that in her greatest
> perfection woman was created to be subject to man ... . But as for
> woman, it is no more possible, that she being set aloft in authoritie
> above man, shall resist the motions of pride, then it is able to be
> weake reed, or to the turning wethercocke, not to bowe or turne at
> the vehemencies of the unconstant wind.[80]

The fact that both Catholics and Protestants honoured these Scriptural defences against the involvement of women in spiritual affairs
shows that the actual role of women in Protestantism was not really
what was at stake. The use of the same repository of language and
stereotypes by Catholics and Protestants alike suggests that misogyny
was a common cultural feature which transcended confessional differences. For example, Nicolas Vignier used the word *femmelette* at the
turn of the seventeenth century to deride the Catholics' constant reference to the councils of the Church: 'But it is the Popes and the clergy of
Rome who despise the holy councils ... as if they were assemblies of

[79] Anon., *Exhortation d'un des Pasteurs de la France à son troupeau* (1561), pp. 9–10.
[80] Knox, *The First blast*, sigs B1ʳ, B2ʳ, B6ᵛ, C2ᵛ.

femmelettes at the baths.'[81] I should like to suggest that the use of this theme in polemic does not necessarily reflect the changing role of women in society but is rather a rhetorical tool.

Bosquet, a Catholic commentator of the first religious war in Toulouse, recounted that, when a minister from Lavaur was challenged by a deacon of Toulouse, he refused to conduct the debate in Latin, but in French, so he could be heard by the *femmelettes* who had come to hear him.[82] Robert Ceneau also argued that the use of the vernacular by Protestant ministers was aimed at the *femmelettes*, not so much to convert but to seduce them.[83] The undertones of sexual desire and adultery permeates this discourse and Catholic theologians often referred to 2 Timothy 3:6–7 describing false prophets: 'For among them are those who make their way into households and captivate silly women, overwhelmed by their sins and swayed by all kinds of desires, who are always being instructed and can never arrive at a knowledge of the truth.'[84] The interchangeability of this image is demonstrated by its use in Protestant writings against the Dominicans and Franciscans at the turn of the century.[85]

Robert Ceneau, for example, points at the Protestant ministers as the real instigators of the women's audacity against Catholic prelates. The pamphlet denies any merit to the Protestant women who are described as the puppets of the ministers who are the real targets of these attacks:

> Yet do not believe that women of this kind ... are the instigators in this unfortunate tragedy. Those who serve as their secretary are worse ... . These [women] only assist and are but present: whereas these [men] preside as masters ... And the femmelettes we speak of are but Arabian flutes ... like puppets ... but the true instigators of the thing, are sound workers, true singers & musicians. They sing too, but the company of women answers in a low voice.[86]

According to Bosquet, the thin end of the wedge was the permissiveness of Catholic husbands towards their wives:

> Having allowed their wives to go to the Minister, and to do all other damnable & apostastic exercises, they disapprove of the

---

[81] Nicolas Vignier, *Apologie Catholique de la doctrine des Eglises Reformees* (Saumur, 1617), p. 28.

[82] Bosquet, *Sur les troubles*, p. 129.

[83] Ceneau, *Response catholique*, sig. D7ᵛ.

[84] D'Espence, *Cinq sermons*, sig. D5ʳ; Lindan, *Discovrs en forme de dialogue*, sig. B2ʳ; Benoist, *Brieve Response a quelque remonstrance*, sig. a5ʳ; Dupuiherbault, *Consolation des catholiques*, sigs. A6ᵛ, A7ʳ.

[85] Nicolas Vignier, *Legende Doree ou Sommaire de l'histiore des freres Mendians de l'Ordre de Dominique, & de François* (Leyden, 1608), p. 62.

[86] Ceneau, *Response catholique*, sigs E6ᵛ–E7ʳ.

husbands who forbid their wives from acting alike, having maintained that they should not be punished, nor coerced by their
husbands to do their will; as if the husband was not the master of
his wife: as if a Catholic wife had license to become a heretic
without his consent and against his will.[87]

Women's role in the Reformation was ridiculed and the emphasis was
placed on the male Reformers or bad Catholic husbands. Catholic
husbands failed to keep their wives in check, and Protestant ministers
were wolves in sheep's clothing, but in both cases men are responsible
for the women's 'mistakes'. Robert Ceneau and Thomas Beauxamis
argued that widows were particularly vulnerable to the arguments of
the Protestants, because they no longer had their husbands to counsel
them.[88] The misogyny implicit in these passages makes appeals to the
consensus values of the intended audience of these works, predominantly urban literate males.

This points to the rhetorical nature of the use of the 'battle of the
sexes' that was made by Catholic theologians. These contradictory
images of women were prejudices that were used indiscriminately to
justify a given argument and, as such, have little bearing on the gender
issues which have been the hallmark of recent historiography.[89] The
theme of the 'battle of the sexes' was a particularly powerful weapon of
propaganda. Femininity was synonymous with disorder and it was used
by the Catholic polemicists to demonstrate that Protestantism was turning the 'world upside down'.

Catholic polemic is characterized by the use of inversion and analogy to
depict Protestantism as a source of divisiveness, chaos and disorder. The
Reformation is depicted as a disease infecting the body social and the
body politic. The theme of the 'battle of the sexes' was turned to
polemical uses to show that Protestantism was particularly attractive to
women on one hand and that it aimed at overturning the traditional
gender roles on the other. By arguing that Protestantism was giving
more power to women, Catholic authors were trying to show that
Protestantism was interested in the overturning of all order. It would
seem that Catholic portrayal of Protestant women, characterized as

---

[87] Bosquet, *Sur les troubles*, p. 157.

[88] Ceneau, *Response catholique*, sig. D7ᵛ; Beauxamis, *Enqueste et griefz*, sig. B5ᵛ.

[89] For conflicting views on Protestantism and Feminism, see I. Backus, 'Marie Dentière:
un cas de féminisne théologique à l'époque de la Réforme', *BSHPF*, CXXXVII (1991),
pp. 177–95; and Keith Moxey, 'The Battle of the Sexes and the World Upside Down', in
L. Coon, K. Haldane and E. Sommer, eds, *That Gentle Strength: historical perspectives
on women in Christianity* (London, 1990), pp. 134–48.

femmelettes, did not reflect an increase in the involvement of women in spiritual affairs: all merit is denied Protestant women and it is clear that the real targets of the polemic were the Protestant ministers or Catholic husbands, in both cases men. Use of the word *femmelette* cannot be used to gauge the effective role that individual women played in the French Reformed movement, since it corresponds to a pre-established stereotype borrowed from the Scriptures. The universality of these stereotypes is shown by the fact that Protestant writers also used these images against Catholicism.[90]

---

[90] *Advertissement a la Royne Mere du Roy*, sig. b3ᵛ; Vignier, *Legende Doree*, p. 62; *Complainte apologique des eglises de France*, sig. C1ʳ; *Exhortation d'un des Pasteurs*, pp. 9–10; Knox, *The First blast*, sigs B1ʳ, B2ʳ, B6ᵛ, C2ᵛ; Vignier, *Apologie Catholique*, p. 28.

CHAPTER SEVEN

The polemical use of
the Albigensian Crusade

In the formal condemnation of Luther's theses issued by the University of Paris, Noël Beda accused Luther of unearthing old heresies which had long been forgotten.[1] He refers in particular to that of the Albigensians or Cathars of Languedoc who lived in the twelfth and thirteenth century. Of all Christian heresies, Albigensianism alone had been the object of a crusade. One of the proclaimed aims of the Albigensian Crusade was to erase all signs that the heresy had ever existed: the heretics and the houses in which they had lived were burned, and later generations were forbidden to honour the memory of their heterodox ancestors.[2] Ironically, it is the inquisitors themselves who perpetuated their memory by committing the story of the Albigensian Crusade to paper. Contrary to what Beda asserted, it was the Catholics who rescued the Albigensians from oblivion in order to use their example against the Reformers.

It was the political dimension of the Albigensian Crusade that made it immediately relevant to contemporary events. The comparison between the emerging Calvinist Church and the Albigensian heresy became commonplace, its purpose being to scare the Court of Catherine de Medici into reversing its policy of conciliation. The emphasis on the retelling of the Albigensian Crusade changed over time to fit new political circumstances. It emerged very strongly in the aftermath of the conspiracy of Amboise and remained strong throughout the reign of Charles IX. The minority of both François II and Charles IX provided the Catholic hardliners with their best argument against the conciliatory policies of Catherine de Medici. After the majority of Charles IX, and during the reign of Henri III, the Catholic opposition to conciliation increasingly turned against the monarch himself. The polemical use of the Albigensian Crusade thus provides an extraordinary insight into the ingenuity of Catholic authors and their ability to rewrite history to fit their needs.

---

[1] Marie-Humbert Vicaire, 'Les Albigeois Ancêtres des Protestants: Assimilations Catholiques', *CF*, XIV (1979), pp. 23–46 (p. 28).

[2] B. Hamilton, *The Albigensian Crusade* (London, 1974), p. 24.

The Albigensian heresy was undoubtedly the most formidable threat to orthodoxy that France had known before the outset of the Reformation. Unlike any other medieval heresy it was highly organized and had been openly adopted by the political élite of Languedoc, led by count Raymond de Toulouse. The organization of the Albigensian Church mirrored that of the Catholic Church, with bishops, archbishops and, allegedly, a Pope.[3] Between the sending of the first papal envoys at the turn of the twelfth century and the last trial in 1329, more than a century was needed to extinguish all traces of heresy.[4] As a consequence of the policy of eradication mentioned above, very little was known about the Albigensians and their doctrine apart from what the Inquisition had reported. Consequently, the Cathar heritage of the areas where Protestantism flourished in the Midi was enough to suggest a connection between the two movements to many authors on both sides of the confessional divide.

The numerous histories of the Albigensian Crusade that were published during the French Wars of Religion were intended to serve as an example of how heretics could be defeated in battle by a decisive monarch. The parallel between Protestantism and the Albigensian heresy first appeared in Catholic polemic on the eve of the French Wars of Religion. Between 1555 and 1562 Calvinism emerged from relative anonymity to become a rallying cry for a whole cross-section of society. At this time, members of the Faculty of Theology, self-appointed champions of orthodoxy, rose to the challenge with unprecedented vigour. Although religious polemic in the vernacular pre-dates 1555, it grew exponentially with the perceived threat of Calvinism and its accompanying flood of books from Geneva.[5] Symptomatic of this growing paranoia is the knee-jerk reaction to the affair of the rue St Jacques in September 1557 described in Chapter 4. In the first decade of the French Wars of Religion the themes which had surfaced during this period were continuously recycled.

Catholic theologians looked for precedents in the history of the Church when orthodoxy had been challenged. The lengthy arguments which had been used against a variety of heretical groups were taken out of context and applied indiscriminately to Protestants, while the Reformed doctrine was grossly misrepresented and compared to earlier heresies which had already been refuted in the great councils of the Church. Although Albigensianism was mentioned in this context, it was

---

[3] René Nelli, *La philosophie du catharisme: le dualisme radical au XIIIe siècle* (Paris, 1975), p. 9.

[4] E. Le Roy Ladurie, *Montaillou: Village Occitan* (Paris, 1982), p. 563.

[5] Kingdon, *Geneva and the coming of the Wars*, p. 93.

but one of many heresies used for the purpose of defaming Protestantism. The reason the Albigensians received special attention from Catholic
polemicists lay in the political specificity of the Albigensian Crusade.
The Crusade provided a precedent for authors who wanted the Crown
to declare an all-out war on Protestantism. Legal arguments of the 'just
war' were recycled in this context to call for further violence on the
Huguenots;[6] for example, Edmond Auger argued that a war fought for
religion was the only just war possible.[7]

The context in which the comparison between Protestantism and
Albigensianism emerged is inextricably linked with the political events
which precipitated the French Wars of Religion. The success story of the
Albigensian Crusade was particularly intended as an inspiration for the
young successors of Henri II: François II and Charles IX. The political
circumstances of the 1560s conjured a comparison with the early thirteenth century when political divisions and the spread of the Cathar
heresy had gone hand in hand. Both had been quashed by Louis IX
who, having defeated heresy in Languedoc, annexed the region to the
Crown of France. St Louis was a powerful symbol of the French monarchy. By conjuring up this symbol, the Crown's supporters were seeking
to resuscitate the moribund crusading spirit in the hope that it would
rid France of the new heresy and unite Christendom once more.

The untimely death of Henri II in 1559 led to the succession of his
15-year-old son François II, who died shortly afterwards to be replaced
by the 10-year-old Charles IX. This situation contributed to the en-
trenchment of the confessional divide, as both Catholic and Protestant
factions accused the other of taking advantage of the young age of the
kings.

This was also a time of directional uncertainty for the Protestants,
torn between patient suffering and active rebellion – as mirrored in the
dilemma of their leader, Jean Calvin. Calvin disapproved of active
rebellion but he nonetheless pleaded with the house of Bourbon to
champion the Protestant cause.[8] Antoine de Navarre's lack of resolve
meant that this would not happen until the outbreak of the Wars of
Religion when his brother the Prince de Condé took Orléans in April
1562.

There was particular controversy between Protestants and Catholics
regarding the age of majority of kings. Protestants, who were trying to

---

[6] Parrow, 'From Defense to Resistance', pp. 27–37; Paul Rousset, 'L'idéologie de
Croisade dans les Guerres de Religion au XVIe siècle', *Schweizerische Zeitschrift für
Geschichte*, XXXI (1981), pp. 174–84.

[7] Yardeni, *Conscience nationale*, pp. 109–10.

[8] Bonnet, ed., *Letters of Calvin*, IV, pp. 67, 69, 91–2, 104, 107.

rid François II of the influence of the Guises, argued that he was not old enough to choose his own advisers and, on those grounds, they asked for the assembly of the Estates General in order to appoint a Council where they would have been represented.

It has been argued that the death of Henri II provoked a transformation of the printing industry. Lack of strong leadership led to the appearance of short works, or *plaquettes*, characteristically in octavo and written in the vernacular, which dealt with affairs of state and religion.[9] Continuous disaffection with the government of Catherine de Medici led Catholic controversialists to write, sometimes openly, against its policy of conciliation. Successive edicts of pacification in 1551, 1560 and 1564 reflect concern for 'seditious pamphlets' which targeted Catholic as well as Protestant works.[10]

This situation came to a head in March 1560 with the tumult of Amboise, a failed Protestant coup that attempted to remove François II from the influence of the Guise faction. References to the reign of Louis IX and the Albigensian Crusade were made in the course of the subsequent polemical exchange between pro-Guise authors and Protestant apologists. In defence of the Protestant cause, François Hotman argued in the *Histoire du Tumulte d'Amboise* that François II was being manipulated by the duc de Guise and renewed the Protestant plea for the summoning of the Estates General. He also pitched the relative merits of the medieval predecessors of the Prince de Condé and his nemesis the duc de Guise. The Bourbons had been dismissed from government because of their Protestant sympathies but Hotman argued that their pedigree gave them as much right as the Guises to be represented at Court. The lineage of the house of Lorraine was allegedly connected to Charlemagne whereas the Bourbons could claim ancestry from Hugue Capet, founder of the Capetian dynasty. Hotman also accused Guise of wanting to usurp the throne on the grounds of his Carolingian lineage, an argument which was turned against the Bourbons who were dubbed 'Huguenots': 'Has the time come ... for the Crown to be transferred from those that the house of Guise call Huguenots: as descending from the race of Hugh Capet, to be given back (as they say) to those who claim descent from Charlemagne?'[11] Faced with the rising danger of factionalism, François II was in a particularly weak position, so the royal archivist, Jean du Tillet, formulated a response that invoked the precedent of Louis IX, who became King at the age of 13 and fought

---

[9] Pallier, 'Les réponses catholiques', pp. 338–9.

[10] Soman, 'Press, Pulpit, and censorship', p. 441.

[11] *Complainte au peuple Francois*, sig. D2^r.

rebellious barons as well as the Albigensian heresy in the early years of his reign.[12]

Jean du Tillet was the secretary of the Parlement of Paris and had been in the employ of the Valois since the reign of François I. His access to the royal charters, combined with his long service to the Crown, made him a perfect advocate for the King. Elizabeth Brown suggests that his allegiance was swayed by Charles (future cardinal) de Lorraine in 1546, at the very beginning of Henri II's reign. In exchange for his reappointment as Clerk of the Parlement, he would have put his knowledge of the charters at the service of the Guises.[13] Moreover, du Tillet had an ulterior motive in writing against the Protestants, as the leader of the conspiracy of Amboise, La Renaudie, was a personal enemy.[14] Du Tillet was aware, as a historian and archivist, that only the unrivalled prestige of St Louis could trump the claims of both the houses of Bourbon and Lorraine.[15]

François Hotman, who was probably the author of a *Responce* to du Tillet, argued in turn that, although Louis IX had come to the throne at an early age, he had remained under the tutelage of his mother, Blanche de Castille, until he was 21.[16] This was a further plea for the calling of the Estates General so that the question of the King's entourage could be settled fairly. At the death of Louis VIII in 1226, Blanche de Castille, having been left with a 13-year-old heir to the throne, had become Regent. The obvious comparison with Catherine de Medici reflected the hope, on the part of the Protestants, that she would be more favourably disposed to their cause than her late husband. This announced the death of François II in December 1560 which led to the succession of

---

[12] Elizabeth A. R. Brown, ed., 'Jean Du Tillet and the French Wars of Religion: Five Tracts, 1562–1569', *Medieval and Renaissance Texts and Studies*, CVIII (1994), pp. 6, 11; Jean du Tillet, *Pour l'Entiere Majorite du Roy Treschrestien, Contre le Legitime Conseil Malicieusement Inventé par les Rebelles* (1560), sig. e3^r.

[13] Brown, ed., 'Jean Du Tillet', pp. 6, 11; Sylvie Le Clech-Charton, 'Le sentiment religieux chez les notaires et secrétaires du roi sous François Ier: un groupe sous influence?', in *Renaissance européenne et phénomènes religieux 1450–1650* (Montbrison, 1991), pp. 219–34 (p. 229).

[14] Donald R. Kelley, *The Beginning of Ideology: Consciousness and Society in the French Reformation* (Cambridge, 1981), p. 268; Donald R. Kelley, *François Hotman: A Revolutionary's Ordeal* (Princeton, 1973), pp. 108–9, 117.

[15] Nicole Cazauran, 'Le roi exemplaire dans quelques pamphlets réformés 1560–1585', *Travaux de Linguistique et de Littérature*, XXII: 2 (1984), pp. 185–200; R. E. Asher, 'Rois légendaires et nationalisme dans la poésie du XVIe siècle français', in F. Simone, ed., *Culture et politique en France à l'époque de l'Humanisme et de la Renaissance* (Turin, 1974), pp. 235–48.

[16] [François Hotman], *Responce au livre inscript, Pour la Majorité du Roy François Second* (Amboise, 1560), sig. B6^r.

Charles IX who was placed under the regency of his mother, Catherine de Medici.

The comparison with the reign of Louis IX, which had originally been intended as a defence of the majority of François II, took on a different meaning during the reign of Charles IX. The example of King St Louis, who had led a crusade to the Holy Land after having defeated the Albigensians in Languedoc, was used to coax Charles IX into leading a crusade against the Protestant heretics.[17] This argument was made more pressing as conciliatory measures were implemented by Catherine de Medici and Michel de L'Hôpital before the outbreak of the Wars of Religion. Not only did these measures provoke the wrath of the leading Catholic nobles led by the duc de Guise, but they also met with unprecedented resistance from the Parlement of Paris and the Faculty of Theology. The theologians and the Parlement expressed their disapproval through the licensing of inflammatory books, often written by members of these two institutions themselves, which called for punitive measures against Protestants.[18]

The first author to mention the Albigensian Crusade in this context was Nicole Grenier in the frequently reprinted work *Le bouclier de la foy* (1547). Even in this early work, published in a very different religious context, St Louis was held up as an example to be followed by the Valois monarchs:

> The King Louis the seventh, father of St Louis, had in his time a big war against the Albigensian heretics, & brought them back within the bosom of the church: of which the son St Louis and his successors the Kings have always been great emulators as true zealots of the honour of God, faith, & the reformation of the abuse arising in the church.[19]

This theme was taken up in 1558 by Antoine de Mouchy, in his *Responce a quelque apologie* published in the wake of the affair of the rue St Jacques. As the first occasion on which Protestants were 'caught in the act' the affair of the rue St Jaques was the catalyst for a flurry of polemic from both sides of the confessional divide: 'under the command of the said king Philip, the French made war on the Albigensians ... in the year 1210. It was reiterated at the time of his son Louis, father of lord St Louis in 1216 so that they were exterminated.'[20]

---

[17] Norman Housley, *The Later Crusades: from Lyons to Alcazar 1274–1580* (Oxford, 1992), pp. 234–66.

[18] Mouchy, *Responce a quelque apologie*, sig. C3ᵛ.

[19] Nicole Grenier, *Le bouclier de la foy* (Paris, 1577), sig. *4ʳ. The 1547 edition is the first edition listed in Higman, *Piety and the People*, p. 235.

[20] Mouchy, *Responce a quelque apologie*, sig. C3ᵛ.

Although these authors praised the medieval monarchs for their efforts to eradicate heresy, they refrained from making a direct comparison between Protestantism and Albigensianism. Quite a different line was taken by Jean Gay's *Histoire des Scismes et Heresies des Albigeois* which openly compared Protestants to Albigensians and called for a crusade against them. This book would probably have escaped the notice of historians if it had not been at the root of a diplomatic incident with the Court of Elizabeth I.[21] Indeed, it earned immediate notoriety by comparing the comte de Toulouse, temporal patron of the Albigensians, with Henry VIII and by making multiple marriages a telling sign of heresy:

> As for the heretics ... please recall the example of a foreign prince ... who changed wives every day, and every day got remarried, having married or kidnapped as many as seven wives: the same happened three hundred and forty five years ago to the count Raymond ... who married and dealt with four wives.[22]

The English ambassador in Paris formally asked for the book to be banned and the Constable de Montmorency published an order forbidding printing without the authorization of the King or his council.[23] The renewed interest in the Albigensian Crusade predictably came from the Parlement of Toulouse for whose members it had particular relevance. The *Histoire des Scismes et Heresies des Albigeois* warned against the danger of allowing temporal patrons to harbour and protect heretics, an allusion which was no doubt intended for the Bourbons: 'The Albigensian heretics were favoured and helped within the lands of the count Raymond of Toulouse, and of the viscount of Beziers his nephew: with the count of Foix, their confederate, they call themselves evangelists like the modern heretics.'[24] The controversy which surrounded the publication of this book illustrates the divergence of interests between the Court, who sought to censor the book, and the Parlement and the Faculty of Theology who had authorized its publication.

The Parlement and the University had worked hand in hand with the government during the ascendancy of the Guises, but were notoriously opposed to the conciliatory measures of Michel de L'Hôpital. The Parlement refused to register the Edict of Pacification of January 1562, and on this occasion, the secretary du Tillet addressed a remonstrance to the King, in which he made a reference to St Louis and the

---

[21] Stevenson, ed., *Calendar of State Papers*, p. 503.

[22] Gay, *Histoire des scismes et heresies des Albigeois*, p. 5.

[23] Guilleminot, 'Religion et politique à la veille des guerres civiles', I, p. 11; Droz, ed., *Chemins de l'Hérésie*, I, p. 375.

[24] Gay, *Histoire des scismes et heresies des Albigeois*, p. 1.

Albigensians: 'King Saint Louis ... under the wise leadership of his mother Queen Blanche, had the good initiative of expelling the heresy of the Albigensians, and chastised Raymond, count of Toulouse, so that by treaty ... he obliged him to purge his lands of the said heresy.'[25] It is clear that du Tillet was referring to the Prince de Condé, who justified the former's fears when he assumed the leadership of the Protestant cause in April 1562.

As Tours and Orléans fell to the Protestants, Jean du Tillet presented a manuscript history of the Albigensian Crusade to Catherine de Medici. This book contained an implicit comparison between the Prince de Condé and the comte Raymond de Toulouse, and echoed the text of the Parlement's remonstrance: 'God reserved his blessings for the king Saint Louis, only fourteen years old, who had followed the advice of his virtuous mother Queen Blanche.'[26] Repeating what he had written after the conspiracy of Amboise, du Tillet appealed to Catherine de Medici through a flattering comparison with Blanche de Castille, to take up arms against the Protestants. Indeed, during the minority of Louis IX (1226–30), Blanche de Castille had quelled the uprisings of no less than three counts.[27] Du Tillet pressed the point that the Catholic Church and the Crown had been in a symbiotic relationship for so long that challenging the one necessarily implied armed rebellion against the other. Furthermore, he observed that the rebellion of the nobles had been encouraged by the young age of the King during the regency of Blanche de Castille:

> The said King St Louis was only 11 years, 7 months and six days on 1 December 1226 when he was crowned under the regency of the Queen Blanche his mother ... the count of Toulouse, scorning the youth of the King & the authority of the Queen, started a war against them.[28]

The whole book could be conceived as a warning to the Protestant nobility, and the Prince de Condé in particular, using the fate of comte Raymond de Toulouse as a deterrent against rebellion: 'The reading of the pitiful falls of great houses, other calamities and mishaps of more powerful than them will possibly hold them back.'[29] In this statement we find the repetition of Jean Gay's argument: 'by which it appears that

---

[25] [Jean du Tillet], *Remonstrances faictes au roy par messieurs de la court de Parlement de Paris, sur la publication de l'Edict du moys de Janvier* (Cambray, 1561), reproduced in Droz, ed., *Chemins de l'Hérésie*, III, pp. 420–32 (p. 431).

[26] Du Tillet, *Sommaire de l'histoire de la guerre*, sig. ã7ʳ.

[27] Polydori Vergilii, *Urbinatis Anglicae historiae libri vigintifex* (Basel, 1546), p. 297.

[28] Du Tillet, *Sommaire de l'histoire de la guerre*, sig. D5ʳ.

[29] Ibid., sig. ã7ᵛ.

several great princes and lords fell in extreme desolation and ruin, for having favoured the heretics'.[30] The history of the Albigensian Crusade also carried a second message: 'But if the rebellion and contempt for the young age of the king persists in taking up religion as an excuse, or attempts to change it, you will have an example to follow.'[31] This passage is an unambiguous call to follow the example of the Albigensian Crusade should the Protestant nobles not heed du Tillet's warning. Throughout the Wars of Religion, histories of the Albigensian Crusade were reprinted by a number of Catholic authors, carrying a similar message in opposition to the royal policy of conciliation.

The second edict of pacification of March 1563 was greeted with as much resistance as the first one, and the Parlement of Paris made the provision that it would not become fully operative until the King had reached his majority.[32] In order to take the reluctant Parlement at its word, Charles IX declared his majority in a *lit de justice* at Rouen in August 1563. The secretary of the Parlement of Paris, Jean du Tillet, had hoped that this event would mark the end of the religious troubles in France: 'waiting for the majority of the King who in one glance, will dissipate all evil according to the saying of Salomon'.[33] On the other hand, he had not expected the majority of the King to be used as a ploy to force the Edict of Amboise on the reluctant Parlement of Paris. Shortly before the promulgation of the Peace of Amboise, du Tillet signed a *privilège* for the publication of another anti-Protestant book by the inquisitor and Dean of the University of Toulouse.[34] Rotier's *Response aux Blasphemateurs de la Saincte Messe* once more referred to the Albigensians and the reign of Louis IX, an argument that had dominated the minority of Charles IX: 'We can surmise that divine providence enabled these monsters and perverse sects to enter in your Kingdom, so that you could have the honour and the glory, in this your young age, to hunt them and expel them from all of your Kingdom forever.'[35]

With the *lit de justice*, Catherine de Medici had demonstrated her unwillingness to compromise, and Charles IX disappointed the expectations

---

[30] Gay, *Histoire des scismes et heresies des Albigeois*, p. 1.

[31] Du Tillet, *Sommaire de l'histoire de la guerre*, sig. ã8ᵛ.

[32] Mack P. Holt, *The French Wars of Religion, 1562–1629* (Cambridge, 1995), pp. 57–8.

[33] Du Tillet, *Sommaire de l'histoire de la guerre*, sig. ã8ʳ.

[34] Robert A. Schneider, *Public Life in Toulouse 1463–1789: From Municipal Republic to Cosmopolitan City* (London, 1989), p. 15.

[35] Esprit Rotier, *Response aux blasphemateurs de la saincte messe: Avec la confutation de la vaine & ridicule coene des Calvinistes* (Paris, 1566), sigs A7ʳ⁻ᵛ.

of the Catholic warmongers. Further appeals were made to Catherine de Medici, who having proved a capable Regent, was compared once more to Blanche de Castille. Blanche de Castille had crushed the rebellion of the barons during the minority of Louis IX, despite being regarded as a foreigner in her own kingdom.[36] In 1565, the Bishop of Montpellier, Guillaume Pellicier, offered the manuscript 'Histoire des prouesses et vaillantises de noble seigneur messire Simon, comte de Montfort' to the Queen Mother who had it bound and marked with her coat of arms.[37] Catherine de Medici acknowledged the comparison between herself and Blanche de Castille in a conversation with the Venetian ambassador, Giovanni Correr, who wrote in 1569: 'in telling me of these things ... she applied them to current affairs'.[38] This indicates that the comparison with the Albigensian Crusade had the desired impact on the ruling élite and might have influenced the policies of the Regent. The Catholic authors who stressed this element of the comparison had probably realized who was in charge at Court and pressed the Regent, rather than the King, for a change in policy. Their prayers were answered, when after the Surprise of Meaux, Catherine de Medici dismissed Michel de L'Hôpital along with his conciliatory policies.

Although the example of Louis IX was continually used, there emerged during the years 1567 and 1568 another contender for the leadership of the Albigensian Crusade in the person of Simon de Montfort. The shift of emphasis from Louis IX to Simon de Montfort prefigures the disillusionment of the ultra-Catholic party with the reign of Charles IX. The leadership of Simon de Montfort was also more historically accurate: he had been designated leader of the Albigensian Crusade by the Pope and offered the lands of the comte de Toulouse as an incentive for victory.[39] Simon de Montfort was therefore an ideal symbol for those advocating the direct involvement of the Pope in the French Wars of Religion.

This development coincided with the first stirrings of the Holy League which appeared in embryonic forms in confraternities and crusading movements in 1567 and 1568.[40] Robert Harding has noted the similarities between the confraternity of the Holy Ghost in Mâcon and a

[36] Jean Richard, *Saint Louis: roi d'une France féodale, soutien de la Terre sainte* (Paris, 1983), pp. 40–46.

[37] Vicaire, 'Les Albigeois Ancêtres des Protestants', p. 36.

[38] Jean Carbonnier, 'De l'idée que le protestantisme s'est fait de ses rapports avec le catharisme ou des adoptions d'ancêtres en histoire', *BSHPF*, CI (1955), pp. 72–87 (p. 83).

[39] Parrow, 'From Defense to Resistance', pp. 28–9.

[40] Crouzet, *Guerriers de Dieu*, I, pp. 379–80, 383–97; Holt, *The French Wars of Religion*, pp. 67–75.

similar movement that had appeared in Languedoc during the Albigensian Crusade.[41] This evolution can be traced in a second publication by Jean du Tillet, *Advertissement a la noblesse* (1568), where he described the Crusade as a confederacy of barons under the leadership of de Montfort: 'We read in the history of the Albigensians, that thriving in their error, and using the same pretexts as our own conspirators, the Nobility took the cross under the banner of one count of Montfort, and warred on them until they were all defeated and exterminated.'[42] Prefiguring developments of the Holy League, in which the Parlement of Paris played a considerable role, du Tillet took the King out of the equation. It was the Catholic nobility, under the leadership of a prominent nobleman following an injunction of the Pope, who had defeated the heretics. This Leaguer reading of the Albigensian Crusade was followed by one of its prominent members, Arnaud Sorbin. Sorbin was the chaplain of the future Henri III to whom he dedicated his work, implying that Henri would succeed where his brother had failed: 'The count of Montfort with the French army ... subdued the Albigensians under foot. ... Henry of Valois harvester of enemies ... will tame the Heresy of the Gauls.'[43]

With his victories at Jarnac and Moncontour in 1569, Henri had become the new champion of orthodoxy, and he soon replaced Charles IX as the potential leader of a crusade against heresy. Simon de Montfort was not exclusively compared to Henri de Valois, however, but also to François, second duc de Guise who had become a martyr and a saint for the Holy Catholic League. A 1569 Parisian edition of Arnaud Sorbin's *Histoire des Albigeois* includes a short companion work entitled *Similitude des regnes du roy Loys IX ... et de celuy du roy Charles* where it is François de Lorraine who is compared to Simon de Montfort: 'Louis IX ordered Simon de Montfort to fight the heretics during his minority ... the king Charles IX fought the rebellious heretics during his minority, through his captain Sir François de Lorraine, duc de Guise, of blessed memory.'[44]

Both these works recognize Simon de Montfort as the real leader of the Crusade, expressing the need for an alternative leadership for the Catholic cause, but disagree as to who should assume that role. The

---

[41] Robert H. Harding, 'The Mobilization of Confraternities Against the Reformation in France', *SCJ*, XI: 2 (1980), pp. 85–107 (p. 86).

[42] Jean du Tillet, *Advertissement a la noblesse, tant du party du Roy, que des Rebelles & Conjurez* (Lyon, 1568), sig. C1ʳ.

[43] Arnaud Sorbin, *Histoire des albigeois, et gestes de noble simon de monfort* (Toulouse, 1568), sig. A4ʳ.

[44] I. D. S. A., *Similitude des regnes du roy Loys IX. par nous nomme s. Loys, et de celuy du roy Charles à present regnant*, bound with Sorbin, *Histoire des albigeois* (1569), sigs AA2ᵛ, AA3ᵛ, AA4ʳ, AA5ʳ.

differences between the *Histoire des Albigeois* and its companion work
the *Similitude des Regnes* thus strangely prefigure the conflict which
pitched Henri III against Henri, duc de Guise in the 1580s. After his
coronation in 1574, Henri III was reminded by the League polemicists
of his oath to rid the country of heresy, and reference was made to the
example of Philippe Auguste leading the Crusade against the Albigensian
heretics.[45] But despite his clever endorsement of the League in 1576,
Henri III came to disappoint those who had seen him as the leader of a
crusade against the Protestants. The duc de Guise came to be seen as its
leading figure and, after his assassination in 1588, became a martyr of
the Holy League, while Henri III became its primary target.

This later period saw the reprinting of the books on the Albigensian
Crusade that had been written during the first three Wars of Religion.
Arnaud Sorbin himself was a notorious Leaguer and his *Histoire des
albigeois* was reprinted in 1569 and 1585 under the evocative title
Histoire de la Ligue Saincte.[46] In addition, the inflammatory *Histoire
des scismes* by Jean Gay was reprinted in Paris in 1589[47] and Jean du
Tillet's manuscript *Sommaire de l'Histoire* was published in 1590 by his
son, who thought that the lessons of the Albigensian Crusade had yet to
be understood:

> Remembering that my late father seeing this kingdom afflicted
> with the same troubles that it had been three hundred years ago, by
> the heresy of the Albigensians ... It seemed to me that the remedy
> that was applied then to heal the wound that was inflicting the
> kingdom ... is now particularly relevant, to heal the same disease
> with which this kindgom is afflicted.[48]

The various versions of the history of the Albigensian Crusade plot
the course of the hopes of a Catholic crusade against Protestantism.
Originally intended as an encouragement for François II and Charles
IX, the comparison with Louis IX soon turned against the Valois monarchs. The later development of the history, after 1568, clearly prefigures
the League where the Guises were designated as the only hope of the
Catholic cause. It is a testimony to the inability of the Crown to control
the printing press, that such inflammatory material was printed

---

[45] Dalia Leonardo, 'In Pursuit of a Godly Kingdom: Kingship and Propaganda during
the Reign of Henry III, 1584–89' (unpublished paper, Sixteenth-Century Studies Conference, St Louis, 1996), 12 pages, p. 9.

[46] Arnaud Sorbin, *Histoire de la Ligue Saincte faicte il y a CCCLXXX ans à la
conduite de Simon de Montfort contre les hérétiques albigeois* (Paris, 1585); Greengrass,
France in the Age of Henri IV, p. 199; Vicaire, 'Les Albigeois ancêtres des Protestants', p.
37.

[47] Vicaire, 'Les Albigeois Ancêtres des Protestants', p. 34.

[48] Du Tillet, *Sommaire de l'histoire de la guerre*, sigs ã3ʳ, ã8ʳ.

throughout the wars. The interest of prominent figures of the Parlement of Paris and the Faculty of Theology in the crusade also illustrates their disagreement with the Crown from the beginning. Although one can suppose that the polemical use of the Albigensian Crusade might have had an influence at Court, its most durable legacy was its impact on Protestant identity.

All the histories of the Albigensians mentioned above portrayed Protestants as offspring of the sect, and the tenets of the Reformed religion were merged with the doctrinal beliefs of the Albigensians. Jean Gay had written that the Albigensians had been exterminated beyond a trace except for 'the Lutherans ... who are their diabolical adopted children',[49] while Jean du Tillet had asserted that it was the seed of the Albigensian heresy that had been at the origin of the evangelical movement: 'In the past 45 years this heresy was reborn in many countries ... and has made more progress in this Kingdom in the past 16 months than ever before, in contempt for the King's young age.'[50] Arnaud Sorbin was no less explicit, in 1569, linking the beliefs of the Albigensians with those of Protestantism: 'Having come across an old manuscript book containing the origin, progress, and end of the Albigensian heresy ... I found the variety of opinions and the acts of the Albigensian heretics to be similar to those of our modern deformed.'[51] But the most radical pamphlet was the *Similitude des regnes*, which made a comparison between Theodore Beza and his Albigensian namesake:

> It is remarkable that the man who was the author of the heresy of the Albigensians was named Theodore: like the one who is author of the heresy of the Huguenots: It is Theodore Beza. Also the heresy that rules at present proceeds from Germany and Bohemia, like that of the Albigensians.[52]

The association between Albigensianism and Protestantism also gave rise to new contenders for the origins of the word *Huguenot*. Gabriel de Saconay linked it with the word *gueux*: 'the heretical soldiers were commonly known as the Ribald, a name that was given to them, the same way that we call them *Gueux* or *Huguenotz*'. This is a contemporary

---

[49] Gay, *Histoire des scismes et heresies des Albigeois*, p. 22.

[50] Du Tillet, *Sommaire de l'histoire de la guerre*, sig. F4ᵛ.

[51] Sorbin, *Histoire des albigeois* (1569), sig. a4ᵛ.

[52] *Similitude des regnes*, sig. AA5ʳ: 'C'est chose digne d'admiration, que celuy qui fut autheur de l'heresie des Albigeois ce nommoit Theodore: comme celuy qui est autheur de l'heresie des Huguenots: aussi l'heresie qui à present regne procede d'Allemagne & Boeme, comme celle des Albigeois. C'est Theodore de Beze.'

reference to the nickname given to the Dutch rebels (Beggars), and possibly to the involvement of Dutch and German Protestants (*Gotz Arriens*) in the war.[53] *Boulgres*, a synonym of *gueux*, was also a name given to the Albigensians who were affiliated to the Bogomils, originating in Bulgaria.[54] The etymology of the word also indicates a connection with buggery which was one of the practices imputed to the Albigensians and the Bogomils. This Bulgarian connection was exploited in the *Similitude des regnes* published in 1569: 'It is remarkable that the heresy of the Albigensians came from Germany ... and came to France and was called the heresy of the Bulgars.'[55] Of course, these associations by name reveal the unwillingness of the polemicists to go into any detail as to what Albigensians and Protestants might really have had in common.

The most significant link is undoubtedly the geographical identity between erstwhile centres of Albigensianism and contemporary hotbeds of Protestant resistance in the Midi. For example, the Cathar heritage of the town of Lavaur was acknowledged by both a Catholic member of the Parlement of Toulouse, and a Protestant minister of Montpellier who reported that Lavaur had been called 'the fountain of heresy' in the thirteenth century.[56] Catholic institutions in Toulouse had been built on the ashes of the Albigensian heresy, by edict of Innocent III who had declared that he would make a 'holy city' out of a 'hearth of pestilence'.[57] It is not surprising to find that many Catholic authors who made the comparison were from Toulouse, for example, Bosquet, Jean Gay and Rotier who was the Dean of the University founded by Innocent III.[58] The wave of iconoclasm and rioting which sprang up in Nîmes, Montpellier, Montauban, and Castres, culminating in the riot of Toulouse in May 1562, was undoubtedly what spurred their involvement. Jean Gay's *Histoire des scismes et heresies des Albigeois* was dedicated to Anne de Montmorency, Governor of Languedoc, and may have been intended as an encouragement to lead the struggle against heresy in this region.

The geographical basis for the comparison between Protestantism and Albigensianism was also noticed by Protestant authors, especially those from Montauban. Jean Fornier (1530–84) was born in Montauban and studied law in Toulouse before trying his hand at poetry in Paris

---

[53] Saconay, *De la providence de dieu*, sigs G2ᵛ, T4ʳ.

[54] Janet G. Gray, 'The Origins of the Word Huguenot', *SCJ*, XIV: 3 (1983), pp. 349–59 (p. 356).

[55] *Similitude des regnes*, sig. AA3ᵛ.

[56] Bosquet, *Sur les troubles*, p. 23; Chassanion, *Histoire des Albigeois*, p. 65.

[57] Schneider, *Public Life in Toulouse*, p. 15.

[58] Rotier, *Response aux blasphemateurs*, sigs A7ʳ⁻ᵛ.

where he was converted to Protestantism in the 1550s.[59] In 1562, he published *l'Histoire des guerres faictes en plusieurs lieux de la France* probably based on the chronicles of Bernard Gui (1262–1331), who had been an inquisitor in Languedoc between 1307 and 1324.[60] Although there is no indication of his sympathy for either the Reformed faith or the Albigensians, Fornier described in great detail the siege of Montauban by Simon de Montfort in 1211. Haag suggested that Fornier would have suffered from persecution and witnessed the siege of Montauban by the Catholics in 1562 in the same year that his account of the Albigensian Crusade was published. One passage might denote irony when he described how the crusaders were absolved of their sins through the sacrament of the Eucharist and the handling of relics.[61]

The affiliation between Protestants and Albigensians was also made by Lancelot du Voisin de la Popelinière in his ambivalent *Histoire de France*:

> the common Faith in France ... was never attacked so fiercely as by the Waldensians and their successors ... the Albigensians ... who, in the face of all Christian powers, spread around the year 1100 and ever since a doctrine not unlike our modern Protestants': not only in France, but almost everywhere else in Europe.[62]

The *Histoire de France* was condemned by the national synod held in La Rochelle in 1581 because the author had deliberately chosen to represent both Catholic and Protestant views impartially.[63]

The predominantly Catholic comparison with Albigensianism went unanswered by the Protestants until the 1580s when, it could be argued, it was too late. The Protestant response to the comparison was to embrace it and make the Albigensians forerunners of the Reformation and members of the true Church. Although French Protestants were aware of a connection with the Albigensians, the Reformed Church did not officially acknowledge it until 1572. As a result of decisions taken

---

[59] Eugene Haag, *La France Protestante*, 6 vols (Paris, 1877–88), VI (1888), pp. 505–6.

[60] Mollat, ed., *Manuel de l'Inquisiteur*, p. vi.

[61] Jean Fornier, *l'Histoire des guerres faictes en plusieurs lieux de la France, tant en la Guienne & Languedoc contre les Heretiques, que ailleurs contre certains ennemis de la couronne: & de la conqueste de la terre saincte: Et de tout ce qui est advenu en France digne de memoire, depuis l'an de grace 1200. jusques à l'an Mil trois cens unze, au quel tous les Templiers furent destruictz* (Toulouse, 1562), sigs B3ᵛ, C4ᵗ.

[62] Popelinière, *L'Histoire de France*, I, fol. 7ᵛ; Guy Bédouelle, 'Les Albigeois, témoins du véritable évangile: l'historiographie protestante du XVIe et du début du XVIIe siècle', *CF*, XIV (1979), pp. 47–70 (p. 55).

[63] J. Aymon, ed., *Tous les Synodes Nationaux des Eglises Reformées de France*, 2 vols (La Haye, 1710), I, p. 151; Kevin C. Robbins, *City on the ocean sea: La Rochelle, 1530–1650* (Leiden, 1997), pp. 178–80.

at national synods held in the south of France, the Albigensians were ultimately included in the Protestant martyrologies. This process was not completed until the end of the French Wars of Religion, where the Albigensians fuelled the new found anti-Popery of the French Reformed tradition.

CHAPTER EIGHT

The Albigensians
as Protestant martyrs

The geographical coincidence of Protestant strongholds in the French Wars of Religion and former bastions of Albigensianism has given some historians food for thought, although few suggest that it was more than accidental.[1] Nonetheless, it has led Michel Jas, a minister and historian of the Midi, to suggest that there was a continuous heterodox tradition between the end of the Albigensian Crusade and the beginning of evangelism in Languedoc.[2] This view is consistent with the Protestant doctrine of the true Church which argued for the parallel existence of two churches from apostolic times to the beginning of the Reformation. The Protestant demand for identity and legitimacy was answered in the shape of martyrologies and histories of the true Church. Protestant martyrologists gradually came to terms with the Catholic comparison with medieval heresy and turned it to their advantage. The adoption by the Protestant Church of the Vaudois, who were thought to descend from the twelfth-century Waldensians, was motivated in part by the need to find historical evidence for this doctrine.[3] The Albigensians, on the other hand, although they presented strong resistance to the rise of the papal monarchy in the thirteenth century,[4] were ignored by the French martyrologists until much later, when they could be considered as indistinguishable from the Waldensians.

Unlike the Hussites and Lollards, who were given ample attention from the Protestant martyrologists of the first and second generation, the Albigensians were largely ignored. Luther is famous for having claimed the Hussites and Lollards as precursors of the Reformation, and these connections were emphasized in both the Lutheran and Anglican Protestant traditions in the face of papal supremacy. The Waldensians,

---

[1] E. Le Roy Ladurie, *Histoire du Languedoc* (Toulouse, 1967), p. 318; J. Garrisson-Estèbe, *Les Protestants du Midi: 1559–1598* (Toulouse, 1980), p. 56.

[2] Michel Jas, *Braises Cathares: Filiation secrète à l'heure de la réforme* (Loubatières, 1992), p. 196.

[3] Euan Cameron, *The Reformation of the Heretics: the Waldenses of the Alps 1480–1580* (Oxford, 1984), pp. 244–5; Gabriel Audisio, *Les Vaudois du Lubéron, Une minorité en Provence 1460–1560* (Mérindol, 1984).

[4] On the rise of the papal monarchy see Colin Morris, *The Papal Monarchy: The Western Church from 1050 to 1250* (Oxford, 1991), pp. 446–7, 453–77.

for their part, had survived medieval persecutions until the beginning of evangelism and were claimed by Swiss and French Calvinists as their religious forebears.[5]

In a way, the Albigensians served the same function for the French Reformation as John Hus and Wycliffe for the Lutheran and Anglican churches. They added a geographical and cultural identity to an otherwise nameless process of association with medieval heretics. It is merely their geographical location which suggested a parentage with the Protestants of the Midi in the same way that the Waldensians had been adopted by Geneva because of their geographical proximity. Neither group had much in common with Protestantism doctrinally, and even the Vaudois of the sixteenth century were described by Euan Cameron as a far cry from the precursors of the Reformation they were made out to be:

> In their doctrines we have seen little evidence to place the Waldenses amongst the precursors of the reformers. In terms of their education and backgrounds, the ministers had more in common with priests (from whom many, for instance in Germany, were converted) than with popular heretics. Since the heretics had traditionally rejected the tutelage of priests and learned religious figures, we are forced to conclude that only their hostility to Rome made the Vaudois suitable subjects for conversion to Calvinism.[6]

This is particularly true of the Albigensians whose radical dualism made them akin to Manichees – an affiliation that was blown up out of all proportion by their Catholic opponents. Although there is some debate as to whether the Albigensians were moderate or radical dualists, the consensus is that they believed the Devil had created the world. Beyond the commonplace view that the Devil was the Prince of this world, the Cathars believed that the true God was a being of pure spirit which had nothing to do with the material world. What made them remotely akin to Protestantism was their Gospel which was translated into Occitan, especially the apocryphal Gospel of Thomas which they interpreted in a dualist light. In this respect they are similar to the Waldensians, Wycliffites and Hussites, although their interpretation of the Gospel was closer to that of the Gnostics of the third and fourth century than of the latter groups.[7]

It is clear that the inclusion of the Albigensians in the Protestant martyrologies stemmed from a confusion between them and the Waldensians that arose in the course of the sixteenth century. This

---

[5] Cameron, *Reformation of the Heretics*, p. 256.

[6] Ibid.

[7] Nelli, *La philosophie du catharisme*, pp. 15–27.

confusion appears to have originated in the near contemporaneity of these two groups which was deliberately exploited by both Catholics and Reformed, although not by the Lutherans. Sebastian Franck was one of the first authors to deal with this question in his *Chronica, zeytbuch und Geschychtbibel* (1531) where he made a clear distinction between Albigensians and Waldensians in two separate entries. One entry described the Albigensian as Manichaean and radical heretics, whereas the second – considerably more substantial – describes the Waldensians' beliefs as close to those of the Anabaptists.[8] A more orthodox contributor to the Magdeburg Centuries, Matthias Flacius Illyricus (1520–75), had stressed the evangelical elements of the doctrine of the Waldensians in his *Catalogus Testium Veritatis* (1556) where the Albigensians are hardly mentioned at all. When they are, it is not in such terms that would suggest the same parentage: 'In the year 1213 the heresy of the Albigensians spread throughout the region and defiled it.'[9]

The affiliation between these two groups was put forward by the Catholics. Indeed, Jean du Tillet asserted in 1562 that the Albigensians had branched off from the Waldensians and that they shared the doctrinal beliefs of the Protestants:

> The Heresy of the Albigensians was born out of two preceding and diverse sects, condemned under the Pope Lucie III, the one and the worst having taken the name of humble, the other the title of poor of Lyon, because they reproved property of goods, and as much as Valdo from Lyon was its author they were also called Waldensians after his name. The Albigensians, although they had other errors by all means conform to those of our times, since they condemn most of what the Roman Church observes, and to lure the Christians from it call it the congregation of hell, and the throne of Rome the beast described in the Apocalypse. ... According to this heresy the sacraments are annihilated, confirmation, extreme unction, auricular confession and imposition of penance are held frivolous things, the Sacred Host of God called bread, Mass abomination, crucifixes and images of the churches idolatry.[10]

These very evangelical views had been associated with the Waldensians by the Protestants with the evident intention of portraying them as members of the true Church.[11] Du Tillet made a reference to the third

---

[8] Sebastian Franck, *Chronica, zeytbuch und Geschychtbibel* (Strasbourg, 1531), pp. 344, 453, 483.

[9] Matthias Flacius Illyricus, *Catalogus Testium Veritatis qui ante nostram aetatem reclamarunt papae* (Basel, 1556), p. 599.

[10] Du Tillet, *Sommaire de l'histoire de la guerre*, sigs A1^{r-v}–A2^r.

[11] Cameron, *Reformation of the Heretics*, p. 256.

Lateran Council of 1179, when Pope Lucius III condemned the Waldensians for the first time; they were condemned again, along with the Albigensians, by Innocent III at the fourth Lateran Council of 1215. This may explain the confusion that emerged, in Protestant martyrologies and Catholic histories alike, between the two. According to Flacius Illyricus, the Waldensians had been ascribed false doctrines by the Catholic Church with the sole purpose of defaming them. The Albigensians had been treated with equal contempt by the Catholics which led Protestant authors to consider them to be as good as the Waldensians.[12]

John Bale wrote about them both on equal terms in his *Image of Both Churches* (1545) where he described them as 'men doubtless of a Godly zeal and spirit'.[13] This view was reiterated and elaborated upon in his *Scriptorum Illustrium maioris Brytanniae ... Catalogus* (1557) where he argued that they had both been upholders of true doctrine in the face of the rise of the papal monarchy.[14] Medieval heretics were interesting to John Bale insofar as they provided him with arguments against the Papacy and the Mendicant Orders. It was thought that the Waldensians and Albigensians had accused the Pope of being the Antichrist. That was enough to justify their good standing among Anglicans and Lutherans. John Bale was undoubtedly responsible for writing the article concerning the Albigensians which appeared in the first vernacular edition of John Foxe's *Acts and Monuments*. It was largely based on the medieval chronicles of Matthew Paris and Roger Wendover, the only sources available to Bale at the time.[15] Matthew Paris's anti-papal stance made him a useful source for the *Acts and Monuments*, but his account of the Albigensians was less than flattering. Bale decided to resolve this conundrum by dismissing these view as false accusations spread by the Papacy:

> What these Albingensis wer, it cannot be wel gathered by the olde popish histories. if there were any that did holde, teache, or maintaine agaynst the Pope ... the histories of that tyme ... doe so deprave them, and misreport them, suppressyng the truthe of theyr artycles, that they make them and paynt them foorth to bee worse then Turkes and infidels. ... Otherwise it is to be thoughte, and so I fynde in some recordes, that the opinions of the sayde Albigenses were sounde ynoughe.[16]

---

[12] For accusations against the Waldensians, see ibid., pp. 108–11.

[13] Henry Christmas, ed., *Select Works of John Bale* (Cambridge, 1849), p. 563. I owe thanks to Dr Tom Freeman (Institute for Historical Research) for the references on Bale.

[14] John Bale, *Scriptorum Illustrium maioris Brytanniae, quam nunc Angliam & Scotiam vocant: Catalogus* (Basel, 1559), p. 308.

[15] Tom Freeman, 'John Bale's Book of Martyrs?': The Account of King John in *Acts and Monuments*', *Reformation*, III (1998), pp. 175–223.

[16] John Foxe, *Actes and Monuments* (London, 1563), fol. 71^v.

Flacius Illyricus had already argued that, because the Waldensians had accused the Pope of being the Antichrist, they had been ascribed false doctrines and persecuted.[17] Bale simply extended this argument to the Albigensians.

The first edition of the *Acts and Monuments* was criticized by contemporary English Catholics writing from the Continent, notably Thomas Stapleton, who attacked Bale's treatment of the Albigensians:

> Now for the other secte of the *Albanenses* or *Albigenses*, springinge of the loynes of the holye brother Waldo, beside the common and usuall errours, of the *Waldenses* ... they preciouse (*sic*) martyrs with M.Foxe. ... Now let Mayster foxe make an accompte of hys holy martyrs, and see howe manie he canne fynde, that have not maynteyned the sayd errours, of these *Albigenses*, *Paterans*, or *Waldenses*: and he shall fynde his holie cataloge altogether voyde and empted.[18]

This direct challenge was answered in the second edition of the *Acts and Monuments* (1570), where an entire chapter was devoted to 'The historie of the Waldenses or Albigenses'.[19] Surprisingly, Foxe treated the Albigensians and Waldensians indiscriminately where his Lutheran predecessors had marked a clear distinction. It was in the interest of martyrologists to blur doctrinal differences and hide discrepancies between Protestant doctrine and that of their adopted forebears.[20]

The thought process that led to the inclusion of the Albigensians in the *Acts and Monuments* preceded the Continental movement. Although Protestant authors relied on Catholic sources, everything that pertained to their beliefs and practices could safely be dismissed. Protestants were encouraged to think so by the fact that Catholic authors tended to ascribe the same villainous crimes to all indiscriminately. Medieval opponents of papal supremacy provided the martyrologists with valuable precedents for resistance. This ideology had emerged with Flacius Illyricus and his historical catalogue of the adversaries of the Papacy. The inclusion of the Albigensians followed the same logic: they too had been persecuted by the Catholic Church for denouncing papal abuses.[21]

As we have seen, the geographical location of the Albigensian movement meant that it had particular relevance in the south of France. The first Huguenot acknowledgement of the Albigensians occurred at the

---

[17] Flacius Illyricus, *Catalogus Testium Veritatis*, p. 930.

[18] Thomas Stapleton, *A Counterblast to M. Hornes Vayne Blaste Against M. Fekenham* (Louvain, 1567), fols 317ᵛ–319ʳ.

[19] Foxe, *Acts and Monuments* (London, 1570), fol. 295ʳ.

[20] E. Cameron, 'Medieval Heretics as Protestant Martyrs', *Studies in Church History*, XXX (1993), pp. 185–207.

[21] Cameron, 'Medieval Heretics', p. 198.

first national synod to be held south of the Loire: at Nîmes in May 1572. It was presided over by Nicolas des Gallars, and Antoine de la Roche Chandieu and Theodore Beza had been sent from Geneva to attend.[22] A Reformed history of the Albigensian Crusade was commissioned and the ministers of Montauban were put in charge: 'Monsieur Berauld, and his colleagues of the Church of Montauban are responsible for getting the History of the Albigensians, written in their language from Monsieur Comerard of Toulouse, and Monsieur d'Acier will translate it into French, and will ... have it printed.'[23] Although nothing immediately came from this decision (probably because of the St Bartholomew's Day massacre) it demonstrates that the French Protestant hierarchy was willing to address the question of the Albigensians.

The massacre of St Bartholomew's Day provoked a transformation of Huguenot identity that favoured the inclusion of medieval predecessors in the *Histoire des Martyrs*. Although Jean Crespin died in 1572, his work was taken up by Simon Goulard who published four editions in 1582, 1597, 1608 and 1619. In a section devoted to the massacre of St Bartholomew's Day, Goulard introduced a distinction between individual and collective martyrdom:

> If we call Martyrs those that were executed one by one by justice, what shall we call so many thousands of excellent figures who were martyred in one fell swoop, not by one executioner, but by a multitude of commoners whose swords were the plaintiffs, witnesses, judges, sentences and executioners of the strangest cruelties that have ever been perpetrated against the Church?[24]

Jean Crespin had primarily been concerned with compiling a list of individual martyrs whose names and examples are consigned in the *Histoire des Martyrs*. By contrast, Simon Goulard extended the status of martyr to anonymous medieval heretics who, like the victims of the St Bartholomew's Day massacre had been persecuted collectively. Unlike individual martyrs who had died at the hand of the king's justice, medieval heretics had died in open defiance of temporal and spiritual authority. Their inclusion in the *Histoire des Martyrs* from 1582 onwards marked the beginning of a new militancy perhaps more eloquent than the tracts of the Monarchomachs.

---

[22] Simon Goulard, *Memoires de l'estat de France, sous Charles Neufiesme* (Meidelbourg, 1576), p. 296.

[23] Aymon, ed., *Tous les Synodes Nationaux*, I, p. 123.

[24] Jean Crespin, *Histoire des Martyrs persecutez et mis a mort pour la verité de l'Evangile, depuis le temps des Apostres jusques à l'an 1574* (Geneva, 1582), fol. 704ᵛ.

This new militancy was no doubt motivated by the perceived involvement of the papacy in the massacre of St Bartholomew's Day, as reflected in Theodore Beza's own words: 'No one can doubt that these events are the result of a plot worked out at the Council of Trent.'[25] Although it is doubtful that the papacy was directly involved in the massacre, this was one of the enduring myths that emerged at this time.[26] As a result, the *Histoire des Martyrs* became increasingly anti-papal, following the lead of those English and Lutheran works that had lambasted the papacy for several decades.

As in the *Acts and Monuments*, anti-popery was a determining factor in the inclusion of the Albigensians in the *Histoire des Martyrs*:

> As regards those they call heretics, namely the enemies of the Papacy, they are accused of the most horrid crimes in the world, in order to tarnish their reputation further ... From the moment the bishop of Rome declared himself to be the universal leader of the Church, there has been people of all kind ... who have denounced ... the corporeal and spiritual tyranny of the Popes.[27]

Although Goulard was at first much more cautious than Foxe: 'Many suffered death for having opposed the traditions of the Antichrist, like the Waldensians or Albigensians.'[28] The caution that was observed by the Huguenot martyrologists can be explained through the political specificity of the French Reformation.

The fact that these arguments had not been used earlier in a French context points to the differences that existed between the Huguenots and the other Protestant traditions. In Germany and England, anti-papal arguments had been instrumental in rallying the political élite to the Protestant cause. The conflict between Pope and secular rulers over the control of Church appointments and revenues, was central to the Lutheran and English arguments. The arguments concerning the Investiture Contest had no clout in France because of the specificity of the Gallican Church, bolstered by the Pragmatic Sanction of 1438 and the Concordat of Bologna in 1516. Whereas the support of secular rulers played a considerable part in the elaboration of Lutheran and 'Anglican' identities, the French monarchy's fluctuating position left the Huguenots to forge their own identity. This might explain both why Huguenots clung for so long to the illusion of loyalty to the Crown and the striking absence of anti-papal arguments before 1572.

---

[25] Pettegree, Duke and Lewis, eds, *Calvinism in Europe*, p. 113.

[26] Kingdon, *Myths about the St. Bartholomew's Day Massacres*.

[27] Crespin, *Histoire des Martyrs* (1582), fol. 25[v]; ibid. (Geneva, 1619), fol. 23[r].

[28] Crespin, *Histoire des Martyrs* (1582), fol. 25[v].

With the accession of Henri IV, a new chapter of Huguenot culture and identity was opened. The onus of Huguenot militancy increasingly fell on the Catholic adversary, not within France, but in Rome. This could now be squared with the new regime which, while not endorsing the Protestant movement, had recognized its right to exist. The arguments of the Monarchomachs, that had been used with much better results by the Catholic League, were no longer relevant to the Reformation debate. Rome became the convenient other against whom both the monarchy and its Huguenot subjects could unite. This choice was no doubt motivated by the impact that Catholic reform was beginning to have in Europe – as is demonstrated by the insistence with which the Huguenot movement identified the Pope as Antichrist at the beginning of the seventeenth century.

Despite numerous Lutheran, Anglican, and Catholic precedents, a Huguenot history of the Albigensians did not materialize until the end of the Wars.[29] Jean Chassanion's *Histoire des Albigeois* (1595) was a product of the new regime, which it salutes in its dedication to Henri IV.[30] Chassanion's history was pitched against the Leaguer Arnaud Sorbin and turned the table round on more than 30 years of Catholic rewriting of history: 'I do not find in my original the first chapter of the history that was published by Arnaud Sorbin in 1569, translated from the Latin ... and his second chapter is full of errors and blasphemies falsely attributed to the Albigensians, that I cannot find in my source.'[31] Like his predecessors, Chassanion reproduced the now familiar argument that what the Catholics had written about the Albigensians could be dismissed as false accusations.[32] His book is remarkable, however, in writing about the Albigensians on their own merits and not connecting them with the Waldensians. It also links the Crusade with the French Wars of Religion, for which he blames the Catholic League, and asserts a direct bond between the Albigensians and the Protestants of the Midi:

> In this we have the portrait ... of things that have occurred in this century in a great part of Europe, in the last sixty years or so in the name of religion, and mainly for the past eight or nine years. ... The Reformed Churches of Languedoc ... are like the harvest of the seed sown by the Albigensians. It is this holy seed that germinated, in those parts of Languedoc & other neighbouring places,

---

[29] Aymon, ed., *Tous les Synodes Nationaux*, I, p. 186.

[30] Theodore Beza, *Histoire Ecclesiastique des Eglises Reformes au Royaume de France*, 3 vols (Antwerp, 1580), I, p. 196; Eugene Haag, *La France Protestante*, 10 vols (Geneva, 1966), III, pp. 351–2.

[31] Chassanion, *Histoire des Albigeois*, pp. 12, 15; Sorbin's source was Pierre des Vallées Cernay.

[32] Chassanion, *Histoire des Albigeois*, pp. 51, 58.

grew forth and flourished in the rays of the sun of justice which pleased God to shine upon us these past times.[33]

These last lines salute the providential end of the wars and reflect the hopes that the new regime of Henri IV held for the Huguenots. In later years the Albigensians were used in conjunction with the Waldensians in anti-papal polemic, particularly in identifying Antichrist as the Pope, heralding a new phase of Huguenot militancy.[34]

The identification of Antichrist as the Pope rested mainly on an apocalyptic interpretation of Revelation. Throughout the Wars of Religion, the French Calvinists remained extremely reluctant to commit themselves on the question of the Antichrist. Calvin, although renowned for his biblical exegesis, avoided the Apocalypse because he had not 'fully understood the text'. Theodore Beza was equally cautious in the preface of a commentary published in 1557.[35] French vernacular bibles, known as the 'Geneva Bibles', preceded the text of Revelation with a paragraph warning the reader against interpreting it too freely.[36] The national synod of Saumur of 1596 even forbade any pastors from teaching or preaching on the Apocalypse without the advice of the Provincial Synod.[37] These precautions, however, were not observed by the Dutch Calvinists or by the English. The 1592 commentary of the Dutchman François du Jon (1545–1602), for example, which clearly identified Antichrist as the Pope, was reproduced in an English edition of a 'Geneva Bible' published in 1607.[38] The following passage is taken from the marginalia concerning Revelation 11:7, describing the persecutions of the two 'witnesses of the truth':

And that this was done to very many godly men, by Boniface and others, the histories doe declare, especially since the time that the

[33] Ibid., pp. 250–51: 'C'est cette Ste Semance laquele en ces quartiers la du Languedoc, & autre lieux circonvoisins a germé, a poussé hors, & s'est epanouie & ejouye aux rayons du soleil de justice qu'il a pleu a Dieu j epandre largement en ces derniers tans.'

[34] Bédouelle, 'Les Albigeois, témoins du véritable évangile', pp. 59–60.

[35] I. Backus, Les 7 Visions et la Fin des Temps: les commentaires Genevois de l'apocalypse entre 1539 et 1584 (Geneva, 1997), p. 6.

[36] I have found it in six different editions published in Geneva, Saumur, Rouen and La Rochelle between 1577 and 1616. I have identified two versions in Le Nouveau Testament c'est à dire, la nouvelle alliance de nostre seigneur Jesus Christ (Geneva, 1577), p. 682, and La Bible qui est toute la saincte escriture du vieil & du nouveau testament (Geneva, 1588), fol. 122ᵛ.

[37] Aymon, ed., Tous les Synodes Nationaux, I, p. 203.

[38] Gerald T. Sheppard, 'The Geneva Bible and English Commentary, 1600–1645', in G. T. Sheppard, ed., The Geneva Bible (New York, 1989), pp. 1–4 (p. 1); fol. 129b.

odious and condemned name amongst the multitude, first of the
brethren Waldonenses or Lugdunenses, then also of the Fraticels,
was pretended, that good men might with more approbation be
massacred.[39]

This clearly interprets Revelation historically, placing the persecution
of the true Church at the hands of the Antichrist in the central Middle
Ages. The witnesses of the truth are identified as medieval heretics,
notably the Waldensians, and the Antichrist as Pope Boniface VIII. The
Flemish Philippe de Marnix also identified the 'two witnesses of the
truth' as the Albigensians and the Waldensians in his 1599 commentary
of *Revelation*.[40] This points to the readiness with which the Antichrist
was identified as the Pope in the Netherlands and in England, whereas
in France, commentators were more cautious.[41]

Lutheran and English Protestants, notably John Bale and Flacius Illyricus,
had for a long time argued that medieval persecutions at the hand of the
papacy had coincided with the reign of Antichrist. The French only
adopted the doctrine of the Papal Antichrist at the end of the wars, when
the different Protestant traditions made common cause against the Catholic
Reformation, and particularly the Jesuits.[42] The doctrine of the Papal
Antichrist was even approved by the national synods of 1603 and 1607,
and would have been adopted as an article of faith had Henri IV not
intervened.[43] The fact that a history of the Albigensian Crusade and a
book on the Antichrist were commissioned by the synod of 1607 points
to the inextricability of these two questions:

> The article concerning the Antichrist inserted at the synod of Gap,
> to be the 31st of our Confession of Faith … has been approved …
> to be … true to what was predicted in the Scriptures. … Monsieur
> Perrin is asked to continue his work on the true history of the
> Albigensians and Waldensians … Monsieur Vignier is asked to put
> pen to paper to deal fully with the matter of the Antichrist, & to
> bring, or to send his work at the next National Synod.[44]

---

[39] Fr du Jon, *Apocalypse ou Revelation de S. Jean Apostre Evangeliste de nostre
Seigneur Jesus Christ* ([Geneva], 1592), p. 208.

[40] Cameron, *Reformation of the Heretics*, p. 249: 'the two olives or the two lamps, of
which St John spoke, whose oil and light spread to the ends of the earth', Revelation
11:4.

[41] Dr David Daniell (Hertford College, Oxford) remarked that the marginalia of the
book of Revelation in seventeenth-century editions of the 'Geneva Bible' was entirely
taken from Jonius's commentary (personal communication, Reformation Studies Colloquium, Warwick, 2000).

[42] Robert Bellarmine, *Disputationes de controversiis Christianae fidei adversus hujus
temporis haereticos*, 3 vols (Ingolstadt, 1586–93).

[43] Soman, 'Press, Pulpit, and censorship', p. 444.

[44] Aymon, ed., *Tous les Synodes Nationaux*, I, pp. 258, 303, 313, 316.

This Vignier was the son and namesake of the surgeon of Henri IV, Nicolas (1530–96), who had described at length the persecutions of medieval heretics at the hands of the papacy in his *Recueil de L'Histoire de l'Eglise* (1601).[45] Although his father converted back to Catholicism in 1579, the younger Nicolas Vignier remained a Protestant and published extensively against Catholic Reformers.[46] His work addressed, in particular, the criticisms of the Jesuit cardinal Bellarmine, against whom he wrote two treatises on the doctrine of the Papal Antichrist in 1606 and 1608.[47] In 1609, the national synod of St Maixent acknowledged his progress on the *Theatre de l'Antechrist* that was sent to Saumur and printed in 1610.[48] This large folio was clearly intended to be the final word on this matter and responded directly to Florimond de Raemond's antimartyrology, François Ribera's commentary on Revelation, and the works of the Jesuits Pierre Cotton and Bellarmine.[49]

In the face of these criticisms, Nicolas Vignier reproduced the view that the medieval persecutions at the hands of the papacy had coincided with the reign of Antichrist. Vignier replicated many arguments found in the works of John Bale against the Mendicant Orders and the rise of the papal monarchy during the central Middle Ages.[50] Unlike his predecessors, however, Vignier argued in *L'Antechrist Romain* that the persecution under the papal Antichrist had been worse than during patristic times:

> Since those times have we seen more horrendous butchery and more cruel persecutions exerted against the Saints? It is true that medieval persecutions cannot be compared to those of Nero, Domitian, Decius or Diocletian: because the latter were but physical, whereas the former were spiritual as well as physical. The first persecutions were interspersed, and lasted but a few months, or a few years. But the medieval ones continued unabated for several centuries. The first ones took several thousand martyrs whereas the

[45] Bédouelle, 'Les Albigeois, témoins du véritable évangile', pp. 55–6.

[46] Nicolas Vignier, *Recueil de L'Histoire de l'Eglise, depuis le Baptseme de nostre Seigneur Jesus Christ, jusques à ce temps* (Leyden, 1601), p. 408.

[47] [Nicolas Vignier], *L'Antechrist Romain, Opposé à l'Antechrist Juif du Cardinal de Bellarmin, du Sieur de Remond & autres* (1606); Vignier, *Legende Doree*.

[48] Aymon, ed., *Tous les Synodes Nationaux*, I, p. 361; Cameron, *Reformation of the Heretics*, p. 249.

[49] Nicolas Vignier, *Theatre de L'Antechrist Auquel est respondu au Cardinal Bellarmin, au sieur de Remond, à Perenius, Ribera, Viergas, Sanderus et autres qui par leurs escrits condamnent la doctrine des Eglises Reformees sur ce subiet: Par Nicolas Vignier* (Saumur, 1610).

[50] Vignier, *Recueil de L'Histoire de l'Eglise*, p. 405; [Vignier], *L'Antechrist Romain*, p. 160; Vignier, *Legende Doree*, p. 66; Christmas, ed., 'Select Works of John Bale', pp. 322, 563; Bale, *Scriptorum Illustrium maioris Brytanniae*, p. 234.

later ones took innumerable multitudes. A chronicler counts 17 thousand Christians killed in one month under Diocletian. While Bellarmine ... counts 100 000 Albigensians killed in one day under the Papacy of Innocent III.[51]

This marks a striking departure from the period of the Wars when the representation of martyrdom had hinged on a comparison with the early Church martyrs. Vignier's emphasis on the medieval martyrs reflects the new-found impact of anti-popery on French Protestant culture. Nicolas Vignier resorted to arguments that had been used in the English and Lutheran traditions, but he gave them a new spin in the face of the attacks of the Catholic Reformation.

Jean-Paul Perrin's history of the Albigensians, commissioned at the same time as Vignier's *Theatre de l'Antechist*, was also instrumental in the polemic surrounding the Papal Antichrist. His progress was recorded at the national synods of 1609 and 1612 and the *Histoire des Vaudois* (including a history of the 'Waldensians called Albigensians') was finally published in Geneva in 1618.[52] The *Histoire des Vaudois* reproduces the interpretation of Revelation found in Dutch commentaries, and clearly identifies the Antichrist as the Pope: 'So that on one hand the Waldensians, and on the other the Albigensians are like the two olives or the two lamps, of which St John spoke, whose oil and light spread to the ends of the earth.'[53]

The developments of the French doctrine of the Papal Antichrist at the turn of the seventeenth century found their way into the *Histoire des Martyrs* under the editorship of Simon Goulard. In 1597 and 1608, Goulard published another two editions of the *Histoire des Martyrs* where medieval heretics feature more prominently than in the previous editions. In the same years, Goulard also published two editions of Illyricus's *Catalogus Testium Veritatis* which he no doubt used as a source for the medieval section of the *Histoire des Martyrs*.[54] This demonstrates unequivocally that the arguments of the Lutheran and Anglican traditions, scorned during the Wars, were now adopted wholeheartedly by the Huguenot tradition. Surprisingly, Goulard seemed to have been unaware of Chassanion's *Histoire des Albigeois* that had been printed in 1595. In the 1608 edition of the *Histoire des*

---

[51] [Vignier], *L'Antechrist Romain*, pp. 159–60.

[52] Aymon, ed., *Tous les Synodes Nationaux*, I, pp. 361, 404: 'Sir Perrin presented his book of the History of the Albigensians and Waldensians ... for which he was given the sum of three hundred pounds.'

[53] Crespin, *Histoire des Martyrs* (1619), fol. 22[r]; Jean-Paul Perrin, *Histoire des Vaudois appelés Albigeois* (Geneva, 1618), p. 64.

[54] Goulard's two editions of the *Catalogus Testium Veritatis* correspond to his second and third editions of the *Histoire des Martyrs*, in 1597 and 1608.

Martyrs, he even laments the lack of material on the Waldensians and Albigensians: 'Their history deserves thorough research, and separate books, having been buried until now, or at the least too summarily or obscurely described.'[55] Goulard used Perrin's *Histoire des Vaudois* instead, in his last edition of the *Histoire des Martyrs* published in 1619, where he reproduces the historical interpretation of Revelation.[56]

Goulard's tribute to the whole debate surrounding the Papal Antichrist lies in the precise dating of its reign, something that had generated a lot of controversy and that most commentators had avoided or approached cautiously. Bellarmine, in his efforts to prove that the Antichrist was not the Pope, had attacked this historical interpretation of Revelation arguing that the reign of Antichrist had not yet taken place. The duration of the reign of Antichrist could be inferred from sibylline indications in Revelation – namely, '42 months', '1260 days', 'three and a half days', and 'a time, times, and half a time'.[57] Bellarmine argued that these indications pointed to a period of three and a half years that would occur before the Last Judgement.[58] For Protestant commentators, this corresponded to the period between the beginning of the papal persecutions and the coming of evangelism. The Dutchman Peter Wesenbec had already asserted in 1585 that there was an unbroken succession between the medieval persecutions and the emergence of evangelism[59] and this view appeared in France in 1603 in Jacques Auguste de Thou's history.[60] By Goulard's reckoning, this time was equal to the 350 years that had elapsed from the beginning of the persecutions of the Waldensians in 1200 and the persecutions of the Vaudois at Mérindol and Cabrières, before the outbreak of the French Wars of Religion:

> They were in the end so harrassed ... that they were finally forced to flee into the deserts ... where their teaching has survived in small groups ... until our century. ... This can be gathered from the declaration of those of Cabrières and Mérindol ... showing that their doctrine and manner of living had been passed on to them from father to son, since the year 1200. ... Following the prophecy of Apocalypse, chapter 12 ... this time of 350 years has passed, from the beginning of the persecutions until the restoration

---

[55] Crespin, *Histoire des Martyrs* (Geneva, 1608), fol. 25ᵛ.

[56] Bédouelle, 'Les Albigeois, témoins du véritable évangile', p. 59.

[57] Revelation 11:2–3, 9, 11; 12:6, 14.

[58] [Vignier], *L'Antechrist Romain*, pp. 199–211.

[59] Petri Wesenbecii, *Oratio De Waldensibus et Albigensibus Christianis* (Iena, 1585), sigs B1ʳ⁻ᵛ.

[60] Jacques Auguste de Thou, *Historia sui temporis libri* (Paris, 1603), p. 459.

of the Church, accomplished in our times by the doctrine of the Gospel.[61]

Goulard perpetuated the story of the true Church that had gone underground as a result of papal persecutions in order to come out into the open with the advent of the Reformation to triumph over the Antichrist. The duration of the battle with Antichrist was not specified but it is clear that upholders of this tradition expected victory, and the end of time, to be imminent. The obvious historical and chronological problems with this tradition meant that it was soon replaced by a Reformed millenarianism where the coming of Antichrist was expected to take place in the future.[62]

The publication of these articles in Perrin's *Histoire des Vaudois appelés Albigeois* and the definitive edition of the *Histoire des Martyrs* ensured that the memory of the Albigensians would be passed on to posterity. Indeed, Agrippa d'Aubigné used Perrin's work for his article on the Albigensians in his *Histoire Universelle*.[63] The English tradition used the medieval martyrs of the true Church to create something akin to an apostolic succession of the true Church. This was elaborated upon by James Ussher, who argued for an unbroken historical link between the Apostles and Luther.[64] An English translation of Perrin even argued for an unbroken succession from the Middle Ages to the sixteenth century:

> And from the Holy Men of that Age the Lamp of pure Doctrine was handed down to Bertram, from him to Peter Bruis to Waldo, from Waldo, to Dulcinus, from him to Marsilius, from him to Wickliff, from him to Hus and Jerom of Prague, and from their Scholars, the Fratres Bohemi, to Luther and Calvin.[65]

The image of the witnesses of the true Church retiring in the desert was perpetuated through the numerous editions of the *Histoire des Martyrs*. It was adopted wholeheartedly by the Camisards who escaped persecution in the hills of Vivarais after the revocation of the Edict of Nantes in 1685 – at which time, it was Louis XIV who was identified as

---

[61] Crespin, *Histoire des Martyrs* (1619), fol. 22[v].

[62] Howard Hotson, 'The Historiographical Origins of Calvinist Millenarianism', in B. Gordon, ed., *Protestant History and Identity in Sixteenth-Century Europe*, 2 vols (Aldershot, 1996), II, pp. 159–181 (pp. 175–6).

[63] Agrippa d'Aubigné, *Histoire Universelle*, 9 vols (Geneva, 1981–95), II, p. 178.

[64] James Ussher, *De Christianorum Ecclesiarum successione et statu Historica Explicatio* (London, 1613).

[65] Jean-Paul Perrin, *The History of the Old Waldenses and Albigenses; Those Two Glorious Witnesses to the Truth of Christianity: In Opposition to the AntiChristianism of Rome, In the several ages preceding the Reformation* (London, 1711), p. 73.

Antichrist. In response to these arguments, Bossuet finally refuted the idea that the Albigensians were indistinguishable from the Waldensians in 1691.[66] To this day, a 'Museum of the Desert' in Millau commemorates the hardship of the Camisards and testifies to the continuing history of a culture that was born out of dialectic with the Catholic adversary.

---

[66] The title of this work is *Histoire abrégée des Albigeois & des Vaudois. Que ce sont deux sectes tres-différentes*, quoted in Bédouelle, 'Les Albigeois, témoins du véritable évangile', p. 65.

Conclusion

Whereas in the case of the Lutheran Reformation, Protestants clearly had the upper hand in the polemical debate with Catholicism, this statement needs to be qualified in the case of French Calvinism. Luther has been described by Reformation historians as a broker of modernity and often praised for his efficient use of the printed word in the vernacular. Catholics, on the other hand, are often depicted by the same historians as unable to exploit this new medium.[1] Although this may have been true of the first half of the sixteenth century, it no longer applies to the latter half where Catholicism had had the time to catch up and strengthen its defences. By the time Calvinism started making inroads into France, the use of the vernacular and printing as a way of reaching the wider audience of those not literate in Latin was well established. Calvinism built on the strength of the Lutheran Reformation but its opponents had had more than 30 years to adjust to the new medium of religious discourse; a completely different situation from the Lutheran Reformation where the Reformers themselves encouraged the production of polemical pieces and vicious attacks against the Papacy. In France, the roles were reversed and it was the Catholic theologians, notably from the Faculty of Theology, who spearheaded the polemical efforts to debase Protestantism.

This extremely inflammatory material should be taken into account when trying to explain the violence of the French Wars of Religion. Although Denis Crouzet has used print culture extensively to depict his 'civilization of eschatological anguish', he has also left out other aspects that are equally revealing. To the rites of violence described by Natalie Davis, I should like to add the repertories of images that crowd the printed polemic of the French Wars of Religion. Print culture is a reflection of the spoken word disseminated in sermons and hearsay, a glimpse of which can be found in print. Concern on both sides of the confessional divide for the opinion of the common man is itself an indication of the growing importance of the printed word. The inability of the Valois to control or to counteract Catholic propaganda was an important factor in their downfall.

The outcome of the use of the 'blood libel' on the eve of the French Wars of Religion points to the interaction between print and public opinion. Although accusations of sexual improprieties and infanticide

---

[1] Mark U. Edwards, *Printing, Propaganda, and Martin Luther* (London, 1994), pp. 76–81.

had been used against religious minorities for centuries, the stereotyping of Protestants on this scale was unprecedented and had a traumatic impact on the relatively new audiences of the vernacular book. After Protestant meetings were held in the open and during the day, however, these accusations did not withstand closer scrutiny, but were turned to the Protestants' advantage and used to reinforce their connection with the first Christian martyrs, against whom the 'blood libel' had also been used. The 'blood libel' then disappeared from Catholic polemic to be replaced by more credible accusations of conspiracy following a change in prosecution from heresy to sedition. It did not vanish altogether, however, as it was used against Italians on the eve of St Bartholomew's Day massacre.

The versatility of Catholic propaganda is shown by its use of the 'battle of the sexes' and the popular topos of the 'world upside down'. In a striking reversal of the German situation, it was the Catholics who appealed to consensus values found in popular culture. Although French Protestants also used these images, they were hampered by the Genevan distaste for crude and inflammatory polemic. Catholics used the full array of medieval stereotypes to good effect, using female attributes to describe heresy. Accusations of sexual improprieties, with which Catholic polemic is replete, can be explained through the association between heresy and adultery. This turns the table on the German situation where it was the Catholics who were usually the butt of crude jokes.

Catholics and Huguenots not only fought doctrinally and physically but also created competing narratives and representations of each other. Huguenot self-perception and identity was born of the dialectic between these competing narratives. In the first instance, a comparison with the early Church emerged on the eve of the French Wars of Religion, providing the Huguenots with their best arguments. With the politicization of the conflict, however, the representation of martyrdom became inoperative as the Huguenots were involved in armed rebellion against the monarch. The massacre of St Bartholomew's Day marked the transformation of Huguenot identity in inspiring a comparison with the collective martyrdom of medieval predecessors. Simon Goulard's four editions of the *Histoire des Martyrs* between 1582 and 1619 illustrate this progression as he included more and more material borrowed from the Lutheran and English traditions. At the turn of the seventeenth century, anti-popery became an essential element of Huguenot self-perception and identity, mirroring a similar phenomenon across the channel.[2]

---

[2] P. Lake, 'Anti-popery: the Structure of a Prejudice', in R. Cust and A. Hughes, eds, *Conflict in early Stuart England: studies in religion and politics, 1603–1642* (London, 1989), pp. 72–106 (p. 82).

This study reflects two communities talking past each other: there is evidence of cross-fertilization between the two discourses but there is no real dialogue. These factors may explain why the French Wars of Religion were so entrenched – only when both parties agreed to disagree could the hatchet of war be buried. Even so, there is evidence that the polemical themes which developed during the French Wars of Religion survived long after the Edict of Nantes and its revocation. A pamphlet published in 1901, *Ce que la France doit aux Protestants*, identifying Catholics as 'enemies of the Republic', testifies to the themes's longevity: 'We know that the enemies of the Republic ... hiding behind the mask of religion in order to deceive the mob, have undertaken ... a violent crusade against religious minorities, against the Protestants and the Jews.'[3] The 'mask of religion' is a turn of phrase that was used on numerous occasions against Protestants during the French Wars of Religion.[4] This example shows how sound-bites which emerged during the French Wars of Religion became embedded in French culture to such an extent that they could be used in 1901 in the context of the separation between Church and State. It has been argued that successful propaganda could be measured by its long-term impact on the culture in which it emerged.[5] It is therefore interesting to note that by 1901 the wheel had come full circle and it was the Catholics who were singled out as enemies of the common weal.

---

[3] Camille Rabaud, *Ce que la France doit aux Protestants* (Paris, 1901), p. 5. It should be noted that the title-page of this pamphlet bears a list of bulk prices: 'Prix: 50 Centimes, pour la propagande, Cinq exemplaires, 1 fr. 50; – dix, 2 fr. 50; – vingt, 4 fr.'.

[4] René Benoist, *Brieve et facile refutation d'un livret divuluge au nom de Jean de l'Espine, se disant Ministre de la parole de Dieu: auquel violentant & detorquant l'escripture saincte, il blaspheme malheureusement le sainct sacrifice Evangelique, dict vulgairement la saincte Messe* (Paris, 1565), sig. E1ᵛ; Durand, *Lettres du Chevallier de Villegaignon*, sig. B7ᵛ; Julius Poggianus, *Oraison funebre, faite a Rome aux obseques & funerailles de feu tres-puissant & magnanime Prince, François de Lorraine Duc de Guise, par le commandement de nostre sainct Pere le Pape PIE IIII* (Reims and Paris, 1563) sig. E2ʳ.

[5] Scribner, *For the Sake of Simple Folk* (1981), p. 9.

Bibliography

Primary Sources

Agrippa d'Aubigné, *Histoire Universelle*, 9 vols (Geneva, 1981–95).
Anon., *Advertissement a la Royne Mere du Roy, Touchant les miseres du Royaume au temps present, & de la conspiration des ennemis de sa Majesté* (Orleans: [Eloi Gibier], 1562).
Anon., *Advertissement au peuple de France*, bound with [Hotman, François], *L'Histoire du tumulte d'Amboyse advenu au moys de Mars, M. D. LX.* (1560).
Anon., *Apologie contre certaines Calomnies mises sus, à la desfaveur & desavantage de l'Estat des affaires de ce Roiaume* (Paris: Pierre Leber, 1562).
Anon., *Complainte apologique des eglises de France, au roy, royne-mere, roy de Navarre, & autres du conseil* (Jaques des Hayes, 1561).
Anon., *Complainte au peuple Francois*, bound with [Hotman, François], *L'Histoire du tumulte d'Amboyse advenu au moys de Mars, M. D. LX.* (1560).
Anon., *Destruction du saccagement, exerce cruellement par le Duc de Guise et sa cohorte, en la ville de Vassy* (Caen, 1562).
Anon., *Discours entier de la persécution et cruauté exercée en la ville de Vaissy* ([Orleans: Eloi Gibier], 1563).
Anon., *Exhortation d'un des Pasteurs de la France à son troupeau* (1561).
Anon., *Histoire memorable de la persecution & saccagement du peuple de Merindol & Cabrieres & autres circonvoisins, appelez Vaudois* ([Geneva, Jean Crespin], 1555).
Anon., *Juste Complainte des fideles de France. contre leurs adversaires Papistes, & autres. sur l'affliction & faux crimes, dont on les charge à grand tort. Ensemble les inconveniens, qui en pourroyent finalement avenir à ceux, qui leur font la guerre* (Avignon: Trophime des Rives, 1560).
Anon., *La Maniere d'appaiser les troubles, qui sont maintenant en France, & y pourront estre cy apres: A la Royne mere du Roy* ([Lyon, Jean Saugrain], 1561).
Anon., *La Polymachie des Marmitons, ou la gendarmerie du Pape. En laquelle est amplement descrite l'ordre que le Pape veut tenir en l'armee qu'il veut mettre sus pour l'eslevement de sa marmite* ([Lyon, Jean Saugrain], 1563).
Anon., *La Suffisance de maistre Colas Durand, dit Chevalier de*

Villegaignon, pour sa retenue en l'estat du Roy. Item, Espoussette des armoiries de Villegaignon, pour bien faire luire la fleur de Lis, que l'estrille n'a point touchee (1561).

Anon., *Le De profundis chante par la France, à la mort & trespas de feu Monsieur le Duc de Guyse* (Paris, Guillaume de Niverd, 1563).

Anon., *Remonstrance a la Roine Mere du Roy sur le discours de Pierre de Ronsard des miseres de ce temps* (Lyon: Francoys le Clerc, 1563).

Aristotle, *Le secret des secretz de aristote pour cognoistre les conditions des hommes et des femmes. Lesquels il filt pour le Roy Alexandre son disciple* (n. p., n. d.).

Auger, Ed., *Sommaire des Heresies, abus, impietez et blasphemes qui sont en la Cene des Calvinistes, & nouvelle Religion pretendue reformee* (Paris: Nicolas Chesneau, 1568).

Augustine, St, 'Six traités anti-manichéens', in R. Jolivet and M. Jourjon, eds, *Oeuvres de Saint Augustin* (Paris, 1961).

Aymon, J., ed., *Tous les Synodes Nationaux des Eglises Reformées de France*, 2 vols (La Haye: Charles Delo, 1710).

Backus, I., ed., *Guillaume Postel et Jean Boulaese: De Summopere et Le Miracle de Laon, 1566* (Geneva, 1995).

Bale, J., *Scriptorum Illustrium maioris Brytanniae, quam nunc Angliam & Scotiam vocant: Catalogus* (Basel, 1559).

Barbier, A., ed., *Pierre de Ronsard: Poèmes* (Oxford, 1972).

Barthélemy, E. de, ed., *Journal d'un curé Ligueur de Paris sous les trois derniers Valois* (Paris, 1866).

Baum, G. and Cunitz, E., eds, *Histoire Ecclésiastique des Eglises Réformées au Royaume de France*, 3 vols (Paris: Fischbacher, 1883–87).

Beauxamis, T., *Enqueste et griefz, sur le sac et pieces, et depositions des tesmoings produictz par les favoriz de la nouvelle Eglise, contre le Pape, & autres Prelatz de l'Eglise Catholique* (Paris: Jerome de Marnef, 1562).

——, *Histoire des sectes tirées de l'armée sathanique* (1st edn 1570; Paris: Guillaume Chaudière, 1576).

Bellarmine, R., *Disputationes de controversiis Christianae fidei adversus hujus temporis haereticos*, 3 vols (Ingolstadt, 1586–93).

Benoist, R., *Brieve Response a quelque remonstrance faicte a la roine mere du Roy, par ceux qui se disent persecutez pour la parolle de Dieu* (Paris: Guillaume Guillard and Amaulry Warencore, 1561).

——, *Claire Probation de la necessaire manducation de la substantielle & reale humanité de Jesus Christ, vray Dieu & vray homme, au S. Sacrement de l'autel* (Paris: Nicolas Chesneau, 1561).

——, *La Manière de cognoistre salutairement Jésus Christ* (Paris: Guillaume Guillard et Amaulry Warencore, 1561).

————, *Epitre a Jean Calvin pour luy remonstrer qu'il repugne a la parole de Dieu en ce qu'il a ecrit des images* (Paris: Nicolas Chesneau, 1564).

————, *Brieve et facile refutation d'un livret divuluge au nom de Jean de l'Espine, se disant Ministre de la parole de Dieu: auquel violentant & detorquant l'escripture saincte, il blaspheme malheureusement le sainct sacrifice Evangelique, dict vulgairement la saincte Messe* (Paris: Guillaume Chaudière, 1565).

————, *Remonstrance aux prestres, religieuses et moynes, qui sous le pretexte d'un licite mariage, ont commis abhominable inceste & sacrilege* (1st edn 1565; Paris: Nicolas Chesneau, 1567).

Beza, T., *Histoire Ecclesiastique des Eglises Reformes au Royaume de France*, 3 vols (Antwerp: Jean Remy, 1580).

Bodin, J., *Les six livres de la république*, 7 vols (Paris, 1583).

Bonnet, J., ed., *Letters of Calvin*, 4 vols (New York, 1972).

————, ed., *Letters of John Calvin* (Edinburgh, 1980).

Bordier, H. L., ed., *Le Chansonnier Huguenot du XVIe siècle* (Geneva, 1969).

Bosquet, M. G., *Sur les troubles advenus en la ville de Tolose l'an 1562* (Toulouse: Raymond Colomiez, 1595).

[Brès, G. de], *Le Baston de la foy chrestienne, Livre tresutile a tous Chrestiens, pour s'armer contre les ennemys de l'Evangile: & pour aussi cognoistre l'ancienneté de nostre saincte foy, & de la vraye Eglise* (Lyon [Antwerp: Christophe Plantin], 1555).

Brès, G. de, *La racine, source et fondement des Anabaptistes ou rebaptisez de nostre temps* ([Rouen]: Abel Clemence, 1565).

Bullinger, H., *Cent Sermons sur l'Apocalypse de Jesus Christ, revelée par l'Ange du Seigneur, veue & escrite par S. Jean Apostre & Evangeliste* (Geneva: François Jaquy, 1564).

Calvin, J., *Institution de la religion chrestienne: en laquelle est comprinse une somme de pieté, et quasi tout ce qui est necessaire a congnoistre en la doctrine de salut* (Geneva, 1541).

[————], *Advertissement sur la censure qu'ont faicte les Bestes de Sorbonne, touchant les livres qu'ilz appellent heretiques* ([Geneva: Jean Girard], 1544).

————, *Declaration pour maintenir la vraie foy … contre les erreurs detestables de Michel Servet* (Geneva, 1554).

————, 'Petit traité montrant que c'est que doit faire un homme fidèle connaissant la verité de l'Evangile quand il est entre les papistes', in O. Millet, ed., *Oeuvres choisies* (Paris, 1995).

————, and Beza, T., *Responses de Jean Calvin et Theodore de Bèze aux argumens et calomnies d'un qui s'efforce de renverser par tous moyens la doctrine de la providence secrete de Dieu* (Geneva, 1559).

Cameron, K., Hall, K. M. and Higman, F., eds, *Théodore de Bèze: Abraham sacrifiant* (Geneva, 1967).

Carion, J., and Melanchthon, P., *Chronique et Histoire Universelle, contenant les choses memorables avenues es quatre souverains Empires, Royaumes, Republiques, & au gouvernement de l'Eglise, depuis le commencement du monde jusques à l'Empereur Charles cinquiesme*, 2 vols (Jean Berion, 1579–80).

Castelnau, M. de, *Mémoires* (Paris: Sebastien Chappelet, 1621).

Castro, A. de, *Adversus Omnes Haereses* (Paris, 1534).

Cazauran, N., ed., *Discours merveilleux de la vie, actions et deportements de Catherine de Medici, Royne-mère* (Geneva: Droz, 1995).

Ceneau, R., *Adversus quendam mali ominis, nullius vero, quod sciri, possit nominis, apologastrum in causa tenebrionum haereticorum, qui hodie cristas erigere coeperunt justa querimonia* (Paris: G. Julien, 1558).

———, *Complainte ou Response catholique contre la defense et le defenseur de la cause des tenebrions heretiques de ce temps* (Paris: Guillaume Julien, 1558).

———, *Response catholique contre les heretiques de ce temps* (Paris: Guillaume Julien, 1562).

Chandieu, A. de la Roche, *Histoire des persecutions, et martyrs de l'Eglise de Paris, depuis l'an 1557. Jusques au temps du Roy Charles neufviesme* (Lyon: [Senneton freres], 1563).

Charbonnier, F., ed., *La Poésie Française et les Guerres de Religion 1560–1574* (Geneva, 1970).

Chassanion, J., *Histoire des Albigeois: touchant leur doctrine & religion, contre les faux bruits qui ont esté semés d'eux, & les ecris dont on les a à tort diffamés : & de la cruelle & longue guerre qui leur a esté faite, pour ravir les terres & seigneuries d'autrui, sous couleur de vouloir extirpé l'hérésie* ([Geneva]: Pierre de Sainctandré, 1595).

Christmas, H., ed., *Select Works of John Bale* (Cambridge, 1849).

Crespin, J., *Histoire des Martyrs persecutez et mis a mort pour la verité de l'Evangile, depuis le temps des Apostres jusques à l'an 1574* (Geneva: Jean Crespin, 1582).

———, *Histoire des Martyrs* (Geneva, 1597).

———, *Histoire des Martyrs* (Geneva: Jean Crespin, 1608).

———, *Histoire des Martyrs* (Geneva: Pierre Aubert, 1619).

De Thou, J. A., *Historia sui temporis libri* (Paris, 1603).

D'Espence, C., *Cinq sermons ou traictez de maistre Claude d'Espence* (Paris: Nicolas Chesneau, 1562).

Des Freuz, R., *Brieve Response aux quatre execrables Articles contre la saincte Messe, escriptz par un autheur incogneu, & publiez à la foyre de Guybray* (Paris: Nicolas Chesneau, 1561).

Désiré, A., *Le Deffensaire de la foy chrestienne* (Paris, 1567).

————, *L'origine et source de tous les maux de ce monde, par l'incorrection des peres & meres envers leurs enfans, & de l'inobedience d'iceux, Ensemble de la trop grande familiarité & liberté donnée aux servans & servantes* (Paris: Jean Dallier, 1571).

[Des Gallars, N.], *Seconde apologie ou defense des vrais chrestiens, contre les calomnies impudentes des ennemis de l'Eglise catholique. Ou il est respondu aux diffames redoublez par un nommé Demochares docteur de la Sorbonne* ([Geneva: Jean Crespin], 1559).

Dolan, J. P., ed., *The essential Erasmus* (New York, 1964).

Dominici, B., *Sermon Funebre fait a Nancy, aux obseques & funerailles de feu Monseigneur, Monsieur François de Lorraine, Duc de Guyse, en l'Eglise des Cordeliers, par l'ordonnance de son Alteze, & de monseigneur le Duc, presens* (Reims: Jean de Foigny, and Paris: Nicolas Chesneau, 1563).

Doré, P., *Anti-Calvin, contenant deus defenses catholiques de la verité du sainct Sacrement* (Paris, 1551).

Du Jon, Fr, *Apocalypse ou Revelation de S. Jean Apostre Evangeliste de nostre Seigneur Jesus Christ* ([Geneva]: Pierre de Sainct-André, 1592).

Du Preau, G., *Des faux prophetes, seducteurs, & hypocrites, qui viennent à nous en habit de brebis: mais au dedans sont loups ravissans,* (Paris: Jaques Macé, 1563).

————, *Histoire de l'estat et succes de l'eglise dresse en forme de chronique generale et universelle* (Paris: Jaques Kerver, 1583).

Du Tillet, J., *Memoires et advis de M. Jean du Tillet, protonotaire et secretaire du Roy tres chrestien, greffier de sa cour de Parlement faict en 1551 sur les libertés de l'église gallicane* (Paris, 1551).

————, *Pour la majorité du Roy trés chrestien contre les escrits des Rebelles* (Paris: Guillaume Morel, 1560).

————, *Pour l'Entiere Majorite du Roy Treschrestien, Contre le Legitime Conseil Malicieusement Inventé par les Rebelles* (1560).

[————], *Pour l'entiere majorite du Roy Treschrestien, Contre le Legitime conseil malicieusement inventé par les rebelles* (Paris: Guillaume Morel, 1560).

[————], *Remonstrances faictes au roy par messieurs de la court de Parlement de Paris, sur la publication de l'Edict du moys de Janvier* (Cambray: Nicolas Lombard, 1561); reprinted in E. Droz, ed., *Chemins de l'Hérésie*, 4 vols (Geneva, 1970–76), III, pp. 420–32.

————, *Advertissement a la noblesse, tant du party du Roy, que des Rebelles & Conjurez* (Lyon: Michel Jove, 1568).

————, *Sommaire de l'histoire de la guerre faicte contre les heretiques Albigeois, extraicte du Tresor des Chartres du Roy par feu Jehan du Tillet Prothenotaire & Secretaire de la maison & Couronne de France,*

Greffier du Parlement de Paris, sieur de la Bussiere (Paris: Robert Nivelle, 1590).

Du Val, A., *Les contrarietez & contredictz, qui se trouvent en la doctrine de Jean Calvin, de Luther & autres nouveaux evangelistes de nostre temps* (Paris: Nicolas Chesneau, 1561).

———, *Mirouer des Calvinistes et Armure des Chrestiens, pour rembarrer les Lutheriens & nouveaux Evangelistes de Genéve (sic)* (1st edn 1559; Paris: Nicolas Chesneau, 1562).

Du Voisin de la Popelinière, L., *L'Histoire de France enrichie des plus notables occurances survenues ez Provinces de l'Europe & pays voisins*, 2 vols ([La Rochelle: Abraham Hautin], 1581).

Dumas, A., *La Reine Margot* (Paris, 1845).

Dupuiherbault, G., *Consolation des catholiques, molestez par Sectaires & Schismatiques* (Paris: Jean de Roigny, 1560).

Durand, N., *Lettres du Chevallier de Villegaignon sur les remonstrances, a la Royne Mere du Roy la souveraine Dame, touchant la Religion* (F. T., 1561).

Eck, J., *Les lieux communs de jean Ekius, contre Luther* (Lyon: Jean Marnax, 1551).

Erasmus, D., *Liber de sarcienda Ecclesiae concordia deque sedandis opinionum dissidiis* (Basel, 1533).

———, *Praise of Folly* (New York, 1989).

Flacius Illyricus, M., *Catalogus Testium Veritatis qui ante nostram aetatem reclamarunt papae* (Basel, 1556).

———, *Catalogus testium veritatis. Historia der zeugen Bekenner und Märterer so Christum und die Euangelische warheit biss hieher auch etwa mitten im Reich der finsternus warhafftig erkennet Christlich und aussrichtig bekennet und dem Bäpstlichen vermeinten Primat irrthumen ergerlichem leben und lastern erstlich widerprochen* (Frankfurt, 1573).

———, *Catalogus Testium Veritatis* (Geneva, 1608).

———, *Catalogus Testium Veritatis qui ante nostram aetatem reclamarunt papae* (Basel, 1608).

Flandrin, J.-L., ed., *Journal d'un bourgeois de Paris sous Henri III par Pierre de l'Estoile* (Paris, 1966).

Fornier, J., *l'Histoire des guerres faictes en plusieurs lieux de la France, tant en la Guienne & Languedoc contre les Heretiques, que ailleurs contre certains ennemis de la couronne: & de la conqueste de la terre saincte: Et de tout ce qui est advenu en France digne de memoire, depuis l'an de grace 1200. jusques à l'an Mil trois cens unze, au quel tous les Templiers furent destruictz* (Toulouse: Jaques Colomies, 1562).

Foxe, J., *Acts and Monuments* (London, 1563).

———, *Acts and Monuments*, 2 vols (London, 1570).

————, *Acts and Monuments* (London, 1610).

Franck, S., *Chronica, zeytbuch und Geschychtbibel* (Strasbourg, 1531).

Gay, J., *Histoire des scismes et heresies des Albigeois, conforme à celle du present: par laquelle appert que plusieurs grans princes, & seigneurs sont tombez en extremes desolations & ruines, pour avoir favorisé aux heretiques* (Paris, 1561).

Glover, T. R. and Rendall, G. H., eds, *Tertullian: Apology* (London: W. Heinemann, 1984).

Goulard, S., *Memoires de l'estat de France, sous Charles Neufiesme* (Meidelbourg: Henrich Wolf, 1576).

Grenier, N., *Le bouclier de la foy* (1st edn 1547; Paris: Nicolas Bonfons, 1577).

Hervet, G., *Discours sur ce que les pilleurs, voleurs, & brusleurs d'Eglises disent qu'ilz n'en veulent qu'aux prestres* (Reims: Jean de Foigny, 1562).

————, ed., *Clementis alexandrini viri longe doctissimi ... omnia quae quidem extant opera* (Paris: Guillaume Guillard and Thomas Bellot, 1566).

[Hotman, F.], *L'Histoire du tumulte d'Amboyse advenu au moys de Mars, M. D. LX.* (1560).

[————], *Responce au livre inscript, Pour la Majorité du Roy François Second* (Amboise, 1560).

Hozius, S., *Des sectes et heresies de nostre temps: traicte composé premierement en Latin, par reverend Pere en Dieu monseigneur Stanislas Hozie, Evesque de Varme en Pouloigne, dedié au roy de Pouloigne, & nouvellement mis en François* (Paris: Vascosan, 1561).

I. D. S. A., *Similitude des regnes du roy Loys IX. par nous nomme s. Loys, et de celuy du roy Charles à present regnant*, bound with A. Sorbin, *Histoire des albigeois, et gestes de noble simon de monfort. Descrite par F. Pierre des Vallées Sernay, Moine de l'Ordre de Cisteaux* (Paris: Guillaume Chaudière, 1569).

Irenée de Lyon, *Contre les Hérésies: Dénonciation et réfutation de la gnose au nom menteur* (Paris, 1984).

Jolivet, R. and Jourjon, M., eds, 'Six traités anti-manichéens', *Oeuvres de Saint Augustin*, XVII (Paris: Desclée de Brouwer, 1961).

Kingdon, R. M., ed., *Registres de la compagnie des pasteurs de Genève au temps de Calvin*, 12 vols (Geneva, 1962–95).

Knox, J., *The First blast of the trumpet against the monstruous regiment of women* (Geneva, 1558).

La Bible qui est toute la saincte escriture du vieil & du nouveau testament (Geneva, 1588).

Labande, E. R., ed., *Guibert de Nogent: Autobiographie* (Paris: Les Belles Lettres, 1981).

Lalanne, L., ed., *Journal d'un bourgeois de Paris sous le règne de François Premier 1515–1536* (Paris: J. Renouard, 1854).

Le Nouveau Testament c'est à dire, la nouvelle alliance de nostre seigneur Jesus Christ (Geneva, 1577).

Le Picart, F., *Les Sermons et instructions chrestiennes pour tous les jours de caresme et féries de Pasques* (Paris: Nicolas Chesneau, 1566).

Leconte, M., *Elegie sur la mort conspiree au seigneur duc de guise, Lieutenant general de la Maiesté du Roy, avec les exhortations faictes par le Clergé aux Citoyens de Paris* (Paris: Guillaume Niverd, 1563).

Legier, B., *Response aux objections et poincts principaux de ceux qui se disent aujourd'huy vouloir reformer l'Eglise, & s'appellent fideles & croyans à l'Evangile* (Paris: Nicolas Chesneau, 1562).

Lérins, V. de, *Petit traite de Vincent Lerineuse pour la verite et antiquite de la foy catholique* (1st edn 1560; Paris: Vascosan, 1563).

Lindan, G., *Discovrs en forme de dialogue, ou histoire tragique en laquelle est nayvement depeinte & descrite la source, origine, cause & progres des troubles* (Paris: Guillaume Chaudière, 1566).

Luther, M. and Melanchthon, P., *De Deux monstres prodigieux, a savoir, d'un Asne-Pape, qui fut trouvé à Rome en la riviere du Tibre, l'an 1496. Et d'un veau-moine nay à Friberg en Misne, l'an 1528* (Geneva: Jean Crespin, 1557).

Luxemburg, B. von, *Catalogus haereticorum omnium* (Köln, 1522).

[Marcourt, A.], *Le Livre des marchans, fort utile a toutes gens pour cognoistre de quelles marchandises on se doit donner garde d'estre deceu* ([Geneva]: Jaquy, Davodean and Bourgeois, [1557]).

[Marlorat, A.], *Remonstrance a la royne mere du Roy, par ceux qui sont persecutez pour la parole de DIEU. En laquelle ils rendent raison des principaux articles de la Religion, & qui sont aujourdhuy en dispute* ([Paris], 1561).

[———], *La Response aux lettres de Nicolas Durant, dict le Chevalier de Villegaignon, addressées à la Reyne mere du Roy. Ensemble la Confutation d'une heresie mise en avant par ledict Villegaignon, contre la souveraine puissance & authorité des Rois* (1561).

Matheson, P., ed., *Argula von Grumbach: A woman's voice in the Reformation* (Edinburgh, 1995).

Maxwell-Stuart, P. G., ed., *The Occult in Early Modern Europe: a documentary history* (London, 1999).

Mayor, J. E. B., ed., *Tertullian: Apologeticus* (Cambridge: Cambridge University Press, 1917).

Migne, J. P., ed., *Patrologia Latina*, 221 vols (Turnhout: Brepols, 1970).

———, ed., *Patrologiae Graecae*, 161 vols (Turnhout: Brepols, 1970).

Millet, O., ed., *Jean Calvin: Advertissement contre l'astrologie judiciaire* (Geneva, 1985).

Mollat, G., ed., *Bernard Gui: Manuel de l'Inquisiteur* (Paris: Les Belles Lettres, 1964).

Mouchy, A. de, *Responce a quelque apologie que les heretiques ces jours passés ont mis en avant sous ce titre: Apologie ou deffence des bons Chrestiens contre les ennemis de l'Eglise catholique* (Paris: Claude Frémy, 1558).

Müller, L. G., ed., *The De Haeresibus of Saint Augustine: a translation with an introduction and commentary* (Washington: Catholic University of America Press, 1956).

New Revised Standard Version Bible (Nashville, 1993).

Nichols, J., ed., 'Narratives of the days of the Reformation', *Camden Society*, LXXVII (1859).

Optat, *Histoire du schisme, blasphemes & autres impietez des Donatiens* (Paris: Frederic Morel, 1564).

Perrin, J.-P., *Histoire des Vaudois appelés Albigeois* (Geneva, 1618).

———, *The History of the Old Waldenses and Albigenses; Those Two Glorious Witnesses to the Truth of Christianity: In Opposition to the AntiChristianism of Rome, In the several ages preceding the Reformation* (London: Joseph Downing, 1711).

Pettegree, A., Duke, A. and Lewis, G., eds, *Calvinism in Europe 1540–1610: A Collection of Documents* (Manchester, 1992).

Poggianus, J., *Oraison funebre, faite a Rome aux obseques & funerailles de feu tres-puissant & magnanime Prince, François de Lorraine Duc de Guise, par le commandement de nostre sainct Pere le Pape PIE IIII* (Reims: Jean de Foigny, and Paris: Nicolas Chesneau, 1563).

Quick, J., *Synodicon in Gallia Reformata: or, the acts, decisions, decrees, and canons of those famous national councils of the Reformed Churches in France*, 2 vols (London, 1692).

Rabaud, C., *Ce que la France doit aux Protestants* (Paris, 1901).

Rabelais, F., *Gargantua and Pantagruel* (London, 1955).

Radice, B., ed., *The Letters of the Younger Pliny* (London, 1969).

Read, C., ed., *François Hotman: Le Tigre de 1560* (Geneva, 1970).

Richer, P., *La Refutation des folles resveries, execrables blasphemes, erreurs & mensonges de Nicolas Durand, qui se nomme Villegaignon: divisee en deux livres* (1561).

Ripa, C., *Nova Iconologia* (Padua, 1618).

Rotier, E., *Response aux blasphemateurs de la saincte messe: Avec la confutation de la vaine & ridicule coene des Calvinistes* (Paris: Jacques Kerver, 1566).

Ruby, C. de, *Discours sur la contagion de la peste qui a esté ceste presente annee en la ville de Lyon* (Lyon: J. d'Ogerolles, 1577).

Sachs, H., *Disputation zwischen einem Chorherren und Schuchmacher darin das wort gottes / und ein recht Christlich wesen verfochten würdt* (1524).

Saconay, G. de, *De la providence de dieu sur les roys de france treschrestiens, par laquelle sa saincte religion Catholique ne defaudra en leur Royaume. Et comme les Gotz Arriens, & les Albigeois en ont esté par icelle dechassés* (Lyon: Michel Jove, 1568).

[————], *Discours Catholique, sur les causes & remedes des Malheurs intentés au Roy, & escheus à som peuple par les rebelles Calvinistes* (Lyon: Michel Jove, 1568).

Sainctes, C. de, *Declaration d'aucuns atheismes de la doctrine de Calvin et Beze* (Paris: Claude Frémy, 1568).

Serres, J. de, *Recueil des choses memorables avenues en France* (1595).

Shaw, H. A., ed., *Conrad Badius and the Comedie du Pape Malade* (Philadelphia, 1934).

Sheppard, G. T., ed., *The Geneva Bible* (New York, 1989).

Sorbin, A., *Histoire de la Ligue Saincte faicte il y a CCCLXXX ans à la conduite de Simon de Montfort contre les hérétiques albigeois* (Paris: Guillaume Chaudière, 1585).

————, *Histoire des albigeois, et gestes de noble simon de monfort* (Toulouse: Arnaud and Jaques Colomies, 1568).

————, *Histoire des albigeois, et gestes de noble simon de monfort. Descrite par F. Pierre des Vallées Sernay, Moine de l'Ordre de Cisteaux* (Paris: Guillaume Chaudière, 1569).

Stapleton, T., *A Counterblast to M. Hornes Vayne Blaste Against M. Fekenham* (Louvain, 1567).

Stegmann, A., ed., *Edits des Guerres de Religion* (Paris, 1979).

Stevenson, J., ed., *Calendar of State Papers, Foreign series, of the reign of Elizabeth, 1561–1562* (London: Public Record Office, 1866).

Talpin, J., *Remonstrance a tous chrestiens qui se sont separez de l'Eglise Romaine* (1st edn 1567; Paris: Nicolas Chesneau, 1572).

Tarbé, P., ed., *Recueil de Poésies Calvinistes, 1550–1566* (Geneva, 1968).

Townsend, G., ed., *Acts and Monuments*, 8 vols (London, 1846).

Ussher, J., *De Christianorum Ecclesiarum successione et statu Historica Explicatio* (London, 1613).

Vacquerie, J. de la, *Catholique remonstrance aux roys et princes chrestiens, a tous magistrats & gouverneurs de Repub. touchant l'abolition des heresies, troubles & scismes qui regnent aujourd'huy en la Chrestienté* (Paris: Claude Frémy, 1560).

Vergilii, P., *Urbinatis Anglicae historiae libri vigintifex* (Basel, 1546).

Vignier, N., *Recueil de L'Histoire de l'Eglise, depuis le Baptseme de nostre Seigneur Jesus Christ, jusques à ce temps* (Leyden: Christoffle de Raphelengien, 1601).

[————], *L'Antechrist Romain, Opposé à l'Antechrist Juif du Cardinal de Bellarmin, du Sieur de Remond & autres* (1606).

————, *Legende Doree ou Sommaire de l'histiore des freres Mendians de l'Ordre de Dominique, & de François* (Leyden, 1608).

————, *Theatre de L'Antechrist Auquel est respondu au Cardinal Bellarmin, au sieur de Remond, à Perenius, Ribera, Viergas, Sanderus et autres qui par leurs escrits condamnent la doctrine des Eglises Reformees sur ce subiet: Par Nicolas Vignier* (Saumur, 1610).

————, *Apologie Catholique de la doctrine des Eglises Reformees* (Saumur: Thomas Portau, 1617).

Vigor, S., *Oraison funebre prononcee aux obseques, de treshaute, trespuissante, & tres-catholique Princesse, ma Dame Elizabeth de France, Royne des Espagnes, prononcee en l'Eglise nostre Dame de Paris, le XXV. du mois d'Octobre 1568* (Paris: Claude Frémy, 1568)

Viret, P., *De la vraye et fausse religion, touchant les voeus et les sermens licites et illicites: et notamment touchant les voeus de perpetuelle continence, et les voeus d'anatheme et d'execration, et les sacrifices d'hosties humaines, et de l'excommunication en toutes religions. Item de la Moinerie, tant des juifs que des Payens et des turcs et des papistes et des sacrifices faits à Moloch, tant en corps qu'en ame* ([Geneva]: Jean Rivery, 1560).

Virgil, *Aeneid* (London, 1956).

Ward, H. R., ed., *Matthew Paris: Chronica Majora*, 7 vols (London, 1876).

Wesenbecii, P., *Oratio De Waldensibus et Albigensibus Christianis* (Iena: Tobias Steinman, 1585).

Westphal, J., *Apologia confesiones de coena contra coruptelas ed calumnias Ioannes Calvini* (Oberursel, 1558).

Wicelius, G., *Libellus de moribus veterum haereticorum* (Leipzig, 1537).

William, K. M., ed., *Shakespeare: Macbeth* (London: Methuen, 1987).

Williams, F., ed., *The Panarion of Epiphanius of Salamis*, 2 vols (Leiden: E. J. Brill, 1987–94).

Witzel, G., *Discours des moeurs tant des anciens hérétiques que nouveaux Lutheriens & Calvinistes auquel leur resemblance est clairement demonstrée* (Paris: Claude Frémy, 1567).

Secondary Sources

Abulafia, A. S., *Christians and Jews in the Twelfth-Century Renaissance* (London, 1995).

Archambault, P., 'The Analogy of the "Body" in Renaissance Political Literature', *BHR*, XXIX (1967), pp. 21–53.

Asher, R. E., 'Rois légendaires et nationalisme dans la poésie du XVIe siècle français', in F. Simone, ed., *Culture et politique en France à l'époque de l'Humanisme et de la Renaissance* (Turin, 1974), pp. 235–48.

Aston, M., 'Corpus Christi and Corpus Regni: Heresy and the Peasants' Revolt', *P&P* CXLIII (1994), p. 3–47.

Audisio, G., *Les Vaudois du Lubéron, Une minorité en Provence 1460–1560* (Mérindol, 1984).

Backus, I., 'Marie Dentière: un cas de féminisne théologique à l'époque de la Réforme', *BSHPF*, CXXXVII (1991), pp. 177–95.

——, *Les 7 Visions et la Fin des Temps: les commentaires Genevois de l'apocalypse entre 1539 et 1584* (Geneva, 1997).

——, ed., *The Reception of the Church Fathers in the West: From the Carolingians to the Maurists* (2 vols, Leiden, 1997).

Bakhtine, M., *L'oeuvre de François Rabelais et la culture populaire au moyen âge et sous la renaissance* (Paris, 1970).

Baumgartner, F. J., *Change and Continuity in the French Episcopate: the bishops and the Wars of Religion, 1547–1610* (Durham, 1986).

Beck, J., *Théatre et Propagande aux débuts de la réforme: 6 pièces polémiques du recueil La Vallière* (Geneva, 1986).

Bédouelle, Guy, 'Les Albigeois, témoins du véritable évangile: l'historiographie protestante du XVIe et du début du XVIIe siècle', *CF*, XIV (1979), pp. 47–70.

Benedict, P., *A City Divided: Rouen during the Wars of Religion* (Cambridge, 1981).

——, 'Of Marmites and Martyrs: Images and Polemics in the Wars of Religion', in *The French Renaissance in Prints from the Bibliothèque Nationale de France* (exhibition catalogue of the Grunwald Centre for the Graphic Arts, Los Angeles, 1995), pp. 108–37.

——, 'The Dynamics of Protestant Militancy: France, 1555–1563', in P. Benedict et al., eds, *Reformation, Revolt, and Civil War*, pp. 35–50.

——, Marnef, G., van Nierop, H. and Vernard, M., eds, *Reformation, Revolt and Civil War in France and the Netherlands, 1555–1585* (Amsterdam, 1999).

Bercé, Y.-M., *Revolt and revolution in early modern Europe: An essay on the history of political violence* (Manchester, 1987).

——, *Fête et révolte: Des mentalités populaires du XVIe au XVIIIe siècle* (Paris: Hachette, 1994).

Betteridge, T., 'Anne Askewe, John Bale, and Protestant history', *Journal of Medieval and Early Modern Studies*, XXVII (1997), pp. 265–84.

——, '"Mete Covers for such Vessels": Sexual Deviancy and the English Reformation' (unpublished paper, Reformation Colloquium, Wadham College, Oxford, 1998), 16 pages.

————, *Tudor Histories of the English Reformations, 1530–83* (Brookfield, 1999).

Bossy, J., 'Some elementary forms of Durkheim', *P&P*, XCV (1982), pp. 3–18.

————, 'The Mass as a Social Institution 1200–1700', *P&P*, C (1983), pp. 29–61.

Bourdieu, P., *Leçon sur la Leçon* (Paris, 1982).

Bourgeon, J.-L., 'Les Guises valets de l'etranger, ou trente ans de collaboration avec l'ennemi (1568–1598)', in Y. Bellenger, ed., *Le mécénat et l'influence des Guises* (Paris, 1997), pp. 509–522.

Brown, E. A. R., ed., 'Jean Du Tillet and the French Wars of Religion: Five Tracts, 1562–1569', *Medieval and Renaissance Texts and Studies*, CVIII (1994).

Burke, P., *Popular Culture in Early Modern Europe* (London, 1994).

Cameron, E., *The Reformation of the Heretics: the Waldenses of the Alps 1480–1580* (Oxford, 1984).

————, 'Medieval Heretics as Protestant Martyrs', *Studies in Church History* XXX, (1993), pp. 185–207.

Cameron, K., 'La polémique, la mort de Marie Stuart & l'assassinat de Henri III', in R. Sauzet, ed., *Henri III et son temps* (Paris, 1992), pp. 185–94.

Carbonnier, J., 'De l'idée que le protestantisme s'est fait de ses rapports avec le catharisme ou des adoptions d'ancêtres en histoire', *BSHPF*, CI (1955), pp. 72–87.

Carroll, S., 'The Guise affinity and popular protest during the Wars of Religion', *FH*, IX (1995), pp. 125–52.

Catach, N., *L'Orthographe française à l'époque de la Renaissance* (Geneva, 1968).

Cazauran, N., 'Le roi exemplaire dans quelques pamphlets réformés 1560–1585', *Travaux de Linguistique et de Littérature*, XXII: 2 (1984), pp. 185–200.

————, ed., *Discours merveilleux de la vie, actions et deportements de Catherine de Medici, Royne-mère* (Geneva, 1995).

Chaix, P., *Recherches sur l'imprimerie à Genève de 1550 à 1564* (Geneva, 1978).

Christin, O., *Une revolution symbolique : l'iconoclasme huguenot et la reconstruction catholique* (Paris, 1991).

————, *La paix de religion: L'autonomisation de la raison politique au XVIe siècle* (Paris, 1997).

————, 'From Repression to Pacification: French Royal Policy in the Face of Protestantism', in P. Benedict, G. Marnef, H. van Nierop and M. Venard, eds, *Reformation, Revolt, and Civil War*, pp. 201–14.

Clark, S., 'Inversion, Misrule and the Meaning of Witchcraft', *P&P*, LXXXVII (1980), pp. 98–127.

———, *Thinking with Demons: The idea of witchcraft in early modern Europe* (Oxford, 1997).

Clifton, C. S., *Encyclopedia of Heresies and Heretics* (Oxford, 1992).

Constant, J.-M., *Les Guise* (Paris, 1984).

Cressy, D., *Bonfires and Bells: National Memory and the Protestant Calendar in Elizabethan and Stuart England* (Berkeley, 1989).

Crouzet, D., *Les Guerriers de Dieu: La violence aux temps des troubles de religion, vers 1525 – vers 1610*, 2 vols (Paris, 1990).

———, *La nuit de la Saint-Barthélemy: un rêve perdu de la renaissance* (Paris, 1994).

Darnton, R., *The corpus of clandestine literature in France, 1769–1789* (New York, 1995).

Davies, C. S. L., 'Peasants revolt in England and France: a comparison', *Agricultural History Review*, XXI (1973), pp. 122–39.

Davies, N., *Europe: A History* (London, 1997).

Davis, N. Z., 'The Rites of Violence: Religious Riot in Sixteenth-Century France', *P&P*, LIX (1973), pp. 51–91.

———, 'The sacred and the body social in Sixteenth-Century Lyon', *P&P*, XC (1981), pp. 40–70.

———, *Society and Culture in Early Modern France* (Oxford, 1995).

Delumeau, J., *Naissance et affirmation de la réforme* (Paris, 1965).

———, *La Peur en Occident, XIVe-XVIIIe siècles* (Paris, 1980).

Diefendorf, B. B., *Beneath the Cross: Catholics and Huguenots in Sixteenth-Century Paris* (Oxford, 1991).

Dipple, G., *Antifraternalism and Anticlericalism in the German Reformation: Johann Eberlin von Günzburg and the Campaign against the Friars* (Aldershot, 1996).

Dompnier, B., 'Les Marques de l'hérésie dans l'iconographie du XVIIe siècle', *Siècle*, II (1995), pp. 77–96.

Droz, E., ed., *Chemins de l'Hérésie*, 4 vols (Geneva, 1970–76).

Durkheim, E., *Les Formes élémentaires de la vie religieuse* (Paris, 1994).

Edwards, M. U. Jr, 'Catholic Controversial Literature, 1518–1555: Some Statistics', *Archiv für Reformationsgeschichte*, LXXIX (1988), pp. 189–205.

———, *Printing, Propaganda, and Martin Luther* (London, 1994).

Eisenstein, E., 'The Advent of Printing and the Protestant Revolt: A New Approach to the Disruption of Western Christendom', in R. M. Kingdon, ed., *Transition and Revolution: Problems and Issues of European Renaissance and Reformation History* (Minneapolis, 1974), pp. 235–70.

El Kenz, D., *Les Bûchers du Roi: la Culture Protestante des Martyrs 1523–1572* (Paris, 1997).

Estèbe, J., 'Debate: The Rites of Violence, Religious riot in Sixteenth-Century France, A Comment'; followed by N. Z. Davis 'A Rejoinder', *P&P*, LXVII (1975), pp. 127–35.

Farge, J. K., *Orthodoxy and Reform in early Reformation France: the Faculty of Theology of Paris, 1500–1543* (Leiden, 1985).

———, *Le Parti Conservateur au XVIe siècle: Université et Parlement de Paris à l'époque de la Renaissance et de la Réforme* (Paris, 1992).

Fédou, R., 'Editions et Traductions du Cardinal Hosius en France', *Collection du Centre d'Histoire du Catholicisme, Université Lyon II*, X (1972), pp. 49–55.

Felsenstein, F., *Anti-Semitic Stereotypes: a paradigm of otherness in English Popular Culture, 1660–1830* (London, 1995).

Feret, P., *La Faculté de Théologie de Paris et ses Docteurs les plus célèbres: Epoque Moderne XVI–XVIIIème siècle*, 6 vols (Paris, 1900–09).

Foster, S., 'Pierre Viret and France, 1559–1565' (unpublished Ph.D. thesis, University of St Andrews, May 2000).

Fragonard, M.-M., 'La détermination des frontières symboliques: nommer et définir les groupes hérétiques', in R. Sauzet, ed., *Les Frontières religieuses en europe du XVe au XVIIe siècle* (Paris, 1992), pp. 37–49.

Freeman, T., 'John Bale's Book of Martyrs?: The Account of King John in *Acts and Monuments*', *Reformation*, III (1998), pp. 175–223.

Garrisson-Estèbe, J., *Tocsin pour un massacre ou la saison des Saint-Barthélemy* (Paris, 1968).

———, *Les Protestants du Midi: 1559–1598* (Toulouse, 1980).

———, *A History of Sixteenth-Century France, 1483–1598: Renaissance, Reformation and Rebellion* (London, 1995).

Gellner, E., 'L'animal qui évite les gaffes, ou un faisceau d'hypothèses', in P. Birnbaum and J. Leca, eds, *Sur L'individualisme* (Paris, 1991), pp. 25–44.

Gibbon, E., *The History of The Decline and Fall of the Roman Empire*, 6 vols (Philadelphia, 1872).

Giese, F. S., *Artus Désiré Priest and Pamphleteer of the Sixteenth Century* (Chapel Hill, 1973).

Gilly, C., 'Das Sprichwort "Die Gelehrten die Verkehrten" in der Toleranzliteratur des 16. Jahrhunderts', in J.-G. Roth and S. L. Verheus, eds, *Anabaptistes et dissidents au xvie siècle, Actes du colloque international d'histoire anabaptiste 1994* (Baden-Baden, 1987), pp. 159–72.

Gilmont, J.-F., *Bibliographie des éditions de Jean Crespin 1550–1572* (Verviers, 1981).

————, *La Réforme et Le Livre: l'Europe de l'imprimé, 1517– v.1570* (Paris, 1990).

————, *Jean Calvin et le Livre Imprimé* (Geneva, 1997).

Ginzburg, C., *Ecstasies: Deciphering the Witches' Sabbath* (London, 1991).

Gow, A. C., *The Red Jews: antisemitism in an apocalyptic age 1200– 1600* (Leiden, 1995).

Gray, J. G., 'The Origins of the Word Huguenot', *SCJ*, XIV: 3 (1983), pp. 349–59.

Greengrass, M., 'The Anatomy of a Religious Riot in Toulouse in May 1562', *Journal of Ecclesiastical History*, XXXIV: 3 (1983), pp. 367– 91.

————, *The French Reformation* (Oxford, 1987).

————, 'The Psychology of Religious Violence', *FH*, V: 4 (1991), pp. 467–74.

————, *France in the Age of Henri IV: The struggle for stability* (London, 1995).

Gregory, B. S., *Salvation at Stake: Christian Martyrdom in Early Modern Europe* (Harvard, 1999).

Guilleminot, G., 'Religion et politique à la veille des guerres civiles: Recherches sur les impressions françaises de l'année 1561', 2 vols (unpublished thesis, Ecole des Chartes, 1977).

Guilleminot-Chrétien, G., 'Le contrôle de l'édition en France dans les années 1560: la genèse de l'édit de Moulins', in P. Aquilon and H.-J. Martin, eds, *Le Livre dans l'Europe de la Renaissance: Actes du XXVIIIe Colloque international d'Etudes humanistes de Tours* (Nantes, 1988), pp. 378–85.

Haag, E., *La France Protestante*, 6 vols (Paris, 1877–88).

————, *La France Protestante*, 10 vols (Geneva, 1966).

Hale, D. G., *The body politic: a political metaphor in Renaissance English literature* (The Hague, 1971).

Hallmark, R. E., 'Defenders of the faith: the case of Nicole Grenier', *Renaissance Studies*, XI: 2 (1997), pp. 123–40.

Hamilton, B., *The Albigensian Crusade* (London, 1974).

Harding, R. H., 'The Mobilization of Confraternities Against the Reformation in France', *SCJ*, XI: 2 (1980), pp. 85–107.

Head, T., 'The Religion of the Femmelettes: Ideals and Experience among Women in Fifteenth- and Sixteenth-Century France', in L. Coon, K. Haldane and E. Sommer, eds, *That Gentle Strength: historical perspectives on women in Christianity* (London, 1990), pp. 149–75.

Heller, H., 'The Italian Saint Bartholomew: Assassins or Victims?' (unpublished paper, Sixteenth-Century Studies Conference, 1999), 17 pages.

Higman, F. M., *Jean Calvin: Three French treatises* (London, 1970).

————, *Censorship and the Sorbonne: a bibliographical study of books in French censured by the Faculty of Theology of the University of Paris, 1520–1551* (Geneva, 1979).

————, *Piety and the People: Religious Printing in French, 1511–1551* (Aldershot, 1996).

————, '"Il seroit trop plus decent respondre en Latin": les controversistes catholiques du XVIe siècle face aux écrits réformés', *THR*, CCCXXVI (1998), pp. 515–30.

————, 'Les genres de la littérature polémique calviniste au XVIe siècle', *THR*, CCCXXVI (1998), pp. 437–48.

————, 'Linearity in Calvin's thought', *THR*, CCCXXVI (1998), pp. 391–418.

————, 'Premières réponses catholiques aux écrits de la Réforme en France, 1525–c.1540', *THR*, CCCXXVI (1998), pp. 497–514.

Hill, C., *The World Turned Upside Down: Radical Ideas during the English Revolution* (London, 1972).

Holmes, C., 'The ritual murder accusation in Britain', *Ethnic and Racial Studies*, IV (1981), pp. 265–288.

Holt, M. P., 'Putting Religion Back into the Wars of Religion', *French Historical Studies*, XVIII (1993), pp. 524–51.

————, *The French Wars of Religion, 1562–1629* (Cambridge, 1995).

Hotson, H., 'The Historiographical Origins of Calvinist Millenarianism', in B. Gordon, ed., *Protestant History and Identity in Sixteenth-Century Europe*, 2 vols (Aldershot, 1996), II, pp. 159–81.

Housley, N., *The Later Crusades: from Lyons to Alcazar 1274–1580* (Oxford, 1992).

Hudson, A., *Lollards and their books* (London, 1985).

Ingram, M., 'Ridings, Rough Music and the "Reform of Popular Culture" in Early Modern England', *P&P*, CV (1984), pp. 79–113.

Jas, M., *Braises Cathares: Filiation secrète à l'heure de la réforme* (Loubatières, 1992).

Joutard, P., Estèbe, J., Labrousse, E. and Lecuir, J., eds, *La Saint-Barthélemy: Ou les résonances d'un massacre* (Neuchâtel, 1976).

Kapferer, J.-N., *Rumeurs: le plus vieux média du monde* (Paris, 1987).

Keen, R., 'The Fathers in Counter-Reformation Theology in the Pre-Tridentine period', in I. Backus, ed., *The Reception of the Church Fathers in the West: From the Carolingians to the Maurists*, 2 vols (Leiden, 1997), II, pp. 701–43.

Kelley, D. R., *François Hotman: A Revolutionary's Ordeal* (Princeton, 1973).

————, *The Beginning of Ideology: Consciousness and Society in the French Reformation* (Cambridge, 1981).

Kim, S.-H., 'Michel de L'Hôpital: The Visions of a Reformist Chancellor during the French Religious Wars', *Sixteenth Century Essays and Studies*, XXXVI (Kirksville, 1997).

Kingdon, R., *Geneva and the coming of the Wars of Religion in France, 1555–1563* (Geneva, 1956).

———, *Geneva and the Consolidation of the French Protestant Movement 1564–1572* (Geneva, 1967).

———, *Myths about the St. Bartholomew's Day Massacres 1572–1576* (London, 1988).

Knecht, R. J., *Catherine De' Medici* (London, 1998).

Lake, P., 'Anti-popery: the Structure of a Prejudice', in R. Cust and A. Hughes, eds, *Conflict in early Stuart England: studies in religion and politics, 1603–1642* (London, 1989), pp. 72–106.

Langmuir, G., 'The Knight's Tale of Young Hugh of Lincoln', *Speculum*, XLVII: 3 (1972), pp. 459–82.

———, 'Thomas of Monmouth: Detector of Ritual Murder', *Speculum*, LIX (1984), pp. 820–46.

———, *Towards a definition of antisemitism* (Berkeley, 1990).

Le Clech-Charton, S., 'Le sentiment religieux chez les notaires et secrétaires du roi sous François Ier: un groupe sous influence?', in *Renaissance européenne et phénomènes religieux 1450–1650* (Montbrison, 1991), pp. 219–234.

Leonardo, D., 'In Pursuit of a Godly Kingdom: Kingship and Propaganda during the Reign of Henry III, 1584–89', (unpublished paper, Sixteenth-Century Studies Conference, St Louis, 1996), 12 pages.

Le Roy Ladurie, E., *Histoire du Languedoc* (Toulouse, 1967).

———, *Carnival: a people's uprising at Romans, 1579–1580* (London, 1980).

———, *Montaillou: Village Occitan* (Paris, 1982).

Lestringant, F., *L'Expérience Huguenote au Nouveau Monde* (Geneva, 1996).

Maag, K., *Seminary or University: The Genevan Academy and Reformed Higher Education, 1560–1620* (Aldershot, 1995).

Matheson, P., 'Breaking the Silence: Women, Censorship, and the Reformation', *SCJ*, XXVII (1996), pp. 97–109.

———, *The Rhetoric of the Reformation* (Edinburgh, 1998).

McLuhan, M., *Understanding Media: The Extensions of Man* (New York, 1964).

Messadié, G., *Histoire Générale du Diable* (Paris, 1993).

Monter, W., *Judging the French Reformation: Heresy Trials by Sixteenth-Century French Parlements* (London, 1999).

Moore, R. I., 'Heresy as Disease', in D. W. Lourdeaux and D. Verhelst, eds, *The Concept of Heresy in the Middle Ages* (Louvain, 1976), pp. 1–11.

————, *The Origins of European Dissent* (Oxford, 1985).

————, *The Formation of a Persecuting Society: Power and deviance in western Europe 950–1250* (Oxford, 1987).

Morris, C., *The Papal Monarchy: The Western Church from 1050 to 1250* (Oxford, 1991).

Moxey, K., 'The Battle of the Sexes and the World Upside Down', in L. Coon, K. Haldane and E. Sommer, eds, *That Gentle Strength: historical perspectives on women in Christianity* (London, 1990), pp. 134–48.

Naef, H., '"Huguenot" ou le procès d'un mot', *BHR,* XII (1950), pp. 208–27.

Naphy, W. G., *Calvin and the consolidation of the Genevan Reformation* (Manchester, 1994).

Nelli, R., *La philosophie du catharisme: le dualisme radical au XIIIe siècle* (Paris, 1975).

Nicholls, D., 'The theatre of martyrdom in the French Reformation', *P&P*, CXXI (1988), pp. 49–73.

Nijenhuis, W., *'Ecclesia Reformata': Studies on the Reformation*, 2 vols (New York, 1994).

Nirenberg, D., *Communities of Violence: Persecution of Minorities in the Middle Ages* (Princeton, 1996).

Nischan, B., *Prince, People, and Confession: The Second Reformation in Brandenburg* (Philadelphia, 1994).

————, *Lutherans and Calvinists in the Age of Confessionalization* (Aldershot, 1999).

Oberman, H., *The Dawn of the Reformation: Essays in Late Medieval and Early Reformation Thought* (Edinburgh, 1992).

Ozment, S., *Reformation in the Cities: The Appeal of Protestantism to Sixteenth-Century Germany and Switzerland* (London, 1975).

Pallier, D., *Recherches sur l'Imprimerie à Paris pendant la Ligue, 1585–1594* (Geneva, 1976).

————, 'Les impressions de la Contre-Réforme en France et l'apparition des grandes companies de libraires parisiens', *Revue Française d'Histoire du Livre*, XXXI (1981), pp. 215–73.

————, 'Les réponses catholiques', in R. Chartier and H.-J. Martin, eds, *Histoire de l'Édition Française*, 3 vols (Paris, 1983), I, pp. 327–47.

Parrow, K. A., 'From Defense to Resistance: Justification of Violence during the French Wars of Religion', *Transactions of the American Philosophical Society*, LXXXIII (1993).

Parry, G. J. R., *A Protestant Vision: William Harrison and the Reformation of Elizabethan England* (Cambridge, 1987).

Pérouse, G.-A., 'De la rumeur à la nouvelle au XVIe siècle Français', in M. T. Jones-Davies, ed., *Rumeurs et Nouvelles au temps de la Renaissance* (Paris, 1997), pp. 93–106.

Pettegree, A., 'Religious Printing in Sixteenth-Century France: the St Andrews project', *Proceedings of the Huguenot Society*, XXVI: 5 (1997), pp. 650–59.

————, *Huguenot Voices: The Book and the Communication Process During the Protestant Reformation* (Greenville, NC, 1999).

Pettegree, A., Nelles, P. and Conner, P., eds, *The Sixteenth-Century French Religious Book* (Aldershot, 2001).

Piaget, A. and Berthoud, G., *Notes sur le Livre des Martyrs de Jean Crespin* (Neuchâtel, 1930).

Po-Chia Hsia, R., *Trent 1475: Stories of a ritual murder trial* (New Haven, 1992).

Polman, P., 'Flacius Illyricus, Historien de l'Eglise', *Revue d'Histoire Ecclesiastique*, XXVII (1931), pp. 27–73.

Prestat, M., 'De la Guerre Psychologique à la Guerre Médiatique', in G. Chaliand, ed., *La Persuasion de Masse: Ses origines contemporaines* (Paris, 1992), pp. 23–81.

Revel, J. and Hunt, L., eds, *Histories: French Constructions of the Past* (New York, 1995).

Richard, J., *Saint Louis: roi d'une France féodale, soutien de la Terre sainte* (Paris, 1983).

Robbins, K. C., *City on the ocean sea: La Rochelle, 1530–1650* (Leiden, 1997).

Roberts, P., *A city in conflict: Troyes during the French Wars of Religion* (Manchester, 1996).

————, 'Huguenot petitioning during the Wars of Religion', in R. Mentzer and A. Spicer eds, *Society and Culture in the Huguenot World, 1559–1665* (Cambridge, forthcoming).

Roelker, N. L., *One king, one faith : the Parlement of Paris and the religious Reformations of the sixteenth century* (Berkeley, 1996).

Rougier, L., *Celse contre les chrétiens: la réaction paienne sous l'empire romain* (Paris, 1977).

Rousset, P., 'L'idéologie de Croisade dans les Guerres de Religion au XVIe siècle', *Schweizerische Zeitschrift für Geschichte*, XXXI (1981), pp. 174–84.

Rubin, M., *Corpus Christi: the Eucharist in Late Medieval Culture* (Cambridge, 1991).

Ruble, Baron de, 'L'arrestation de Jean de Hans et le tumulte de Saint-Médard', *Bulletin de la Société de l'Histoire de Paris et de l'Ile de France*, XIII (1886), pp. 85–96.

Rushkoff, D., *Media Virus! Hidden Agendas in Popular Culture* (New York, 1991).

Santschi, C., *La Censure à Genève au XVIIe siècle* (Geneva, 1978).

Sawyer, J. K., *Printed Poison: Pamphlet Propaganda, Faction Politics, and the Public Sphere in Early Seventeenth-Century France* (Oxford, 1990).

Schneider, R. A., *Public Life in Toulouse 1463–1789: From Municipal Republic to Cosmopolitan City* (London, 1989).

Scribner, R. W., *For the Sake of Simple Folk: Popular Propaganda for the German Reformation* (Cambridge, 1981).

———, *For the Sake of Simple Folk: Popular Propaganda for the German Reformation* (Oxford, 1994).

———, 'Heterodoxy, literacy and print in early German Reformation', in P. Billen and A. Hudson, eds, *Heresy and Literacy 1000–1530* (Cambridge, 1994), pp. 255–78.

Shennan, J. H., *The Parlement of Paris* (London, 1968).

Simone, F., ed., *Culture et politique en France à l'époque de l'Humanisme et de la Renaissance* (Turin, 1974).

Smith, M. C., *Ronsard and Du Bellay versus Bèze: Allusiveness in Renaissance Literary Texts* (Geneva, 1995).

Soman, A., 'Press, Pulpit, and Censorship in France before Richelieu', *Proceedings of the American Philosophical Society*, CXX (1976), pp. 439–63.

Taithe, B. and Thornton, T., eds, *Propaganda: Political Rhetoric and Identity 1300–2000* (Sutton, 2000).

Tallon, A., *La France et le Concile de Trente, 1518–1563* (Rome, 1997).

———, 'Le Cardinal de Lorraine et la Réforme Catholique' (unpublished paper, Reims, October 1999), 8 pages.

Taylor, L., *Soldiers of Christ: Preaching in the Late Medieval and Reformation France* (Oxford, 1992).

———, *Heresy and Orthodoxy in Sixteenth-Century Paris: François Le Picart and the Beginnings of the Catholic Reformation* (Leiden, 1999).

Telle, E., *L'oeuvre de Marguerite d'Angoulême Reine de Navarre et la Querelle des Femmes* (Geneva, 1969).

Thompson, K., *Moral Panics* (London, 1998).

Tillyard, E. M., *The Elizabethan world picture* (London, 1972).

Turchetti, M., 'Religious Concord and Political Tolerance in Sixteenth- and Seventeenth-Century France', *SCJ*, XXII: 1 (1991), pp. 15–25.

Venard, M., 'Catholicism and Resistance to the Reformation in France, 1555–1585', in P. Benedict, G. Marnef, H. van Nierop and M. Venard, eds, *Reformation, Revolt, and Civil War*, pp. 133–48.

Vicaire, M.-H., 'Les Albigeois Ancêtres des Protestants: Assimilations Catholiques', *CF*, XIV (1979), pp. 23–46.

Walker Bynum, C., *Fragmentation and Redemption: Essays on Gender and the Human Body in the Medieval Religion* (New York, 1991).

Wanegffelen, T., *Ni Rome ni Genève* (Paris, 1997).

Weber, A., *Teresa of Avila and the Rhetoric of Femininity* (Princeton, 1990).

Weber, H., 'La Boétie et la tradition humaniste d'opposition au tyran', in F. Simone, ed., *Culture et politique en France à l'époque de l'Humanisme et de la Renaissance* (Turin, 1974), pp. 355–74.

Weber, M., *L'éthique Protestante et L'esprit du Capitalisme, Les Sectes Protestantes et L'esprit du Capitalisme* (Paris, 1965).

Wylie Sypher, G., 'Faisant ce qu'il leur vient a plaisir: The image of Protestantism in French Catholic Polemic on the Eve of the Religious Wars', *SCJ*, XI (1980), pp. 59–84.

Yardeni, M., 'The attitudes to the Jews in literary polemics during the religious wars in France', *Zion*, XXVIII (1963), pp. 70–85.

————, *La conscience nationale en France pendant les guerres de religion (1559–1598)* (Louvain and Paris, 1971).

Index

Chassanion, Jean 122, 126
Châteaubriant, Edict of (1551) 8
Chesneau, Nicolas 38
Christ 18, 33–4, 45, 53, 64, 83, 85, 87
Christendom 27, 31–2, 57–8, 60, 69, 84, 101
Christians 31–3, 49, 53–5, 63–6, 70–71, 75, 80, 84–5, 99, 113, 117, 126
Church
  Apostolic 33, 46, 63, 85, 115, 128
  Councils 58, 95, 100
  early 84, 131
  Fathers 28, 55–6, 58
  History 36, 58, 100
  true 34, 115, 117, 124, 128
  see also Catholic; France, Gallican Church
civil disobedience 23–4, 29, 32, 35, 37, 47, 66–9, 71, 79, 101, 103, 106, 108
  accusations of 52, 67–9, 71, 77, 79, 86–8, 97, 131
  and Catholic polemicists 7, 10–12
  fear of 17, 20, 45, 70
  and the Reformation 13–14, 16, 18–19, 47, 52, 68–70
Civil Wars, see France, and Spain, Wars of Religion
Coligny, Gaspard de 30, 32, 77
'common folk' 24, 46, 63, 93
  concern for the opinion of the 17–19, 45–9, 63, 130
  and illiteracy 17, 20, 21, 41–2, 93, 96
Compiègnes, Edict of (1557) 65, 67
conciliation 6, 9–11, 29, 36, 39, 45–7, 52–3, 67, 99, 102, 104–5, 107–8
concord, religious 6, 9, 11, 59–60
Condé, Prince de 32, 67, 79, 101–2, 106
Corpus Christi day, feast of 18, 31–2, 83; see also Eucharist
Counter-Reformation, see Catholic Reformation
Court, see France, Crown
Crespin, Jean
  Histoire des Martyrs 14, 63, 66, 68, 78, 80, 120

see also Goulard
Crouzet, Denis 1, 25–8, 30–31, 130; see also eschatology; historiography
crusade 36, 132; see also Albigensian
Cyprian, St 64, 66

Des Gallars, Nicolas 15–16, 45, 50, 65–6, 71, 73, 75, 78–80, 120
Désiré, Artus 5, 11–12, 18–19, 44, 79, 87, 89, 91, 94
disease
  heresy as 56–7, 70–71, 85–6, 97
  and spreading of ideas 49–50
Donatists 36, 64
Du Bourg, Anne 9, 70, 72, 75
Durand, Nicolas, Chevalier de Villegagnon 59, 69, 76–7
Du Tillet, Jean 86, 102–3, 105–7, 109–11, 117
Du Val, Antoine 5, 18, 28, 42, 60, 87
Du Voisin de la Popelinière 62, 113

Eck, John 20, 33, 93
Edicts of pacification 8, 10–11, 16, 39, 67, 72, 102, 105, 107
  Catholic polemicists reaction against 9–12, 67, 99, 102, 105, 107
  see also heresy, laws
effigies, vicarious executions of 30, 32, 40, 92
Elizabeth I, Queen of England 95, 105
Empire, Holy Roman 3, 47, 70, 81
England 32, 34, 47, 81, 89, 93, 105, 121
Erasmus, Desiderius 59–60, 84, 92
eschatology 26–9, 32, 128, 130
d'Espence, Claude 38–9, 44
Estates General, see France
Eucharist 12, 18, 31–3, 53–5, 59, 77, 83–4, 107, 113, 117; see also Corpus Christi
execution, see 'theatre of martyrdom'

femmelette 17, 35, 81, 90, 92–3, 95–6, 98
Flacius Illyricus, Matthias 117–19, 124, 126
Flügschriften 3, 19–20